THE WRITING STUI
STORIES ABOUT

PERSPECTIVES ON WRITING
Series Editors, Susan H. McLeod and Rich Rice

The Perspectives on Writing series addresses writing studies in a broad sense. Consistent with the wide ranging approaches characteristic of teaching and scholarship in writing across the curriculum, the series presents works that take divergent perspectives on working as a writer, teaching writing, administering writing programs, and studying writing in its various forms.

The WAC Clearinghouse, Colorado State University Open Press, and University Press of Colorado are collaborating so that these books will be widely available through free digital distribution and low-cost print editions. The publishers and the Series editors are committed to the principle that knowledge should freely circulate. We see the opportunities that new technologies have for further democratizing knowledge. And we see that to share the power of writing is to share the means for all to articulate their needs, interest, and learning into the great experiment of literacy.

Recent Books in the Series

Kristine L. Blair and Lee Nickoson, *Composing Feminist Interventions: Activism, Engagement, Praxis* (2018)

Mya Poe, Asao B. Inoue, and Norbert Elliot (Eds.), *Writing Assessment, Social Justice, and the Advancement of Opportunity* (2018)

Patricia Portanova, J. Michael Rifenburg, and Duane Roen (Eds.), *Contemporary Perspectives on Cognition and Writing* (2017)

Douglas M. Walls and Stephanie Vie (Eds.), *Social Writing/Social Media: Publics, Presentations, and Pedagogies* (2017)

Laura R. Micciche, *Acknowledging Writing Partners* (2017)

Susan H. McLeod, Dave Stock, and Bradley T. Hughes (Eds.), *Two WPA Pioneers: Ednah Shepherd Thomas and Joyce Steward* (2017)

Seth Kahn, William B. Lalicker, and Amy Lynch-Biniek (Eds.), *Contingency, Exploitation, and Solidarity: Labor and Action in English Composition* (2017)

Barbara J. D'Angelo, Sandra Jamieson, Barry Maid, and Janice R. Walker (Eds.), *Information Literacy: Research and Collaboration across Disciplines* (2017)

Justin Everett and Cristina Hanganu-Bresch (Eds.), *A Minefield of Dreams: Triumphs and Travails of Independent Writing Programs* (2016)

Chris M. Anson and Jessie L. Moore (Eds.), *Critical Transitions: Writing and the Questions of Transfer* (2016)

THE WRITING STUDIO SAMPLER: STORIES ABOUT CHANGE

Edited by Mark Sutton and Sally Chandler

The WAC Clearinghouse
wac.colostate.edu
Fort Collins, Colorado

University Press of Colorado
upcolorado.com
Louisville, Colorado

The WAC Clearinghouse, Fort Collins, Colorado 80523–1040

University Press of Colorado, Lousville, Colorado 80027

ISBN 978-1-64215-017-9 (PDF) | 978-1-64215-014-8 (ePub) | 978-1-60732-896-4 (pbk.)

Printed in the United States of America

Library of Congress Cataloging-in-Publication Data

Names: Sutton, Mark, 1974– editor. | Chandler, Sally W., editor.
Title: The writing studio sampler : stories about change
 / edited by Mark Sutton and Sally Chandler.
Description: Fort Collins, Colorado : The WAC Clearinghouse, [2018]
 | Series: Perspectives on writing | Includes bibliographical references and index.
 | Identifiers: LCCN 2018036251 (print) | LCCN 2018058049 (ebook)
 | ISBN 9781642150179 (pdf) | ISBN 9781642150148 (ePub)
 | ISBN 9781607328964 (pbk. : alk. paper)
Subjects: LCSH: English language—Rhetoric—Study and teaching (Higher)
 | Writers' workshops. | Critical pedagogy.
Classification: LCC PE1404 (ebook) | LCC PE1404 .W7347 2018 (print)
 | DDC 808/.0420711—dc23
LC record available at https://lccn.loc.gov/2018036251

Copyeditor: Don Donahue
Designer: Mike Palmquist
Series Editors: Susan H. McLeod and Rich Rice

This book is printed on acid-free paper.

The WAC Clearinghouse supports teachers of writing across the disciplines. Hosted by Colorado State University, and supported by the Colorado State University Open Press, it brings together scholarly journals and book series as well as resources for teachers who use writing in their courses. This book is available in digital formats for free download at wac.colostate.edu.

Founded in 1965, the University Press of Colorado is a nonprofit cooperative publishing enterprise supported, in part, by Adams State University, Colorado State University, Fort Lewis College, Metropolitan State University of Denver, Regis University, University of Colorado, University of Northern Colorado, Utah State University, and Western State Colorado University. For more information, visit upcolorado.com. The Press partners with the Clearinghouse to make its books available in print.

For Nancy Thompson and Rhonda Grego

CONTENTS

THE WRITING STUDIO SAMPLER: STORIES ABOUT CHANGE

CHAPTER 1.

WRITING STUDIOS AND CHANGE

Sally Chandler and Mark Sutton

Kean University (retired) and Midlands Technical College

Writing Studio is a methodology articulated by Rhonda Grego and Nancy Thompson (1995, 1996, 2008) which enables writers to develop proficiency in the use and critique of discourses that constitute and surround the academy. Studio approaches have existed in both the fine and the practical arts, including rhetoric, since ancient times (Macauley, 1999). While studios differ widely by context, both in terms of the skills they model and the products they create, a defining feature has always been their emphasis on mentored learning-through-doing. In studios, apprentice learners master their craft through directed group participation. In Grego and Thompson's model for Writing Studios, learning-through-doing involves working on writing in small, facilitated groups. Participants in these mentored groups engage in collaborative reflection and interactional inquiry about writing and how writing is taught at their institution. Writing Studio's position in a thirdspace, outside-alongside the institutions and programs they serve, is a third feature of Writing Studies' version of studio.

The Writing Studio Sampler is a collection of essays about Writing Studio. These essays are, among other things, "I was there" stories: narratives told by individuals who designed, worked in, or administered a studio; or who used their studio's outside-alongside position to challenge and transform the institutional structures which framed it. Individual essays tell the story of a particular Studio: how it emerged at a specific institution; how it grappled with local economic, political, and social contexts; how it strove to meet the needs and purposes of its (varied!) stakeholders. Taken together, these essays illustrate the myriad ways collective reflection and interactional inquiry function to create what is most powerful about Studio: its ability to initiate change.

The fact that Writing Studio is a methodology—not simply a way to do things but a process for reflecting on, critiquing, and re-envisioning the way things are done—means that studios can serve many different pedagogical and administrative purposes. Studios described in this collection function outside-alongside community colleges (Leach and Kuhne), small liberal arts colleges (Fraizer), small urban universities (Cardinal and Keown), state colleges (Matzke and Garrett; Gray), and large state universities (Santana, Rose, and LaBarge).

While most studios described in this collection support courses in first-year writing programs, others act as sites for learning and change within a writing center (Miley), a service-learning program (Johnson), an Accelerated Learning Program (Ritola et al., Leach and Kuhne), or a training site for graduate teaching assistants (Korsnack). It is our intention that *The Writing Studio Sampler's* varied, detail-rich representations of what Studio can do will provide useful models and provoke questions for individuals interested in setting up or revising studio programs at their home institutions.

This introduction provides a brief overview of Writing Studio's history and theory, along with a discussion of why studio methodology is so important in today's changing educational environment. For readers who are new to Studio, these discussions can fill in the story of how and why Studio became part of Writing Studies, clarify definitions of unfamiliar terms, and direct readers to theorists important to Studio's on-going development. For readers more familiar with studio methodology, these sections can clarify the particular interpretation of Writing Studio set forward in this book. The final section of the introduction provides an overview of the collection's remaining chapters.

THOMPSON AND GREGO'S WRITING STUDIO

Nancy Thompson and Rhonda Grego's Writing Studio was designed for the University of South Carolina's first-year writing program. It emerged from a complex web of political exigency, economic pressure, and sociological circumstance. In 1990, the South Carolina Commission on Higher Education forbid four-year state colleges and universities from offering credit-bearing developmental courses. This, of course, did not prevent schools from admitting students needing extra support to pass first-year writing. During this time period, the University of South Carolina was working to increase its profile as a research institution. These shifts created a situation where the need to support underprepared writers was likely to increase and commitment to that support was likely to decrease.

As these changes were occurring, Grego and Thompson were full-time composition faculty in the Department of English at The University of South Carolina. Their working-class backgrounds made them well aware of the impacts these changes would have on their program. Departmental policies for funding composition further complicated the situation: "[The] English department's history of using the Writing Center and other kindred activities as a financial buffer . . . made it clear to us that further departmental funding cuts would soon disproportionately affect composition's work" (Grego & Thompson, 2008, p. 2). Taken together with changes at the state and university level, this policy made it clear to Grego and Thompson that their program was in danger of losing its connection to "our discipline's narrative of progressive social action" (2008, p. 2).

In response, Thompson and Grego, along with other colleagues from the basic writing program, spent the fall 1991 semester gathering data on their classes and reviewing relevant composition scholarship and available literature on institutional and government support for basic writing programs (Grego & Thompson, 2008, pp. 2–3). Their findings suggested that factors influencing the support for and success of basic writing students extended far beyond the classroom. As they report in *Teaching/Writing in Thirdspaces: The Studio Approach*, "[Composition instructors'] work with student writing (both products and processes) was influenced by institutional politics, preferences, and power relations at many more levels than currently attended to" (2008, p. 5). Additionally, they found that while scholarship on college writing in general—and on basic writing in particular—recognized the importance of factors outside classroom, it did not propose a solution, or even a plan, to address the larger, structural factors that shaped the teaching of writing. According to Grego and Thompson, scholarship merely

> acknowledge[d] the institutional power relations and politics
> that . . . dominated our work as compositionists and affected
> the lives of writing teachers and students. In composition
> research and accompanying pedagogies, the classroom as
> institutional space/place was often neutralized, while the rest
> of the institution's geography seemed typically only a general-
> ized part of the picture provided—if it was attended to at all.
> (2008, p. 5)

In other words, researchers understood that pressures outside the classroom affected the success of basic writers, but they were not really working on addressing those pressures.

Studio was a response to these realizations. It was designed to create a means to study relationships between learning and institutional contexts; to challenge the discourses, structures, and material circumstances which create and maintain those contexts; and to support all stakeholders in learning to navigate those contexts and discourses. As Grego and Thompson put it, the studio approach positioned participants to act on "(a) our heightened awareness of the institutional power relations that defined not only 'basic writing' but also 'student writing' and (b) our desire to engage in local action, to explore a very located (in place) and situated (in space) view of student writing" (2008, pp. 5–6). Defining features of Grego and Thompson's Writing Studio included studio's position in thirdspace, a place/space outside-alongside the institution it served; interactional inquiry as its central methodology; and all participants' engagement in collaborative reflection.

Grego and Thompson's original Studio, and most studios that trace their lineage from their work, organize "small groups of students to meet frequently and regularly . . . to bring to the table the assignments they are working on for a writing course, another English course, or a disciplinary course or undergraduate research experience that requires communication products" (2008, p. 7). In the original Studio, these groups were generally made up of students from different sections of English 101. Talk within the studio group helped students see beyond their individual course to the larger patterns of how communication was taught and used at the University of South Carolina at that time. The facilitator helped

> by explicating assignments not only in terms located within
> the assignment itself . . . but also . . . in terms of the history
> of the course at that institution, in terms of what the [facilita-
> tor] knows about the disciplinary background of the students'
> teachers, in terms of the history of such courses overall, and,
> sometimes most important, in terms of [the facilitator's] own
> experiences as a writer who has negotiated similar assignments
> or teachers in his or her academic career." (Grego & Thomp-
> son, 2008, p. 95)

Rarely was a facilitator the student's classroom instructor, and even if they were, studio's positioning lessened their ability to enforce grading policies. Studio's "grade" was based on attendance and participation, and its effect on the student's English 101 grade was determined by the classroom instructor, not the facilitator. This allowed the facilitator to act as a guide instead of an evaluator. Grego and Thompson theorized this positioning using a theory of thirdspace, where the Studio exists outside but alongside traditional institutional and disciplinary structures.

This outside but alongside positioning helps create space for collaborative reflection which is not driven by dominant power structures. Collaborative reflection is a group process, and for it to emerge, studio groups must meet together over a defined period of time. Deep familiarity among participants—understanding of each other's personal contexts, habits of speech, interests, and aspirations—lays the foundation for successful collaboration. The reflective element, often modeled or prompted by the facilitator, heightens awareness of patterns in ideas, talk, and writing. Ultimately, as collective reflection becomes more comfortable and proficient, participants notice, name, and begin to comment on discursive structures which make certain patterns inevitable and block others. Grego and Thompson called this process interactional inquiry.

Interactional inquiry has roots in feminist discourses and action research. It comes into being when "group participants (whether students or staff) engage in regular sessions in which they share, largely through talk and stories, their experiences, letting the life of their weekly everyday work gather force by finding similarities and common ground through a cross-sectional analysis" (Grego & Thompson, 2008, p. 175). Interactional inquiry's reflection on and analysis of structures permeating participants' experiences with the academy takes place primarily through talk. This talk, however, was supplemented by writing: writing produced for assignments, writing reflecting on assignments, and writing prompted by experiences surrounding both the assignments and life within academic culture. Ideas raised in all these different forms of writing are discussed and revisited, accepted and challenged, combined and recombined, discarded and picked up again over weeks of studio meetings by all participants, both students and staff. New experiences provide more data and refine the group's analysis. This process of mining group experience for patterns, trying those patterns in the fire of group reflection and critique, and then re-casting them in light of group identities, questions, and interests is the heart of interactional inquiry. More in-depth discussion of interactional inquiry and thirdspace can be found in the "Theoretical Roots" section of this introduction.

Studio's positioning outside but alongside traditional academic structures and its use of interactional inquiry laid the ground for the success. From 1992 to 2001 (the program's last year), at least eighty percent of students who regularly attended studio meetings in Grego and Thompson's program passed their first-year composition courses. These pass rates either matched or slightly exceeded passing rates for all first-year composition students (Thompson & Fosen, 2002). Grego and Thompson continued to develop the studio model in their on-going work as compositionists. When Grego joined the faculty at Benedict College in 1997, she developed the Bridges Writing Program, a version of Studio for Benedict's first-year writing program. The Bridges' program lasted a little longer than the original Studio, persisting in a limited form from 2002 through 2005. Thompson also expanded on the original project, designing a studio for the University of South Carolina's College of Engineering. This Studio supported engineering students' capstone projects (Thompson et al., 2005). Grego and Thompson's experiences with both of these programs are described in the *Teaching/Writing in Thirdspaces,* the major theoretical text on Studio.

Beyond Grego and Thompson's work, studio methodology has been responded to and modified by others. Early on, Peter Elbow (1996) praised it as a "seemingly utopian approach" that has allowed those involved in it to see basic writers not "so much through the lens of basic and nonbasic. . . . Instead, they are beginning to see a range of students with particular locations in a complex universe of strengths and weaknesses" (p. 91). Elbow believes this focus on individuals benefits students by resisting the restrictive labels traditionally associated with basic writing. William Lalicker (1999) supported this judgment in his overview of approaches to teaching basic writing. He stated the approach "enforces the notion that basic and standard composition students are all working collaboratively toward fluency in academic discourse and critical discourse consciousness (rather than segregating basic writers in a simplistic linguistic world where grammatical conformity dominates." (1999, "Alternative 2: The Studio Model") Others (Contugno, 2009; EEO/EOF, 2011; Gill, 2003; Greshman & Yancey, 2004; Kim & Carpenter, 2017) wrote about how they implemented Studio in a variety of institutional spaces and for a variety of different populations. In April 2005, John Tassoni started a listserv to discuss studio theory and practice, and a Special Interest Group (SIG) dedicated to the approach began meeting at the Conference on College Composition and Communication (CCCC) in 2007. The SIG has sponsored two workshops at CCCC: one (2015) focused on different studio sites and strategies for implementing a program, and the other (2017) shared pedagogical strategies used at various studio sites. Materials from both workshops are available online; see the references for the URLs. More importantly, both the listserv and SIG act as a studio space, a place where experienced practitioners can discuss their home sites and where newcomers can receive support for creating their own Studio.

WHAT MAKES A WRITING STUDIO UNIQUE?

Grego and Thompson intentionally designed Studio as a "highly adaptable approach" made up of "a configuration of relationships that can emerge from different contexts" (2008, p. 7). In other words, Studios occupy spaces appropriate to their purposes, adapt to the agendas of their stakeholders, and reflect and subvert the discursive structures of the particular institutions where they are housed. This flexibility leads to the question: What features make a Writing Studio a Studio and not a writing group, or a writing center, or a workshop? The easy answer is that a studio positions itself outside-alongside the program it is attached to, and that it engages participants in collaborative reflection and interactional inquiry. But what does that mean? And what does it look like? Outside-alongside programs can take many different forms, in both theory and practice. And reflection and critique can take place in writing centers, workshops, and writing groups as well as in studios. So then, what makes a Writing Studio unique?

As pointed out by Grego and Thompson (2008, p. 7), the small, facilitated group is the most important component of Writing Studio. Interactive, mentored feedback loops within and among studio groups allow Studios to function as communities of practice: groups of people who share a concern or a passion for something, and who learn how to do it better as they interact regularly (Wenger-Trayner & Wenger-Trayner, 2015). A community of practice may or may not include facilitation, but for studio groups, the focused reflection orchestrated by a facilitator is essential. Depending on institutional context, facilitators may be undergraduates, graduate students, faculty, or academic specialists. Facilitators are not so much teachers as moderators, group members responsible for focusing the flow of discussion. In general, facilitators do not come to a group meeting with lesson plans, or even a fixed idea of what the group will do on a particular day. Rather, they respond to what participants say about their writing, about class experiences or experiences with school in general, and about all the personal and political circumstances surrounding writing process. Spontaneous discussion often suggests the group's agenda for the day, and students may accept or reject any topic or focus proposed by the facilitator. The facilitator then keeps the group moving in a timely fashion, offering support as needed. While the group's facilitator may have more experience with writing and with academia, it is a benchmark of studio methodology that discussion takes its direction through interaction, using interactional inquiry to explore the conventions of academic discourse and the institution in which students are enrolled.

For example, suppose a studio group is made up of students who have different classroom instructors, but who are all working on an assignment which involves analysis. Even if instructors use the same textbook, they will almost always design and teach a genre slightly differently. These small differences can confuse students, who bring their own particular histories with any given writing genre to the course. Studio groups' use of interactional inquiry—talking through the many different kinds of analyses their teachers have asked them to construct—helps studio participants identify and characterize what analytic process is and how it works. The facilitator may share experiences teaching or writing analysis, but these experiences are only additional data, not The Answer provided by "an authority figure." This unfolding characterization of analysis as a genre gives students the opportunity to select, orchestrate, and modify general analytic features as needed to produce their individual compositions. When students receive instructor comments and other types of feedback on their work, they can bring this data back to the studio group to refine their thinking. Interactional inquiry does not require that all group members are working at the same place on the same assignment. It only requires that participants bring data and reflect on language features. The features they explore might come from assignments, from class discussions, from the structure of institutional practices, really any language interaction of importance to the group.

This focus on cooperation and critical reflection on discourse creates a clear parallel between Writing Studios and Writing Centers. Both use guided learning through doing, and both (in different ways) place students in (different kinds of) outside-alongside spaces. Yet Studios differ from Writing Centers in several important ways. First, studios are meant to be "attached to any course or experience in the academy that requires students to produce communications" (Grego & Thompson, 2008, p. 9), and they work with groups rather than individuals. Writing centers support an entire institutional community, and while writing center coaches are sometimes attached to individual courses, they generally work in one-on-one sessions on an as-needed basis. In contrast, Studio's learning dynamics center on relationships among a mentor and a group of students who work with one another over a prolonged period of time. Another difference is that writing centers often end up providing support that can sometimes become scripted. This script tends to direct the writer to his or her writing resources with attention to the writer's process and the immediate writing context. In contrast, Studio's prolonged conversation among multiple participants means that studio groups will have less stable scripts. The different perspectives within the group generally include scripts and discursive patterns from more than one assignment, classroom, or program. This broader perspective provides a different kind of support, discussions which ultimately lead to the interrogations of writing products and processes. The one-on-one structure of many writing center sessions is less often directed toward this end.

Writing workshops also have features in common with Studio, especially when they develop interactive, reflective discussions among a core group of participants. At the same time, writing workshops are almost always driven by an upfront, clearly defined agenda, and they generally do not engender the long-standing relationships seen within Studio. Even in a workshop series involving the same group of participants, workshops' fixed agenda and the hierarchical flow of knowledge from leaders to participants is quite different from Studio's interactive, emergent flow. Writing groups, with their long-term membership and egalitarian patterns for communication, can and do position members to reflect on and critique discourses associated with their writing (Chandler, 2001; Gere, 1987). At the same time, writing groups are generally not linked to institutional structures in the same way as Writing Studios; they are more outside than alongside, and more often than not writing group participants bring self-sponsored, rather than assigned, writing. In general, even when writing groups include a facilitator, procedures for presenting and responding to writing are directed toward the agendas of individual writers, rather than toward reflection on and critique of an institutional writing context.

While this collection focuses on Studio, we do not mean to imply that Studio is better or more important than other approaches. Studios, writing centers, writing workshops and writing groups all provide support that is empowering, effective, and important while each being distinctly different. Studio's uniqueness comes from its creation of a longstanding group, and the engagement of that group in interactional inquiry within the outside-alongside position of a thirdspace.

THEORETICAL ROOTS

If Writing Studio's most important practical feature is the group, studio's position in a thirdspace is its most important theoretical feature. Grego and Thompson's use of thirdspace draws from multiple sources, including architect Edward Soja's (1996) *ThirdSpace: Journeys to Los Angeles and Other Real-and-Imagined Places*. They use Soja's definitions of first, second, and thirdspace to theorize equivalent spaces for Writing Studies. Soja defines firstspace as concrete physical space, the world that can be mapped (1996, pp. 74–75). Grego and Thompson (2008) connect firstspace to student writers' "everyday work to produce their assignments" (p. 82), as well as the teaching practices and material conditions of a specific school. In other words, firstspace for Writing Studio is reality.

Soja defines secondspace as a theorized interpretation of reality. For Grego and Thompson (2008), secondspace is embodied in the scholarship representing Writing Studies' disciplinary doctrine. According to Grego and Thompson, this scholarship creates and codifies the language and concepts used to define "good" writing, as well as appropriate writing genres and pedagogies. Disciplinary scholarship sets up the right (and wrong) ways for teaching based on shared assumptions about appropriate forms and practices for academic writing, students' and teachers' identities, and the contexts in which writing for takes place. Grego and Thompson argue that because most scholarship is conducted at elite research universities, composition theory tends to be based on assumptions based in experiences and material realities associated with that very particular set of universities. When theory based on elite contexts is applied at non-elite institutions with radically different material conditions, economic resources, and student bodies, mismatches are inevitable. While applying scholarship based on conditions at research universities as institutions with radically different teaching contexts may "[allow] teachers to feel that they are at least providing their students with an education similar to that at institutions of a higher class" (Grego & Thompson, 2008, p. 159), methods derived from

11

this research rarely address or even recognize the very real needs within local, non-elite contexts. In general,

> [t]he further away the faculty and institution are from the upper end of the scale/hierarchy of knowledge making in any discipline, the more generic the curriculum and view of writing handed down from loftier spaces/places may become— not because of any lack of faculty expertise but because the curriculum forged at the upper end of the scale will be ill-equipped to deal with firstspace life at other places. (p. 186)

Writing Studio is a thirdspace, a space designed to bridge the differences between a particular school (firstspace) and what composition scholarship theorizes as "the right way" to teach writing (secondspace). Soja (1996) states that thirdspace "can be described as a creative recombination and extension, one that builds on a firstspace perspective that is focused on the 'real' material world and a secondspace perspective that interprets this reality through 'imagined' representations of spatiality" (p. 6). Because thirdspace is liminal, the norms of communication required in first and second spaces become available for critique, analysis, and re-creation. In thirdspaces, composition scholarship's secondspace of best practices can be reconsidered and modified in light of faculty expertise and material conditions at a particular institution.

A second source for Studio's thirdspace theory comes from Kris Gutierrez, Betsy Rymes, and Joanna Larson's (1995) study of classroom power reflected in discourse. They posit that students and teachers use different scripts, defined as "particular social, spatial, and language patterns . . . that members use to interpret the activity of others and to guide their own participation" (1995, p. 449). Teachers control the dominant, culturally powerful script (Gutierrez, Rymes & Larson, 1995, p. 446). Students have their own scripts which draw on and twist the teacher's statements into ideas that "relate simultaneously to the teacher's words and to [the students'] own cultural perspective" (Gutierrez et al., 1995, p. 461). These counterscripts enable students "to assert their difference from the assigned role" given to them by the dominant script (Gutierrez et al., 1995, p. 451). The different scripts can co-exist in ways that allow the classroom's work to go on as usual, limiting possibilities for change (Gutierrez et al., 1995, p. 452).

Gutierrez and her co-researchers argue "that the potential for change exists in the dynamic interrelation between the official and unofficial scripts; it is in this interaction that a sustainable challenge to the social and political functions of the teaching relationship and the transcendent script can be created" (1995, p. 452). As both sides work towards mutual understanding, students and teachers "must let go of [their] scripts and communicate across them, [creating] a third space for unscripted improvisation, where the traditionally binary nature of the student and teacher script is disrupted" (Gutierrez et al., 1995, p. 453). Thirdspace thus allows for the possibility of interrogating and changing identities.

Gutierrez and her co-researchers argue that creating thirdspace in a classroom is difficult; but as observed by Grego and Thompson, "the 'outside-but-alongside' positioning of studio groups can be a kind of 'safe house' for risk taking on the part of students and teachers" (2008, p. 74). When everything goes as it should, Studio does not eliminate or suppress students' counterscripts. Rather, the way Studio opens

> different writing courses, teachers, and assignments for weekly discussion can put [the counterscripts'] distancing activities on the table for discussion . . . [T]he script (and thereby the counterscript) enacted across more than one classroom [will be] more openly examined by students and group leaders in Studio groups as they meet to discuss not just the students' writing but the contexts in which the writing is being assigned and assessed. (Grego & Thompson, 2008, pp. 74–75)

By opening up the scripts, students and teachers are able to change in ways that can benefit both groups.

If thirdspace provides a philosophy for Studio, then interactional inquiry represents its methodology. As explained earlier, interactional inquiry functions as action research; it is made up of conversation and writing produced through an on-going series of reflective interactions where participants examine and re-think their experiences. Thompson links this process to "the extended time of a semester that gives us the opportunity to think about the good places and the rough spots in our program; the extended time to bring them up, leave them a while, come back to them after we've lived a little more, had a few more experiences, and bring them up again with a new perspective to a group of other people whose perspectives have also changed" (Grego & Thompson, 2008, p. 180). This process, through which the group as a whole develops and tests hypotheses about academic writing in general and about how academic writing works at their institution in particular, is central to studio work.

Grego and Thompson explicitly state that "Studio and interactional inquiry are not interpretative models so much as productive ones" (2008, p. 172). They reference Gilles Deleuze and Michel Foucault's analyses of how divisions between theory and practice have collapsed to explain how interactional inquiry creates points of connection between different spaces that are normally kept rigidly separate (2008, p. 173). By bringing conflicting, and sometimes ignored, discourses into conversation with each other, "[s]tudio looks for ways to help

13

unheard voices speak into the silences more immediately and directly located within their own institutional spaces/places" (Grego & Thompson, 2008, p. 188). Grego and Thompson point out that "too often it is organizationally easier (or less dangerous) to find fault with what students do or do not bring in their writing than to find fault with the harsh realities that the institutional setting wants us to ignore" (2008, p. 158), such as the quantity and quality of support for struggling learners, the curriculum's effectiveness, or the faculty's conception (or misconception) of best practices. In other words, students get blamed because faculty will not, or cannot, admit that the system within which their students are taught is the real obstacle to good learning. Studio's recursive cycles of interactional inquiry create a safe space for everyone involved to openly discuss these obstacles and to develop ways to respond to and change them. Interactional inquiry opens up "the thirdspace that lies between the collapse of firstspace perceptions and secondspace conceptions, in part by 'listening' to persistent local problems that, by their persistence, seem to be 'telling us' something, either about ourselves or about student writing, or about both" (2008, p. 178). The "listening" made possible by thirdspace is able to "tell" staff about their studio's and their institution's workings through the application of interactional inquiry.

While research findings produced through interactional inquiry may not always produce traditional academic scholarship, Grego and Thompson "propose that 'theorizing the cross-section' of multiple Studio programs can help compositionists generate a body of knowledge about academic writing that reflects different kinds of higher education institutions" (2008, p. 25). Because findings derived from "theorizing the cross-section" are grounded in a broad range of institutional contexts, they would be both more inclusive and more particular than traditional scholarship, and well suited as a basis for local, context-based change. Grego, for example, describes how faculty in the Bridges Writing Program "came to see the institution's role in constructing and maintaining distance between students and writing/learning" as a result of a lack of clear communication (Grego & Thompson, 2008, p. 198). Grego created lines of communication to administrators higher up the institutional hierarchy so that the administrators could see what was already working in classrooms, things they had previously been ignorant of or ignored. More importantly, the community created through interactional inquiry led to the faculty "coming together . . . in advocating with the upper administration for smaller class sizes and additional pay for increased classroom hours of teaching, as well as lobbying for our own writing program assessment design" (Grego & Thompson, 2008, pp. 199–200). These changes were meant to persuade administrators to use the expertise of Benedict's faculty to better benefit students.

Our discussion of thirdspace and interactional inquiry here and elsewhere in this introduction has been designed as an overview. While all of the studio programs described in this book use thirdspace as a philosophy and interactional inquiry as their guiding methodology, each program tweaks and adapts both to meet the needs of their institutional space. These modifications, fully encouraged by Grego and Thompson throughout almost all studio-related discussions they have ever participated in, increase the chances of creating a program that will work at a particular site and lead to positive change.

WRITING STUDIOS AND CHANGE

Studio scholarship has persistently identified Studio's potential to effect institutional critique and change as one of its central strengths (Grego, 2002; Grego & Thompson, 1996; Rodby, 1996; Rodby & Fox, 2000; Tassoni & Lewiecki-Wilson, 2005). In light of today's changing landscape for higher education, Studio's power to identify, reflect on, and articulate paths for local change are sorely needed. Over the last twenty years, institutions of higher education have undergone economic, administrative, and pedagogical reorganizations with deep-reaching consequences for teaching and learning. Former provost of the University of Southern California and higher education researcher Lloyd Armstrong (2014) notes that

> the economic picture has been dominated by two recessions in the past decade, with an accompanying significant repositioning of the role of the United States in the world. Real family income has been flat or decreased over that period for the vast majority of families, and family wealth has taken a significant dip. As a result, the ever-increasing real costs of higher education have become ever more onerous. (Section 1)

Rocky economics and governments' changing commitment to educational funding have contributed to changes both in the way students go to school and in how institutions of higher education are structured and administered.

Across all economic classes, an increasing percentage of students pursuing four-year degrees are choosing schools close to home (Eagan et al., 2014; National Center for Education Statistics, 2015). This means they often commute, work part-time, or have family responsibilities in addition to being students. Increasing numbers of students also begin their education by taking classes part-time, or they start at a less prestigious school with plans to transfer (Eagan et al., 2014). This new pattern means lost revenue for the schools these students would have traditionally attended, and it compounds problems posed by decreases in federal and state funding for education. In many cases, colleges and universities have responded by adapting models from business and industry. As discussed at length by scholars and in the popular press, these models fundamentally redefine roles for administrators, faculty, and students; and they often measure institutional success in terms of efficiency, economic return, or other measures which can conflict with traditionally established or research-based best practices for teaching and learning. In general, higher education's on-going response to these changing times has resulted in increased numbers (and varieties) of administrators and professional staff; decreased roles for and numbers of full-time, tenure track faculty; increased reliance on contingent and part-time faculty; reduced and "commodified" course offerings which have moved away from the liberal arts and towards vocationally-focused curricula; and the adoption of assessments which value efficiency and standardization (Ginsberg, 2011). Because of these shifts, writing programs are often called upon to do more for a larger number of students with fewer faculty, fewer courses, and less support.

Unsurprisingly, this shift is taking place within vigorous and unresolved conflicts over what services or products higher education is supposed to deliver, what students need, what practices constitute good teaching, and what administrative structures will ensure good learning and teaching (Berrett, 2011; Chomsky, 2014; Eberly & Martin, 2012; Klausman, 2013; Mendenhall, 2014). This debate over how best to re-imagine education is discussed more fully in other places. For the purposes of this introduction, it is sufficient to point out that the changing social, economic, and communication structures in the contemporary United States have created a moment in education where past assumptions about educational practices and goals must be reassessed with a critical eye.

The Writing Studio Sampler does not provide concrete answers to questions faced by writing teachers and administrators. Neither is it a volume of research which quantifies and correlates paths to success. While most of the essays present a kind of "hero" story, they are not all successes, so neither is it a collection of exemplars for meeting today's changing educational demands. Studios operate within particular contexts, and contexts change. Historically, writing studios have been created to solve institutional problems, usually on short notice and with limited funding. In doing so, they have also contributed valuable information about the cultural contexts they serve and why a given pedagogical approach will (or will not) work in that context. *The Writing Studio Sampler* comes from this tradition. The contributors describe situations where they find themselves in more than one role. They are often asked to act at odds with their training as compositionists, or they are otherwise positioned outside their comfort zones. Nonetheless, they take on the tasks placed before them; set forward their stories; and reflect on the ways Studio can support constructive interactions, relationships, value systems, and discourses within what are otherwise very trying situations. These stories provide the institutional histories which precede reorganizations and demands for change, they describe the process of change created through studio practices, and they report the outcomes of applications of studio methodologies, regardless of whether the outcome was a success or a failure. Most importantly, each essay illustrates the important role Studio can play in the re-examination of the culture of teaching and learning. When taken together and cross referenced, they present an opportunity to "theorize the cross-section": to notice, reflect on, and interrogate what Studio does and how it does it. Throughout, readers can consider the roles studio methodology can play in the re-visioning of writing pedagogies that can serve the many different and always changing needs of today's students.

OVERVIEW OF THE CHAPTERS

The Writing Studio Sampler's opening chapter sets the stage for those to follow by reminding us how cultural narratives shape our thinking and actions. In "Story Changing Work for Studio Activists: Finding Points of Convergence," Alison Cardinal and Kelvin Keown draw readers' attention to stories that frame our beliefs and shape our participation in educational practices. Using their experiences piloting several writing studios at a small urban university as data, they interrogate local and global stories which shape studio stakeholders' expectations: expectations that will influence whether they will authorize (or block) a studio's development. Within their own context, the authors report how their strategic, interactive responses to cultural stories led to increasing effectiveness in their studio's successive iterations.

This chapter is particularly important because, as Cardinal and Keown point out:

> little has been written about how to strategically tell the story
> of studio work to administrators and students. We argue that
> strategically engaging in what Linda Adler-Kassner (2008)
> calls "story-changing work" will increase the likelihood of
> success.

Their chapter documents how studio advocates can readily enlist cultural stories about learning transfer and acceleration in efforts to promote writing studios, and cautions that we must not get drawn in by our own stories so that we fail to notice the pragmatic interests and specific identity stories brought to Studio by students. This last idea may be the chapter's most useful point: the warning to studio advocates not to become caught up in utopic dreams of what Studio is "supposed" to be, and as a result, miss opportunities to create programs more grounded in stakeholders' actual needs.

As made clear by Cardinal and Keown, studios are engendered both by the cultural stories which frame and sustain them and by the contextual realities where those stories materialize. The next three chapters pay particular attention to the ways context can influence new program's development, or the maintenance and adaptation of an existing program.

In the first of these chapters, "Studio Bricolage: Inventing Writing Studio Pedagogy for Local Contexts," Aurora Matzke and Bre Garrett relate their different experiences starting new studio programs as they began their careers as writing program administrators at two different institutions. Using bricolage as a theoretical lens, they provide separate, but interrelated, reflections on how material and discursive affordances can shape Writing Studios. In particular, the authors use two concepts from bricolage, uptake and "not talk," as tools for recognizing and assessing available resources for program design. Uptake is the interactive, in-context process of interrogating the material landscape to discover what is available for the bricoleur's project, in this case, the development of Writing Studios. The uptake process is inclusive, and it emphasizes taking in all that is at hand before assessing its purpose or usefulness. In contrast, "not talk" assesses the particular ideas and discursive structures that frame a project in terms of what is NOT wanted, imagined, or desirable. Within this chapter, "not talk" clarified what was "not useful, needed, or wanted" by stakeholders who would participate in studio programs.

Through the use of uptake and "not talk," Matzke and Garrett dissect and re-think features of their institutional contexts, and then use this information in the development of their Writing Studios. In many ways, the use of uptake and "not talk" is a particular elaboration on interactional inquiry. Incorporating these two concepts when assessing a context can help focus and manage the often overwhelming challenge of accurately perceiving and analyzing studio sites. As might be expected, the development of Matzke and Garrett's Studios was not seamless, and difficulties encountered by the authors, especially difficulties with student buy-in, may cause readers to reflect back to Cardinal and Keown, or to look forward to chapters by Santana, Rose, and LaBarge, and by Ritola et al., chapters which further elaborate connections between context and the processes and practices which foster a successful Studio.

While Matzke and Garrett focus on the development of new or repurposed writing studios at schools with more or less traditional administrative structures, Tonya Ritola, Cara Minardi Power, Christine W. Heilman, Suzanne Biedenbach, and Amanda F. Sepulveda describe the challenges of developing a writing studio at a school with less standard structures and expectations. They were challenged to: meet pre-existing conditions set by funding sources, respond to the state of Georgia's larger political focus on retention, and create a process for developing and administering a Writing Studio that could function within Georgia Gwinnett College's flat structure while simultaneously providing support for developmental writing which met the team's professional standards. Their chapter, "The Politics of Basic Writing Reform: Using Collective Agency to Challenge the Power Dynamics of a Flat Administration," focuses on how they capitalized on their collective agency as composition teachers and scholars to both resist and comply with these contextual requirements.

Specifically, Ritola et al., strove to create programmatic support in keeping with composition theory's best practices (practices and concepts which sometimes were not readily understandable to the administrators making programmatic decisions) without either making unsustainable demands on writing faculty or failing to meet institutional requirements. Implicit to the story of their negotiations are questions similar to those raised by Cardinal and Keown, questions about what happens when utopian stories of Writing Studio and writing pedagogies are simply not feasible within a given institutional context. As writing teachers and program administrators, we all face contexts which demand negotiation or even compromise. This chapter suggests collective agency as an approach for achieving a long-term course of action which preserves professional standards in keeping with local contexts.

Dan Fraizer's chapter, "Navigating Outside the Mainstream: Our Journey Sustaining Writing Studio," traces how the studio program at Springfield College, a small liberal arts college in Western Massachusetts, has responded to changing student and administrative attitudes and needs over two decades. This reflective discussion also focuses on how contextual factors shape and reshape writing studios' structures and practices with a focus on the importance of on-going conversations among teachers, administrators, and students as a factor in bringing about programmatic change.

Fraizer's chapter tracks two important, but traditionally problematic, aspects of studio programs: development of systems for placement and enrollment in studio programs; and systems for communication among studio facilitators, course instructors, and students. Each of the three placement systems Fraizer describes functioned well enough in a particular time and place, and it is not clear that movement from one system to the next represents progress in the usual sense of the word. Rather, Fraizer shows how his studio's placement practices necessarily respond to on-going changes in student identities and family dynamics which in turn shape how students make decisions about school, all of which contribute to changing conceptions of what placement standards should do and how they should do it. As a result, Fraizer suggests that looking for a "best" way to place students may be essentially untenable. This observation sets up the importance of his second reflection, which is presented within a story about the need for regular dialog among teaching faculty, studio staff, and students. He concludes that the productivity of these on-going conversations can provide a basis for effective programmatic change. Fraizer's observations about how to support useful faculty-studio-student dialog can help program directors build strong studio programs despite the all too human, less than perfect personnel who usually staff (and administer!) writing courses and studios.

Like Fraizer, Christina Santana, Shirley K. Rose, and Robert LaBarge's "A Hybrid Mega Course with Optional Studio: Responding Responsibly to an Administrative Mandate" is also a meditation on relationships between studio placement decisions and studio success. The authors discuss a hybrid program with directed-self placement. The program included requirements for face-to-face class attendance and for completion of asynchronous online course assignments; it also included an optional Writing Studio which students could chose to attend up to five times a week.

Santana et al.'s Writing Studio was underpinned by a utopian narrative which allowed that students can best decide what kind and how much help they need with their writing. The accuracy of that narrative played out in complicated ways. The writing studio component, unsurprisingly, was plagued by poor attendance. Yet the chapter's analysis of student reflections on why they did (or did not) attend studio sessions and what they got out of sessions they did attend clearly illustrates that correlations between pass/fail rates, or even grades for the supported course, do not tell the whole story. A closer look shows some of the reasons why such data don't necessarily reflect what students learn from Studio, or for that matter, what they learned from making uncoerced decisions about whether or not to attend studio sessions. In their analysis, the authors "[draw] an important distinction between self-placement (which allows students to determine the level of difficulty of the material they are required to master) and required attendance (which structures student choice regarding elements within a course)." In making this distinction, the chapter demonstrates "that though students may seek out extra attention when they need it, they may only do what is required for a number of pragmatic and very rational reasons." Tension between these two different impulses is evident in the presentation of this studio's story, and it sets up important questions for much needed research on "students' abilities to make efficacious and strategic choices regarding their supplemental writing instruction." In addition to taking a much needed look at the ramifications of optional attendance, utopian stories, and material circumstances, this chapter also illustrates studio's potential to re-shape context. Like Ritola et al., Santana et al., point out how their program's structures for gathering data and formulating plans for change were integral to the outside-alongside positioning and interactional inquiry of Writing Studio itself.

The next three chapters deepen the exploration of context by exploring how studio methodologies might revise or work in tandem with courses or functions not traditionally associated with Writing Studios. In this grouping, we see writing studio methodologies elaborated as: a vehicle for communication among a cohort of writing teachers; a feature of teacher training; and a synergistic element within service learning courses.

In "Professional Development, Interactional Inquiry and Writing Instruction: A Blog Called 'Accelerated English @ MCTC,'" Jane Leach and Michael Kuhne describe how a collaborative blog set up for studio program staff at Minneapolis Community and Technical College (MCTC) functioned as a space for interactional inquiry. The blog was open to all MCTC Accelerated Developmental English instructors and selected colleagues. The blog allowed for the "continual to-and-fro between action and reflection" (Grego & Thompson, 2008, p. 72) which led to "trying out approaches, actions or changes discussed within the inquiry group in their daily lives at the site." The blog's support for interactional inquiry was particularly important at MCTC, a public, urban, two-year comprehensive college where faculty have heavy teaching loads and little time to sit down together to talk. Use of the blog allowed staff to participate in a kind of collaborative, in-process professional development; it also provided space for collective, reflective problem solving in order to meet program goals.

Leach and Kuhne report most frequently discussed topics (ascertained from the word cloud in the blog's tag directory) and reflect on the kind and amount of resolution produced through online interactional inquiry among blog participants. The authors' discussion of faculty posts about poor student class attendance deepens Santana et al.'s, discussion of poor attendance. Where Santana et al., present an analysis of student perspectives on attendance and experiences with Studio by excerpting statements from interviews, Leach and Kuhne provide selections from blog entries where staff write about how they felt about and responded to issues in students' lives which affected attendance. Similar to Santana et al.'s, observations that traditional markers of "what students got out of studio" did not reflect what more intimate, grounded reflection revealed, Leach and Kuhne note that a blog used for collaborative reflection allowed participants "to discuss matters that too frequently are left unwritten or unspoken in our work." In their conclusion, they point out the value of what can happen in a teaching community when such disclosures are subjected to interactional inquiry.

Kylie Korsnack's chapter "GTAs and the Writing Studio: An Experimental Space for Increased Learning and Pedagogical Growth" opens up another application of studio methodologies. Her chapter illustrates how Studios can serve a vital role in training graduate students to become effective teachers, something that has become more important as the job market grows both more demanding and more competitive. As she points out, even those graduate students who go through a rigorous training program can feel unprepared for classroom teaching. Her chapter documents the experiences of graduate teaching assistants (GTAs) who were eased into teaching responsibilities through spending mentored time as studio group facilitators and by observing experienced teachers.

The chapter centers on Korsnack's examination of program documents and interviews with studio facilitators and faculty directors. Analysis of these documents illustrates how a studio apprenticeship both supports GTAs in developing nuanced, grounded teaching philosophies, allows them to study student writing and helps them learn how to plan and manage class activities. Korsnack describes how studio's liminal space positions the new graduate student as a more experienced guide for a small number of students instead of as the authority figure over a traditional class. This different relationship with students, outside-alongside the perspective of the classroom teacher, provides GTAs with an inside view of how students think through their writing processes and positions them to learn lessons about teaching that they could not learn as easily within the role defined for instructors. The required observations of experienced teachers further supported GTA's growth as writing instructors, allowing them to "'learn to see what works and what doesn't work [for the teacher they are observing] on the way to developing their own personal pedagogy."

Like Korsnack, Karen Gabrielle Johnson describes a program which extends the reach of writing studio methodology. In "Multiplying Impact: Combining Third and Fourthspaces to Holistically Engage Basic Writers," she documents the form and function of a studio program linked to service learning. She describes this program as a service learning/studio combination, and her analysis focuses on the synergistic effects for student learning when thirdspaces (Writing Studios) and fourthspaces (service learning) interact. Specifically, Johnson observes that while service learning courses can increase student engagement through their community-based, experiential components, students may need spaces both to articulate those experiences in language and to practice, discover, and invent the forms for writing about them. Her discussion illustrates how Writing Studio, with its facilitated discussions and on-going interactional inquiry, can provide such spaces. Because of this and despite the work-intensive demands of both Studios and service learning projects, Johnson concludes that the two approaches, when combined, help basic writing students better integrate learning.

In many ways, the two final chapters draw together and extend earlier discussions about the importance of context; the intentional, reflective use of studio methodologies to respond to and push back against those contexts; and the use of studio methodologies within new contexts and for new purposes. Each of these last two chapters, in its own way, presents a writing studio story which suggests new possibilities for studio methods. Michele Miley's "Writing Studios as Countermonument: Reflexive Moments from Online Writing Studios in Writing Center Partnerships" documents how online studios can make visible "moments of resistance to innovation influenced by disciplinary discourse and institutional relationships." Mary Gray's "Something Gained: The Role of Online Studios in a Hybrid First-year Writing Course" describes a Writing Studio that is entirely online. In both cases, online features of these programs revise and reconfigure interactional inquiry, the outside-alongside placement of studios, and communication dynamics already present within studio methodology. These "new studios" also draw on theory and practice from digital writing and new media, and extend possibilities for the reflective, analytic, and interpersonal practices which energize face-to-face studio conversations.

Miley uses Paul Butler's discussion of countermonument theory to frame her discussion of Writing Studios associated with The University of Houston Writing Center's Writing in the Disciplines (WID) program. In the chapter's introduction, she paraphrases Butler's observation that "countermonuments require a great amount of self-assessment and reflection and, importantly, a willingness to allow viewers to share authority in the construction of identity" (Butler, 2006, p. 15). She points out that a countermonument's willingness "to open itself to its own violation" (Butler, 2006, p. 15) can allow us to see ourselves from multiple perspectives and in new ways, and then illustrates how a writing studio's positioning outside-alongside mainstream discourses creates the ideal space for a countermonument. As she puts it, she uses "Butler's metaphor of the countermonument and its possibilities for creating reflexive spaces to describe my experience with online writing studios both in a WID partnership and in the larger first-year composition partnership." This discussion draws from nearly four years of data and includes countermonumental reflections which consider "how online writing studios can help writing teachers . . . to resist disciplinary calcification and to work within and against the institution . . . [and] . . . how studios make visible the moments when, without the willingness to take the structural risks that Butler calls for, we [can] become 'monolithic or static'" (2006, p. 11), despite our motivation to be innovative." Miley's elaboration of the metaphor of countermonument in terms of one online studio program suggests a way to conceptualize learning within the always changing contexts of studio programs that have not yet been fully invented.

Gray describes an online hybrid/studio-supported model for first-year composition, a studio developed through collaboration among the University of Houston's Department of English and the Writing Center. She tracks program development over several years, and her analysis of data to assess student reception and program success illustrate how a hybrid/studio approach can be used to comply with institutional demands for alternative delivery methods while still supporting the National Council of Teachers of English's statements on the benefits of first-year writing courses. In discussing the success of the online studio, she observes that the fact that studio groups met online added multiple layers of complexity for student participation, facilitator training, and various communication issues. In light of these complexities, she reflects that the project could not have been successfully maintained "without the Writing Center's role as the site for studio development and implementation." The chapter concludes by suggesting that the hybrid/studio supported model "may offer possibilities for retaining important elements of traditional first-year writing courses that might be diminished or lost in the rush to new delivery methods and credit alternatives," and in doing so, they "may hold the potential to mitigate those losses and realize unexpected gains."

AN INVITATION

Taken together, the chapters in *The Writing Studio Sampler* suggest the range of the Studio model's potential. As emphasized throughout this introduction and Grego and Thompson's work, writing studios respond to the contexts in which they are created. It is not a pedagogy in a box that can be used unmodified anywhere. As a result, the chapters in this collection bring issues "to the table," a phrase Nancy Thompson frequently used in staff meetings. All authors raise points grounded in circumstances at their home institutions. At the same time, they do not present responses formulated through their studio work as the only answer to their situation. It is up to readers to continue to explore studio's possibilities in light of their own experiences as they create programs and propose actions specific to their particular contexts.

REFERENCES

Armstrong, L. (2014, December 12). A business model view of changing times in higher education. [Web log post]. Retrieved from http://www.changinghigheredu cation.com/2015/01/the-problem-with-ca-higher-education-mission-expense.html.

Berrett, D. (2011, July 14). The fall of faculty. *Inside Higher Ed.* Retrieved from https://www.insidehighered.com/news/2011/07/14/fall-faculty.

Butler, P. (2006). Composition as countermonument: Toward a new space in writing classrooms and curricula. *WPA: Writing Program Administration, 29*(3), 11–25.

Chandler, S. (2001). *Interpretation in context: A feminist ethnographic study of a women's writing group.* (Unpublished doctoral dissertation). Wayne State University, Detroit.

Chomsky, N. (2014, October) Corporate business models are hurting American universities. *Salon*. Retrieved from https://www.salon.com/2014/10/10/noam_chomsky_corporate_business_models_are_hurting_american_universities_partner/.

Contugno, M. (2009). Encouraging students writing now! *Adult and Basic Education and Literacy Journal, 3*(3), 171–174.

Eagan, K., Stolzenberg, E. B., Ramirez, J. J., Aragon, M. C., Suchard, M. R. & Hurtado, S. (2014). The American freshman: National norms fall 2014. *Higher Education Research Institute, UCLA*. Retrieved from https://www.heri.ucla.edu/monographs/TheAmericanFreshman2013.pdf.

Eberly, J. & Martin, C. (2012) The economic case for higher education. *The U.S. Department of Treasury*. Retrieved from http://www.treasury.gov/connect/blog/Pages/economics-of-higher-education.aspx.

Elbow, P. (1996). Writing assessment in the 21st century: A utopian view. In D. Daiker & L. Z. Bloom. *Composition in the twenty-first century: Crisis and change* (pp. 83–100). Carbondale, IL: Southern Illinois University Press.

Gere, A. R. (1987). *Writing groups: History, theory, and implications*. Urbana, IL: National Council of Teachers of English.

Gill, M. (2013). *Implementing writing studio at a secondary institution*. (Unpublished master's thesis). Kean University, Hillside, NJ.

Ginsberg, B. (2011). *The fall of faculty: The rise of the all administrative university and why it matters*. Oxford, UK: Oxford University Press.

Grego, R. (2002). Community archaeology: An historically black college deconstructs basic writing. In S. B. Fowler & V. Vitanza, *Included in English studies: Learning climates that cultivate racial and ethnic diversity* (pp. 53–69). Washington, D.C.: American Association of Higher Education/National Council of Teachers of English.

Grego, R. C. & Thompson, N. (2008). *Teaching/writing in thirdspaces: The studio approach*. Carbondale, IL: Southern Illinois University Press.

Grego, R. C. & Thompson, N. (1996). Repositioning remediation: Renegotiating composition's work in the academy. *College Composition and Communication, 47*(1), 62–84.

Greshman, M. & Yancey, K. B. (2004). New studio composition: New sites for writing, new forms of composition, new cultures of learning. *WPA: Writing Program Administration, 28*(1/2), 9–28.

Gutierrez, K., Rymes, B. & Larson, J. (1995). Script, counterscript, and underlife in the classroom: James Brown versus Brown v. Board of Education. *Harvard Educational Research, 65*, 445–471.

Kim, M. & Carpenter, R. (2017). Writing studio pedagogy: Space, place, and rhetoric in collaborative environments. Lanham, MD: Rowman & Littlefield.

Klausman, J. (2013). Toward the definition of a writing program at a two-year college: You say you want a revolution? *Teaching English in the Two Year College, 40*(3), 257–273.

Lalicker, W. B. (1999, November 19). A basic introduction to basic writing program structures: A baseline and five alternatives. Retrieved from *Basic Writing e-Journal*: https://bwe.ccny.cuny.edu/Issue%201.2.html#bill.

Lave, J. (1991). Situating learning in communities of practice. In J. L. L. Resnick, *Perspectives on socially shared cognition* (pp. 63–82). Washington, D.C.: American Psychological Association.

Mendenhall, A. S. (2014). The composition specialist as flexible expert: Identity and labor in the history of composition. *College English, 77*(1), 11–31.

Macauley, W. J., Jr. (1999). *Studio pedagogy and first-year composition: A qualitative study of studio-based learning, student empowerment, and the application of studio pedagogies to college-level composition.* (Unpublished doctoral dissertation). Indiana University of Pennsylvania, Indiana, PA.

National Center for Education Statistics, Institute of Education Science (2015, May). Characteristics of postsecondary students. *The Condition of Education.* Retrieved from https://nces.ed.gov/programs/coe/pdf/Indicator_CSB/coe_csb_2015_05.pdf.

Rodby, J. (1996). What it's worth and what's it for? Revisions to basic writing revisited. *College Composition and Communication, 47*(1), 107–111.

Rodby, J. & Fox, T. (2000). Basic work and material acts: The ironies, discrepancies, and disjunctures of basic writing and mainstreaming. *Journal of Basic Writing, 19*(1), 84–99.

Soja, E. W. (1996). Thirdspace: Journeys to Los Angeles and other real-and-imagined places. Cambridge, UK: Blackwell.

Studio PLUS Special Interest Group. (2015). *Writing studio tools and strategies across contexts.* Retrieved from https://sites.google.com/site/studioworkshopc2015/.

Studio PLUS Special Interest Group. (2017). *Writing studio pedagogy: Cultivating student voice and capacity for change.* Retrieved from https://sites.google.com/site/studioworkshopc2017/.

Tassoni, J. P. & Lewiecki-Wilson, C. (2005). Not just anywhere, anywhen: Mapping change through studio work. *Journal of Basic Writing, 24*(1), 68–92.

Thompson, N. E., et al. (2005). Integrating undergraduate research into engineering: A communications approach to holistic education. *Journal of Engineering Education, 94*(3), 297–307.

Thompson, N. & Fosen, C. (2002, May 3). Some informal results. *The Writing Studio.* Retrieved from http://www.cas.sc.edu/engl/studio/.

Thompson, N. & Grego, R. (1995). The writing studio program: Reconfiguring basic writing/freshman composition. *WPA: Writing Program Administration, 19*(1), 66–79.

Wenger-Trayner, E. & Wenger-Trayner, B. (2015). *Introduction to communities of practice.* Retrieved from http://wenger-trayner.com/introduction-to-communities-of-practice/.

CHAPTER 2.

STORY-CHANGING WORK FOR STUDIO ACTIVISTS: FINDING POINTS OF CONVERGENCE

Alison Cardinal and Kelvin Keown

University of Washington-Tacoma

In *Teaching/Writing in Thirdspaces*, Rhonda Grego and Nancy Thompson (2008) offer an aspirational narrative of Studio's potential to transform students and institutions. They imagine Studio as a place where the teacher acts as a guide rather than authority, and students collaborate in a workshop-like environment. The Studio also provides space to critique the institution and challenge the assumptions about identity and ability that institutions and faculty impose upon students (Gutierrez, Rymes & Larson, 1995). This liberatory narrative Grego and Thompson (2008) tell about the Studio is what John Paul Tassoni and Cynthia Lewiecki-Wilson (2005) describe as the "utopian dream" of a subversive studio thirdspace.

It comes as no surprise that this counter-hegemonic studio narrative comes into conflict with the narratives of institutions concerned with "buildings and budgets" (Grego & Thompson, 2008, p. 28). With small class sizes and organic curricula, studios appear to operate in opposition to institutions' focus on measurable outcomes and efficiency. These conflicting narratives result in material consequences for studio programs, including programs being enervated, defunded and cancelled (Grego & Thompson, 2008; Warnick, Cooney & Lackey, 2010). To further complicate matters, studio creators must contend with students' own engagement—and resistance—to our utopian studio narrative (Matzke & Garrett, this volume; Santana, Rose & LaBarge, this volume). These localized narratives play out amidst the backdrop of larger cultural narratives of writing and writers. While several accounts describe studio programs (Grego & Thompson, 2008; Tassoni & Lewiecki-Wilson, 2005; Warnick et al., 2010), little has been written about how to strategically tell the story of studio work to administrators and students. This chapter, alongside Matzke and Garrett (this volume), address this needed area of theorization. We argue that strategically engaging in what Linda Adler-Kassner (2008) calls "story-changing work" will increase the likelihood of success for studio programs.

To illustrate this story-changing work in action, we (Alison Cardinal, a full-time lecturer; and Kelvin Keown, a staff TESOL specialist) narrate our studio story to demonstrate how the interaction of narratives played out in our context. Through an analysis of our experience piloting several iterations of Studios at a small urban university, we illustrate how our engagement with institutional narratives shaped our studio program. Gleaning insights from our experience, we offer story-changing strategies for reframing studio work.

THE IMPORTANCE OF STORY-CHANGING WORK

In popular culture, the narrative of an ongoing literacy crisis persists (Holland, 2013; Leef, 2013).These stories, however wrongheaded, carry weight. They can lead to legislators determining basic writing's place on college campuses (Grego & Thompson, 1996, pp. 62–63; Ritola et al., this volume) and administrators deciding to fund writing programs. These stories also determine students' perception of the value of their writing courses (Bergmann & Zepernick, 2007).

How exactly do we begin transforming these stories? Adler-Kassner (2008) argues that any story-changing work must start from a place of principle, which she describes as a set of strongly held values that serve as the basis for action (pp. 22–23). Studio pedagogy is motivated by the post-process ideals of democratizing the classroom and critiquing hegemonic power structures (Grego & Thompson, 2008; Paul-Tassoni & Lewiecki-Wilson, 2005). As Adler-Kassner (2008) points out, however, strongly held principles are not enough: "Ideals without techniques, values without tactics" result in "a mess" (p. 127). To avoid the mess caused by unmoored ideals, Adler-Kassner (2008) encourages Writing Program Administrators (WPAs) to preemptively engage with dominant narratives as they play out in one's local context.

In many ways, studios already employ story-changing strategies that work from ideals. Beginning locally, studios seek to challenge and reshape dominant stories about writers and writing through interactional inquiry. This method, where studio participants collectively explore what writing is and how it is defined, could even be called a story-changing pedagogy. While Studio has had great success enacting story-changing work in the classroom, studios have had difficulty effecting lasting change on the institutional level (Grego & Thompson, 2008, p. 171). Considering the challenges of starting and sustaining studio programs, communicating studio work to outside audiences benefits from a strategic approach.

A story-changing approach begins with understanding how institutional change works. Drawing from his observations about moments when black people made gains in civil rights, critical race theorist Derrick Bell (2004) argues that change only happens when the interests of "white folks" and "black folks" converge and that granting rights to black people somehow also benefits whites (p. 49). While some of this convergence is out of our control, Bell suggests that activists can harness interest convergence by using "interest-converging arguments," which he argues "can extract a measure of victory from what otherwise would be almost-certain defeat" (2004, p. 159).

Studio activists can also use this strategy by preemptively demonstrating how studio interests converge with the interests of administrators to make the success of the program more likely. However, in order to have a more transformative effect, studio administrators should strive to reframe the conversations around writing. Appropriating institutional arguments is the first step, and the second is to use that appropriation to redirect the argument by reframing the interests of the institution in ways that reflect studio values. Steve Lamos (2011), who also uses interest convergence, suggests that finding places of convergence as the basis of story-changing work "can help us both alter old stories and to tell new stories" about writing programs to demonstrate to our institutions that these programs "remain relevant and important—even essential—to the success of both under-represented minority students and mainstream institutions themselves in the present day" (p. 163).

It is important to acknowledge that finding story convergence is not cut and dry. When we talk about changing the stories of "the institution," we are actually discussing a complex mix of interests represented by individual departments, administrators, legislators, teachers, and students (Ritola et al., this volume). And as Matzke and Garrett (this volume) describe, studio activists can begin this story-changing work by first "interacting with community stakeholders, accumulating resources from different locations, and situating claims and appeals within local discourses." Making Studios successful relies on first being attuned to the various discourses, locating multiple points of convergence among stakeholders, and then working from these convergences to begin story-changing work at those intersections.

STORIES ABOUT WRITING AND WRITERS

Before addressing possible points of conversion or diversion of interests among the various players involved in higher education, we describe two stories that Studios seek to tell that we find most salient for finding points of interest convergence. Following a description of the story-changing efforts already present in studio work, we will describe institutional stories of higher education that are pervasive on a national scale that most, if not all, studio activists will need to contend with. Finally, we will offer two examples of the way compositionists have already attempted to find places of convergence between studio's interests and the interests of larger institutional and societal forces in an effort to advocate for the ideals Studios inhabit.

THE NARRATIVE POSITIONING OF STUDIOS

Studios have gained in popularity in the last ten years, partly out of a need to promote new stories about so-called "basic writers." Studio, like other recent models (Adams et al., 2009; Glau, 1996; Ritter, 2009), resists characterizing students as "basic writers," since this term implies a deficiency (Horner & Lu, 1999). Because Studio is a supplement to other courses rather than a course taken prior to "real college," Studio reframes the story of students from deficient to novice writers. This shift in narrative is important: "Basic writer" is a fixed identity, but novice is a role all writers necessarily inhabit when learning something new. As Gutierrez, Rymes, and Larson (1995) argue, a thirdspace such as a studio is uniquely positioned to challenge the "normative patterns of life" (p. 449) inherent in traditional classroom spaces by creating the conditions necessary to create counterscripts about student identities. And because Studio can be placed at any point in the curriculum, not just as a basic writing course (Miley, this volume), Studio emphasizes that students need support whenever they encounter new writing situations. For students, the repositioning of one's writing identity to novice can have powerful effects on learning (Reiff & Bawarshi, 2011; Sommers & Saltz, 2004). Studio has a potentially transformative narrative effect on how institutions and students understand how one learns to write in ways that benefit student learning.

In addition to the narrative of novice writers, Studios emphasize the importance of metarhetorical awareness. Grego and Thompson (2008) position metarhetorical awareness as an essential tenet to studio work, since it encourages students to develop a greater awareness of the stories the institution and the larger society tells about them. In addition to helping students develop a classroom-specific awareness of genre, disciplinary norms, or academic discourse, metarhetorical awareness "encourages us to attend . . . to the complexity and influence of the institutional location" (Grego & Thompson, 2008, pp. 63–64). By collectively identifying the "gaps and fissures" (Grego & Thompson, 2008, p. 25) where change is possible, students and studio facilitators become co-partners in story-changing work (Gutierrez, Rymes & Larson, 1995).

NATIONAL/INSTITUTIONAL STORIES: EFFICIENCY

There are many stories about education that Studio must contend with, but we will focus on the pervasive educational narrative of *efficiency* that we argue most impacts studio work at both public and private institutions. Efficiency, according to Williamson (1994), is rooted in the capitalist value of return on investment and pervades every aspect of American education, from teacher training to assessment. Williamson (1994) argues that the efficiency narrative emphasizes efficient use of funds, efficient teacher labor, and efficient student achievement (p. 58). These efficiency narratives are naturalized and easy to overlook. After all, who would claim that higher education should be less efficient? This narrative, however, belies the complexity of learning to write. As composition research has shown, students' writing development is a complex process and does not progress in a linear, efficient fashion (Haswell, 2000; Sternglass, 1997). However, the idea that writing is a general skill that can be learned efficiently and uniformly assessed persists (Williamson, 1994). The focus on financial efficiency, and even learning efficiency, seems at odds with studio programs that rely on small course caps and emphasize the difficult-to-measure aspects of learning. The challenge for studio programs is figuring out how to contend with efficiency narratives without sacrificing the progressive principles Studio espouses.

CONVERGING INTERESTS

In this section, we describe strategic ways Studios can engage with efficiency narratives to further the interests of studio programs without sacrificing their principles. By finding points of convergence between Studio and efficiency narratives, studio programs can engage in story-changing work. We specifically identify narratives of acceleration and transfer of learning as useful narratives that frame studio work around narratives of efficiency while also reframing efficiency on our own terms.

Acceleration

In the last 20 years, the interests of Studios, institutions, venture philanthropy, and students converged to shorten the developmental pipeline common at many institutions. This convergence has led to the expansion of studio-like programs nation-wide, replacing traditional BW sequences with other models. However, none rival the wide-reaching influence of the Accelerated Learning Program (ALP) out of the Community College of Baltimore. The Accelerated Learning Program is a notable example of how harnessing the converging interests of studio principles and efficiency narratives have led to story-changing about basic writers.

At first glance, ALP appears vulnerable to the critique of financial inefficiency. In their model, students take a studio-like course, capped at 11, alongside first-year composition (FYC), both of which are taught by the same instructor.

31

Despite the appearance of an expensive program, Adams et al. (2009) have been able to argue that ALP increases financial efficiency. Adams et al. (2009) use pass rate statistics to tell the story that eliminating the traditional sequence is cheaper for institutions. Because more students are retained, tuition dollars increase, and this makes student time in studio courses an efficient use of students' time and money. They also frame ALP in terms of efficient student achievement. The term *accelerated* suggests a slow, inefficient curriculum has been replaced with a sleek, streamlined model. Here we see how progressive ideals of access to education and capitalist ideals of financial efficiency converge. Harnessing a narrative of efficiency, ALP reframes basic writers as capable of handling college-level work, which upholds the studio ideals of treating students as novices.

It is important to note, however, that not all ALP courses use studio pedagogy. While there are significant overlaps between ALP and Studio, ALP's argument for replacing the traditional BW sequence does not advocate for a particular pedagogical approach (Adams, 2013). In contrast to Studio, ALP does not promote itself as a counter-hegemonic space that challenges institutional norms. This points to some of the dangers of interest convergence: How do studio programs find convergence of interests without sacrificing ideals? Ritola et al.'s (this volume) description of the Segue program at Georgia Gwinnet College is a notable example of the blending of these two approaches. While a focus on financial efficiency and retention has been successfully used as a point of interest convergence in studio program development (Fraizer, this volume; Ritola et al., this volume; Matzke & Garret, this volume), Studio needs to find ways to reframe student learning in addition to using quantitative and monetary measures of student success.

Transfer of Learning

Another possibility for finding convergence between efficiency narratives and studio work comes from transfer of learning. Transfer, the ability to take something learned in one context and repurpose it for use in another context, has gained prominence in composition research in the last seven years. One of the key motivators for researching transfer of learning is to figure out how to help students make efficient use of their writing knowledge. In a time of shrinking budgets, it makes sense that composition would be drawn to research that helps WPAs make First-Year Composition (FYC) as efficient as possible.

In convergence with Studios, transfer scholarship has identified metarhetorical awareness as a key component to helping students transfer their writing knowledge across contexts (Beaufort, 2007; Yancey, Robertson & Taczak, 2014). Transfer research has also shown the unique power of thirdspaces for helping students see and make connections across contexts (Fraizer, 2010). However, most transfer research focuses on using metarhetorical awareness (also referred to as metacognition or reflection) to move between contexts rather than critique them. However, some theories, like DePalma and Ringer's (2014; 2011) adaptive transfer, account for how the dynamic process of repurposing knowledge plays out amidst the unstable power dynamics within an institution. Similarly, Nowacek (2011) offers a model of transfer that emphasizes using metarhetorical awareness not just as a tool for writing efficiency but also as a means for selling one's rhetorical choices in a new writing context that may or may not value a writer's chosen approach. Both of these orientations towards transfer can potentially be used to harness narratives of efficiency while also offering ways metarhetorical awareness can be used for resistance within new learning contexts rather than just encouraging only assimilation. By harnessing the convergence of efficiency and metarhetorical awareness, Studio can use transfer of learning theories as an avenue for story-changing work.

STORY-CHANGING WORK IN ACTION

Finding points of convergence necessitates grappling with local stories alongside national conversations. Writing programs contend with intersections of a multitude of stories, some of which may echo national stories and others which represent the positioning of the institution. In this section, we describe how this mix of stories played out at our university and how we, like Matzke and Garrett (this volume) and Ritola et al. (this volume), used available resources and discourses to develop and evolve our Studio program. Our goal in describing the interplay of narratives is to demonstrate how we negotiated these stories to begin our own Studio program.

HISTORY OF UNIVERSITY OF WASHINGTON TACOMA

At our institution, stories of efficiency played out within local stories of *excellence* and *access*. Our institution, the University of Washington Tacoma (UWT), is a small urban university that has historically promoted itself as providing quality, affordable education to an urban population. From its founding in 1990, UWT has narratively framed itself in mission documents as a regional university that sought to offer students *access to excellence*.

UWT's mission statement on diversity states that the university "seeks out and supports individuals who may experience barriers in gaining access to college" (UW Tacoma, 2015, sec. "Diversity"). UWT has taken its commitment to access seriously throughout its history and accepts students from a wide range of backgrounds and educational experiences. This move on the part of admissions has not been without controversy, and many faculty see this focus on access as a threat to the excellence promised by the institution. Students, both transfer and first-year, are commonly described as deficient, and professors find themselves teaching what they consider "remedial" skills to students who they thought should have entered college more prepared. In the meantime, the institution, for the sake of monetary efficiency, increased enrollment to compensate, further reinforcing the perception of an increase in "underprepared" students, many of whom are multilingual. As the mission statement promises, access would be coupled with support. In the current moment where efficiency and access appear to threaten excellence, Studio found a moment of interest convergence to capitalize on. While an increase in students helped with the budget, with limited support, students were struggling, leading to fewer tuition dollars in the long run. In this climate, Keown advocated for a studio course by harnessing the narratives of access, excellence, and efficiency.

PILOT STUDIO MODEL 1: DISCOURSE FOUNDATIONS

As the number of multilingual (ML) students has grown on our campus, so has a chorus of dichotomous, contentious narratives about ML writers at UWT. Multilingual writers add to "diversity," but they aren't "ready"; faculty complain that they don't have time to teach "language skills," but more often than not will grade on "perfect grammar." In piloting the first Studio, Keown found that the Studio soldered together the competing narratives of access, excellence, and efficiency. Discourse Foundations, a Studio conceived in response to the institutional inefficiencies faced by ML students at UWT, told a new story on campus: that the prerequisite to excellent academic writing for ML students is, in part, the explicit instruction of novice writers in the grammatical and lexical features of a new discourse.

In the spring of 2011, Keown, the staff TESOL specialist in UWT's Writing Center, proposed a Studio that specifically focused on the needs of ML novice academic writers. The concept for the course came out of Keown's concern that student struggles with grammar and vocabulary in academic discourse could not be addressed only by visits to the Writing Center. About one-third of UWT students are ML writers, but at the time Keown proposed the Studio, there were no courses with the stated goal of teaching the grammar and lexis of academic discourse. Though interaction and feedback in the Writing Center is a productive opportunity for ML writers to test their hypotheses about how English works (Aljaafreh & Long, 1994; Goldstein & Conrad, 1990), it was clear to Keown that the campus should be doing more to augment its support for ML writers. Thus, proposing the Studio capitalized on the convergence of student narratives and institutional interests.

It was (and remains) our conviction that offering credit for the study of academic language addresses the fairness gap that occurs when students are welcomed into academia as they are in accordance with the narrative of access and financial efficiency. However, written feedback from faculty signals that many of these writers do not meet faculty expectations of "excellence." Keown hoped that a studio model would promote the more efficient transfer of academic discourse knowledge, so that UWT could "stop punishing students for what they do not bring with them" (Matsuda, 2012, p. 155). Keown used the available discourse of efficiency to argue for serving ML students, thus contributing to excellence through the support that the Studio offered.

For many writers new to academia, especially non-native speakers of English, one of their most pressing needs is an orientation in the linguistic features of academic discourse (Hinkel, 2004; Holten & Mikesell, 2007). This pulling back of the veil on the lexical and grammatical details of academic writing is crucial work because students' relative lack of linguistic capital (Bourdieu, 1977, p. 657) plots for them a more treacherous course through the academy. Practically speaking, novice writers benefit from a tour guide through academic discourse, or what Powers (1993) referred to as a "cultural informant" (p. 41). A thirdspace specifically for ML writers, therefore, would profit from a facilitator trained in applied linguistics. For Keown, trained in TESOL, the focus on developing metarhetorical awareness through interactional inquiry naturally gravitated toward analysis of language features that academic writers use as a means to accomplish their rhetorical objectives. Leading students in this kind of inquiry necessitates facilitator awareness of the lexicogrammatical features of academic discourse, thereby engaging students in the noticing of those features with inductive teaching approaches, and prompting students to connect discourse conventions to their own writing.

The major challenge of the course, from Keown's perspective, was the lack of students' common, concurrent writing experiences. The Studio was not tied to any one course, so students came from a broad range of courses, some that required writing and some that did not, which made discussions of writing difficult. In addition, because the Studio was only offered as a two-credit course with no letter grades, Keown did not feel there would be sufficient student incentive to produce new writing; besides, the original idea was for students to improve writing external to the Studio. However, the disparate nature of student writing assignments in external courses, combined with no collaboration with the instructors of those courses, rendered the Studio difficult to manage. For Keown, those were the fundamental weaknesses in the course's design. Despite these weaknesses, the first iteration of the Studio confirmed that multilingual and novice writers at UWT can benefit from a studio that encourages interactional inquiry into academic discourse. Furthermore, Discourse Foundations helped to spark a shift away from the narrative at UWT that faulted multilingual writers for lacking college readiness towards a narrative about institutional responsibility to students beyond mere access. The momentum for Studio at UWT generated by this narrative shift is apparent in the subsequent growth and adaptation of Studio within the writing curriculum.

PILOT STUDIO MODEL 2: WRITING ACROSS THE CURRICULUM

During the 2011–2012 academic year, when Keown was developing and piloting the first sections of Discourse Foundations, Cardinal was in her first year as a full-time lecturer at UWT. Keown and Cardinal decided that she would develop a curriculum more targeted towards all students while Keown would continue his ML-targeted curriculum.

Cardinal's version of Studio could be taken by any student at any level, from freshman to senior, as long as they were enrolled in a writing-intensive (W) course. We thought offering the Studio to any student helped to change the narrative of the basic writer, since all writers, regardless of their experience, are novices when faced with unfamiliar writing contexts. It was our hope that this model would offer the support needed by freshmen and incoming transfer students, two of the groups that struggle the most as they transition into our university.

The curriculum also played into the institution's efficiency narrative, since we framed the two-credit class as a transitional course that would require minimal class time. We imagined a course where students of all levels could gain a deeper metarhetorical awareness of writing across the curriculum, experienced writers could mentor novices, and all would benefit from a weekly discussion of the wide variety of genres written in the academy. In the spring of 2012, Keown and Cardinal were able to convince the department to offer six sections of the Studio the following year, two each quarter.

Drawing on recent research on transfer of learning (Fraizer, 2010; Nowacek, 2011; Reiff & Bawarshi 2011; Wardle, 2007) Cardinal developed a studio model that was rooted in both studio principles and transfer of learning scholarship. This allowed her to capitalize on the story convergence of efficiency and metarhetorical awareness. She hoped that by designing a transfer-inspired model, the Studio could fulfill its promise of helping students more efficiently repurpose their prior writing knowledge. Cardinal developed several assignments that emphasized metarhetorical awareness, including a weekly reflective journal, along with a genre taxonomy in which students categorized the types of writing they have done in the past. Cardinal envisioned a utopic thirdspace marked by engagement, vitality, and co-construction of writing knowledge

(Winzenreid et al., 2017). She imagined a studio where one student brought a paper from psychology, another from biology, and yet another from a FYC course, and students collaborated to develop a deeper metarhetorical awareness of academic discourse.

What she did not anticipate was how much students' own ideals of efficiency would determine the effectiveness of the curriculum. Because 14 students self-selected to be in Studio, Cardinal assumed her students would be a highly engaged group. This was not the case. She found that efficiency narratives pervaded students' attitudes towards learning. Students thought workshopping was an *inefficient* use of time, and they were more concerned with their own projects and were not invested in the work of the other students. She thought students would be intrigued by the writing done in other disciplinary contexts, but in reality students saw discussions about an assignment in another discipline from their own as irrelevant or, at worst, a distraction from their own writing projects. The portfolios revealed that students were able to use principles from genre awareness to analyze their own work, but the engagement Cardinal tried to encourage through interactional inquiry was met with ambivalence. This problem occurred in part because Cardinal's utopic studio narrative diverged from student interests.

In winter quarter, five freshmen enrolled in Cardinal's section. Cardinal found that students' concurrent enrollment in FYC was vital to the Studio's successful functioning. With shared content, students saw interactional inquiry as an efficient use of their effort, and this convergence of interests led to a more fruitful writing community. This time around, Cardinal and her students did their own story-changing work by becoming more metarhetorically aware of how language in academia influenced the identities of learners. The winter course convinced Cardinal and Keown that WAC Studios are difficult to make successful because most students don't see the value in studying writing in other disciplines outside of their own.

In preparation for arguing for a more extensive studio program the coming year, Cardinal attended the 2013 Conference on College Composition and Communication, including the Studio Special Interest Group led by Rhonda Grego, to gain a better national perspective on the story-changing work around studios and basic writers currently under way. We found that conversing nationally with other studio activists provided an important way to discover which narrative strategies were effective for sustaining studios.

Ultimately, we decided to retool the Studio for freshmen to take with FYC to better negotiate the stories of efficiency coming from students and administrators. Because the problems of student engagement were a result of the Studio's placement in the curriculum, we made the argument that we needed a more coordinated rollout of the class for first-year students. In meetings with administrators, we argued that first-year students were the ones who would benefit the most from developing metarhetorical awareness since they would use this awareness for the remainder of their college career. We were able to capitalize on these converging interests with the hopes that Studio would accelerate the learning of freshmen while also helping with retention. Using the quantitative data provided by the ALP team that showed the model's efficiency, we were able to capitalize on this institutional exigency when making our case for a more expansive studio program.

STUDIO MODEL 3: FIRST-YEAR COMPOSITION

The administration asked Cardinal and Riki Thompson, an Associate Professor in the Writing Studies department, to design and roll out a writing support program for first-year students. The program had two components: a two-credit pre-autumn writing-intensive course and a Studio taken concurrently with FYC. Unlike ALP, each studio contained students from many FYC sections. We retained some elements of the WAC studio model by requiring students to bring in writing from all their courses. To avoid the stigma attached to support classes and help students make the best choice for themselves, UWT used Directed Self-Placement. With a total of around 400 incoming freshmen, 40 students chose the Studio that autumn.

Cardinal found that a smaller class size and linking the course to FYC improved the effectiveness of the Studio. Buy-in was higher due to the converging interests of students and studio leaders. Once students had common content, the interactional inquiry was more efficacious, and students were more willing to offer feedback on drafts to other students. The WAC portion of the Studio was also more effective. Because students were not yet solidified in a major, many students commented in their reflections how useful it was to investigate writing across the disciplines and that Studio gave them the opportunity to preview writing they would be doing in future disciplinary courses.

In the following year, Cardinal collaborated with several other writing faculty members to design a mixed methods assessment that engaged in story-changing work. By qualitatively describing metarhetorical awareness demonstrated in the portfolios, the assessment reframed basic writing students as novices on a journey to writing excellence. And following ALP's lead, we collected quantitative retention, which demonstrated the increased retention of students who took the basic writing sequence over those that did not. By combining qualitative with quantitative data, we gained a full picture of studio's impact on student learning and student success at UW Tacoma.

CONCLUSION

Our narrative illustrates how converging interests can help start and sustain a studio program. This requires attention to both local and national stories. From our experience, many of these points of interest convergence can be predicted prior to beginning a studio program by examining institutional discourse around support courses, including the statements by administrators, mission statements, and institutional histories that have local significance. As Ritola et al. (this volume) similarly argue, reading the "compositional situation" necessitates "attention to localized contexts as a necessary first step in studio design." We suggest, however, that certain points of convergence are applicable across most contexts. Transfer of learning provides a nexus of convergence between Studios and efficiency narratives that every institution could employ for story-changing work. Because the transfer of writing ability across contexts is a fundamental justification for the existence of all writing courses and programs regardless of context, studio activists would benefit from its use. Acceleration, in contrast, is more institution-specific. This convergence is most likely more applicable to public, access-oriented institutions like our own where shortening the developmental pipeline is state or institutionally-mandated (Ritola et al., this volume).

Our narrative also points to the necessity of attention to the material conditions alongside the discursive as the basis of story-changing work. In our particular context, the story-changing work was targeted towards administrators and students. Because there was no established basic writing program at UW Tacoma at the time, we did not face the challenge of having to argue for a change in pre-existing courses. We also had the advantage of having a relatively stable workforce who, while contingent, held full-time contracted positions, which other authors in this volume did not (Matzke & Garrett, this volume; Fraizer, this volume). In other contexts, more energy might be needed to story-change with faculty more so than administrators. Placement into studios also emerges in this volume as a local issue (Fraizer, this volume; Santana et al., this volume). We encourage special attention to the stories that placement tells about students (Hassel et al., 2016). Without creating a carefully-crafted placement mechanism, Studio risks reinscribing students as deficient even as third-space principles require studio activists to do the opposite (Gutierrez, Rymes & Larson, 1995).

It is important to note, however, that studio activists cannot perfectly predict all the stories they will encounter. As several chapters in this volume emphasize, studio activists must be attuned to the kairotic moments and exigencies that emerge and nimbly seize on those opportunities (Matzke & Garrett, this volume). Matzke and Garrett describe this process as *bricolage* where studio program developers piece together discursive and material resources for development of Studio as they emerge. While we recognize that not every institution has the luxury of trying out several models due to administrative structures and local resources, the unanticipated kairotic moments point to the importance of piloting a studio to account for the dynamic landscape of shifting interests. Running several models allowed us to examine the points of divergence that affected the impact of studio work and make adjustments before rolling out our FYC studio program.

As a final note, it's important to emphasize that this story-changing work is never finished but is an ongoing process that is continuously negotiated over time. Interests of institutions are in flux and shift depending on economic, political, and ideological circumstances. And while we have so far described interests between administrators and studio programs, campus-wide interests are much more complex. We must contend with a network of interests held by disciplinary faculty, students, and other writing faculty. With a strategic approach, however, we can feel empowered to pursue studio agendas on our campuses using interest convergence to engage in story-changing work.

REFERENCES

Adams, P. (2013, March). *Thinking our way toward a pedagogy for basic writing.* Paper presented at the meeting of the Conference on College Composition and Communication, Las Vegas, NV.

Adams, P., Gearhart, S., Miller, R. & Roberts, A. (2009). The accelerated learning program: Throwing open the gates. *Journal of Basic Writing, 18*(2), 50–69.

Adler-Kassner, L. (2008). *The activist WPA: Changing stories about writing and writers.* Logan, UT: Utah State University Press.

Aljaafreh, A. & Lantolf, J. P. (1994). Negative feedback as regulation and second language learning in the zone of proximal development. *The Modern Language Journal, 78*(4), 465–483.

Beaufort, A. (2007). *College writing and beyond: A new framework for university writing instruction.* Logan, UT: Utah State University Press.

Bell, D. (2004). *Silent covenants: Brown v. Board of Education and the unfulfilled hopes for racial reform.* Oxford, UK: Oxford University Press.

Bergmann, L. & Zepernick, J. (2007). Disciplinarity and transfer: Students' perceptions of learning to write. *WPA: Writing Program Administration, 31*(1–2), 124–149.

Bourdieu, P. (1977). The economics of linguistic exchanges. *Social Science Information, 16*(6), 645–668.

The Community College of Baltimore County. (n.d.). *The Accelerated Learning Program.* Retrieved from http://alp-deved.org.

DePalma, M. J. & Ringer, J. M. (2011). Toward a theory of adaptive transfer: Expanding disciplinary discussions of "transfer" in second-language writing and composition studies. *Journal of Second Language Writing, 20*(2), 134–147.

DePalma, M. J. & Ringer, J. M. (2014). Adaptive transfer, writing across the curriculum, and second language writing: Implications for research and teaching. In M. Cox & T. Zawacki (Eds.), *WAC and second language writers: Towards linguistically and culturally inclusive programs and practices* (pp. 43–67). Fort Collins, CO: The WAC Clearinghouse and Parlor Press/Boulder, CO: University Press of Colorado. Retrieved from https://wac.colostate.edu/books/perspectives/l2/.

Fraizer, D. (2010). First steps beyond first year: Coaching transfer after FYC. *Writing Program Administration, 33*(3), 34–57.

Glau, G. (1996). The "stretch" program: Arizona State University's new model of university-level basic writing instruction. *WPA: Writing Program Administration, 20*(1–2), 79–91.

Goldstein, L. & Conrad, S. (1990). Student input and negotiation of meaning in ESL writing conferences. *TESOL Quarterly, 24*, 443–460.

Grego, R. & Thompson, N. (1996). Repositioning remediation: Renegotiating composition's work in the academy. *College Composition and Communication, 47*(1), 62–84.

Grego, R. & Thompson, N. (2008). *Teaching/writing in thirdspaces: The studio approach*. Carbondale, IL: Southern Illinois University Press.

Gutierrez, K., Rymes, B. & Larson, J. (1995). Script, counterscript, and underlife in the classroom: James Brown versus Brown v. Board of Education. *Harvard Educational Review, 65*(3), 445–472.

Hassel, H., Klausman, J, Toth, C., Swyt, W., Griffiths, B., Sullivan, P. & Roberts, L. (2016). TYCA White Paper on Placement Reform. *Teaching English in the Two-Year College, 44*(1), 135–157. Retrieved from http://www.ncte.org/library/NCTEFiles/Resources/Journals/TETYC/0423-mar2015/TETYC0423White.pdf.

Haswell, R. (2000). Documenting improvement in college writing: A longitudinal approach. *Written Communication, 17*(1), 307–352.

Hinkel, E. (2004). *Teaching academic ESL writing: Practical techniques in vocabulary and grammar*. Mahwah, N.J.: Lawrence Erlbaum Associates.

Holland, K. (2013, November 11). Why Johnny can't write, and why employers are mad. *CNBC*. Retrieved from http: //www.cnbc.com/id/101176249.

Holten, C. & Mikesell, L. (2007). Using discourse-based strategies to address the lexicogrammatical development of generation 1.5 ESL writers. *The CATESOL Journal, 19*(1), 35–52.

Horner, B. & Lu, M. (1999). *Representing the "other": Basic writers and the teaching of basic writing*. Urbana, IL: National Council of Teachers of English.

Lamos, S. (2011). *Interests and opportunities: Race, racism, and university writing instruction in the post-Civil Rights era*. Pittsburgh, PA: University of Pittsburgh Press.

Leef, G. (2013, Dec 11). For 100K, you would at least think college grads could write. *Forbes.com*. Retrieved from https://www.forbes.com/sites/georgeleef/2013/12/11/for-100k-you-would-at-least-think-that-college-grads-could-write/.

Matsuda, P. K. (2012). Let's face it: Language issues and the writing program adminis-trator. *WPA: Writing Program Administration, 36*(1), 141–163.

Nowacek, R. (2011). *Agents of integration: Understanding transfer as a rhetorical act.* Carbondale, IL: Southern Illinois University Press.

Powers, J. K. (1993). Rethinking writing center conferencing strategies for the ESL writer. *The Writing Center Journal, 13*(2), 39–47.

Reiff, M. J. & Bawarshi, A. (2011). Tracing discursive resources: How students use prior genre knowledge to negotiate new writing contexts in first-year composition. *Written Communication, 28*(3), 312–337.

Ritter, K. (2009). *Before Shaughnessy: Basic writing at Yale and Harvard, 1920–1960.* Carbondale, IL: Southern Illinois University Press.

Sommers, N. & Saltz, L. (2004). The novice as expert: Writing the freshman year. *College Composition and Communication, 56*(1), 124–149.

Sternglass, M. (1997). *Time to know them: A longitudinal study of writing and learning at the college level.* London, UK: Routledge.

Tassoni, J. P. & Lewiceki-Wilson, C. (2005). Not just anywhere, anywhen: Mapping change through studio work. *Journal of Basic Writing, 24*(1), 68–92.

University of Washington-Tacoma Office of the Chancellor. (2015). *Mission, values and vison.* Retrieved from https://www.tacoma.uw.edu/chancellor/mission-values-and-vision.

Wardle, E. (2007). Understanding "transfer" from FYC: Preliminary results of a longi-tudinal study. *Writing Program Administration, 31*(1–2), 65–85.

Warnick, C., Cooney, E. & Lacky, S. (2010). Beyond the budget: Sustainability and writing studios. *Journal of Basic Writing, 29*(2), 74–96.

Winzenried, M., Campbell, L., Chao, R. & Cardinal, A. (2017). Co-constructing writing knowledge: Students' collaborative talk across contexts. *Composition Forum, 37.*

Williamson, M. (1994) The worship of efficiency: Untangling theoretical and practi-cal considerations in writing assessment. In B. Huot & P. O'Neill (Eds.), *Assessing writing: A critical sourcebook* (pp. 57–80). Boston, MA: Bedford/St. Martin's.

Yancey, K. B., Robertson, L. & Taczak, K. (2014). *Writing across contexts: Transfer, composition, and sites of writing.* Logan, UT: Utah State University Press.

CHAPTER 3.

STUDIO BRICOLAGE: INVENTING WRITING STUDIO PEDAGOGY FOR LOCAL CONTEXTS

Aurora Matzke and Bre Garrett
Contributors: Kelsey Huizing and Justin McCoy
Biola University and University of West Florida

In this chapter, two new Writing Program Administrators (WPAs), from very different universities, collaborate with studio facilitators to describe surprisingly similar experiences starting up studio programs. We argue that studio designers must perform as bricoleurs: interacting with community stakeholders, accumulating resources from different locations, and situating claims and appeals within local discourses. We use bricolage concepts of "uptake" and "not talk" to investigate our institutional studio narratives. While the two experiences contain moments of overlap, we also point out the nuances and different moves we made in order to "sell" studio curricula at our institutions.

Aurora and Bre are both newly hired WPAs at universities on opposite U.S. coasts. Aurora serves as co-director of the English Writing Program at Biola University, a small, private university in southern California; Bre directs the Composition Program at the University of West Florida (UWF), a mid-size, public university in Florida. Both Aurora and Bre accepted positions as WPAs right out of their Ph.D. programs, and both launched studio curricula in the first years of their jobs. Neither of their studio experiences easily aligned with studio best practices, and both required considerable negotiation, re-purposing, re-identifying, and transformation of locally available first-year writing models.

As we write, contributors Kelsey Huizing and Justin McCoy serve, respectively, as a Teaching Assistant at Biola and as an Instructor at UWF. Kelsey and Justin write as facilitators of Writing Studio classes. Narratives from all three perspectives (WPA, Teaching Assistant, and Instructor) allow us to uniquely highlight moments of bricolage from multiple perspectives. The multiplicity of viewpoints provides a view of Studio that is fairly unique to *The Writing Studio Sampler*. Ultimately, we hope our contribution highlights an array of possible moves for the plethora of stakeholders involved in most studio ventures.

Throughout this chapter, we document both administrative and pedagogical practices that illustrate how we continue to work within situated constraints to invent studio models particular to our respective local contexts.

STUDIO AND BRICOLAGE IN THEORY

An allocated writing environment, such as Studio, can provide a place that enables students to identify themselves as writers and to work with differences among home, school, and civic communities. In this volume, Alison Cardinal and Kelvin Keown provide a succinct overview of the liberatory potential of studio spaces, while acknowledging through Grego and Thompson "that this counter-hegemonic studio narrative comes into conflict with the narratives of institutions concerned with 'buildings and budgets.'" Consequently, how might teachers and administrators imagine sustainable physical realities for these studio spaces? As called for in the work of Cardinal and Keown, we hope our use of bricolage, as a practical theoretical frame to apply to Studio and the ways teachers and administrators engage in facilitator training, course design, marketing, classroom pedagogy, and program assessment, might begin the work of "strategically tell[ing] the story of studio work to administrators and students" (this volume).

At both institutions, studio development emerged at moments of kairos and exigence—key components of administrative uptake. By kairotic moments, we mean opportunities that arise that may be beyond the scope of one's originally identified goals and objectives. By exigence, we mean an articulated need or demand for change, system-wide—many of the chapters within this collection make note of such opportunities often being connected to Studio (Cardinal & Keown; Gray; Leach & Kuhne; Ritola et al.; and Santana, Rose & LaBarge). At UWF, for example, opportunities arose for faculty and programs to receive retention funding. At Biola, writing faculty were abandoning a potential studio site, while campus conversations focused on accreditation concerns related to writing, critical thinking, and information literacy abounded. Consequently, these curricular openings, combined with administrative focus, allowed for positive redirections in campus writing practice.

As a theoretical grounding for invention, bricolage was first defined and related to knowledge acquisition by Claude Levi-Strauss (1972) in *The Savage Mind,* and further investigated by Jacques Derrida (1978), and Gilles Deleuze and Félix Guattari (1984). Christopher Wibberley (2012), Cynthia Selfe and Dickie Selfe (1994), and Rebecca Nowacek (2013) offer some of the more recent work on bricolage in institutional landscapes. Wibberley agrees with Levi-

Strauss, Derrida, and others when he states bricolage "starts with what is at hand/what is available" (2012, p. 3). He further argues that, "[w]ith academic bricolage . . . the consideration of the process by which the bricolage is built—however emergent—is an important aspect of the overall work. This process must be articulated, both in terms of the 'mechanisms' of production and also in terms of any philosophical approach underpinning its production" (2012, p. 6). Wibberley's focus on "the consideration of the process" allows us, as authors, to more objectively view the work we've undertaken at our respective institutions. What might be viewed as a piecemeal approach to institutional intervention is, on further reflection, seen as a negotiation of local opportunities. Bricolage, then, becomes a useful frame for the sometimes baffling and complicated web of educational affordances present at many institutions. In other words, before change can take place, one must note what is available.

In "Politics of the Interface," Cynthia L. Selfe and Richard J. Selfe (1994) identify bricolage as a means by which computer designers "can support alternative approaches to constructing meaning" (p. 493). Drawing on Turkle and Papert, Selfe and Selfe specify that the construction of meaning happens through "the arrangement and rearrangement of concrete, well known materials, often in an intuitive rather than logical manner" and "by interacting with [a subject] physically" (1994, p. 493). Such "well known materials," in curricular design, constitute project discourse; course and institutional histories; policies; location in the form of buildings and spaces; pedagogies; and a range of students, teachers, administrators, and staff. Studio opportunities may thus not proceed from a strongly articulated plan outlined by major university stakeholders. Instead, arrangement schemes may arise from the "physical" interactions of the stakeholders in the available institutional spaces.

In her 2013 Conference on College Composition and Communication address, "Transfer as Bricolage: Assembling Genre Knowledge Across Contexts," Nowacek defined bricolage much as Wibberley. She also argued bricolage occurs through a negotiation of "uptake" and "not talk." Uptake happens when bricoleurs first examine "what is at hand" before deciding what will be useful, or "taking up" the available means. For example, when Bre arrived at UWF, retention discussions were already underway; she was able to "uptake" retention concerns in her studio initiative. During this time of "uptake," bricoleurs spend a significant amount of time theoretically and practically engaged in "not talk": defining what is *not* useful, needed, or wanted. For Aurora, "not talk" occurred when instructors discussed their frustrations with the lack of structure in the potential studio space. "Not talk" allows organizers to locate clarity and exigence that rest separately from pre-established norms. We found ourselves defining what Studio is not while reaching out to make connections with established programs at our universities. As practitioners, we are not willing to be stymied by arguments that overly simplify studio practices, purposes, and the individuals making use of the courses; thus, we must engage in "not talk" in order to clarify our goals.

When participating in "on the ground" course design, curricular designers must look, as Wibberley (2013) and Selfe and Selfe (1994) argue, to the available means and physical affordances of production. Before action takes place, steady uptake enables bricoleurs to survey "what is at hand" (a neglected course in Aurora's case, a retention initiative in Bre's) prior to assessing usefulness or outcome. During "uptake," one must reflexively practice "not talk" (solid learning was not occurring in Aurora's case; students were not getting enough support in Bre's), identifying what is *not* useful, needed, or wanted (Nowacek, 2013). Uptake is a collaborative, hands-on process that requires one to, quite literally, traverse the physical landscape and become intimately familiar with campus resources (Selfe & Selfe, 1994). In our work, we use Nowacek's concepts of "uptake" and "not talk" to help us define "the mechanisms of production" operating in both institutional contexts. Through "not talk," bricoleur administrators are able to find openings for "uptake" that acknowledge joint purposes with other programs, misidentified or misused resources already in place, and/or new practices in line with university goals or missions. Another place to view the type of studio emergence that may be connected with bricolage is that described by Dan Fraizer within "Navigating Outside the Mainstream" (this volume). Fraizer outlines similar moments that could be labeled as "not talk" and uptake at his own institution—Studio is not remedial nor basic (the "not talk"); Springfield needed someone to assist struggling writers (the uptake).

Bricolage also functions as a theoretical frame to define studio pedagogical approaches. Organizers can shapeshift studio curricula depending upon the model that most suits local contexts, learning outcomes, and student needs; Studio "is not limited to a course per se but is a configuration of relationships that can emerge from different contexts" (Grego & Thompson, 2008, p. 7). The main purpose of studio curricula is a central and extensive one-on-one focus on writing instruction, but what this looks like and how it fits within a university curriculum may significantly differ.

STARTING THE YEAR AT A NEW LOCATION: OPENINGS FOR NEW INITIATIVES, NEW COMMUNITIES

Joining new university communities may open opportunities for designing and reshaping writing pedagogy and writing culture, something both Aurora and Bre experienced. In addition, our initial work to make a case for Studio transpired quite smoothly, because we framed our purposes within university initiatives and discourses. For Bre, university-wide attention toward retention efforts created prime opportunities for administrators to listen to and try out new programs centered on student learning. Bre's experiences resonate with Christina Santana, Shirley K. Rose and Robert LaBarge's (this volume).

While new, young, feminist WPAs might wish to pause, watch, and gather intel during their first years, we jumped to take advantage of institutional momentum for communal, positive change. Yet even in the face of opportunity, we worked to remember two pieces of advice and one overwhelming truth. The advice: 1) New program development always requires "cost-analysis," and 2) Opportunities are most successfully crafted from local sites of flux best known by those with on-the-ground experience. The overwhelming truth: As a new WPA, it's impossible to perform a strong cost-analysis, and you have little to no local experience.

While building relationships constitutes a survival skill for how WPAs become part of institutional communities, it does not always happen without tension and the acknowledgement of differences, which is where uptake and not-talk come into play. We strove to channel new relationships into mutual partnerships and alliances, a rhetorical task that involves a combination of spontaneous decision making and goal shifting, deliberate cross-campus conversations, professional development, and WPA work boldly and loudly cast as "intellectual and scholastic activity." For Aurora, this relationship building needed to occur at a grassroots level: The time and money were there, but no one understood how to use them. These actions required a quickly established ethos predicated on relational uptake. Credibility intricately links to and evolves from relationship building and a keen awareness of time and moment. This situational preparedness is most aptly demonstrated in this volume by Santana, Rose, and LaBarge. Somewhat differently for Aurora and Bre, they were new to their home institutions. Yes, starting/rejuvenating programs at our new institutions could have been risky, if we attempted to assert dominance in these spaces, instead of promoting a model of shared responsibility. Sure, we could have lost funding. However, as students with need were already underserved at our new homes, there was much more to gain—even in fits and starts—than there was to lose.

For us, seizing these opportunities was the first step toward actively embracing bricolage. In the following section, we provide detailed narrative accounts of our positionalities in order to show "not talk" and "uptake" overlaps and differences among positionalities and between institutions, providing a Venn-like opening with which others might situate differing university contexts.

SITUATED NARRATIVES AND INSTITUTIONAL CONTEXTS

SMALL, PRIVATE, LIBERAL-ARTS UNIVERSITY—AURORA'S STORY

When I arrived at Biola's roughly 4,000-student campus, tucked up against the hills of La Mirada, California, I understood my job was to work as a Co-Director of the English Writing Program (EWP). The EWP included two courses taught to all incoming students in their first and second semesters. These courses were called "Critical Thinking and Writing I" and "Critical Thinking and Writing II." Yet, I noticed something curious during my first semester. There was another course with "Critical Thinking and Writing" in the title—ENGL 100.

At Biola, the accelerated-stretch composition (ASC) course, ENGL 100, arose over a decade ago out of a perceived need related to student preparedness. The ASC courses carried the same units toward graduation as the non-stretch, but with twice as much course time set aside. A non-stretch course meets twice a week for two-and-a-half hours of instruction; the stretch meets for five hours spread out over a four-day period. Different than most "intensive English courses" designed almost exclusively for English language learners, students are placed in ENGL 100 if they have SAT/ACT scores lower than Biola's cutoff for reading and writing, are in the completion stages of the university's intensive English program, are returning to the institution after a long absence from school, are ear-marked by administrators as needing "extra assistance," or self-select as wanting additional time with an instructor. In other words, the population is highly mixed for reasons that aren't entirely clear or in line with best practices in writing instruction. My impression upon entering the university? The course worked as a "catch-all."

The other interesting wrinkle: ASC courses were taught exclusively by part-time faculty and undergraduate teaching assistants (TAs). The part-timers would teach two of the four meeting times, and a TA would teach the other two. In addition, the same semester I began to investigate ENGL 100, or "Basic Studies in Critical Thinking and Writing," the veteran adjuncts teaching the course moved to graduate programs and/or different work. Consequently, only brand new teachers—all without formal post-secondary training in the teaching of writing, let alone work with students deemed "at risk" by the university—were assigned to ENGL 100. If the part-time faculty were not prepared, the level of preparedness for the TAs assigned to ENGL 100 was even sparser. I immediately thought, "Could this be studio space?"

Learning about studio pedagogy from John Tassoni while earning my doctorate taught me the importance of investigating university purposes with first-year students outside and alongside first-year writing. At the same time, I knew that the small, one-unit courses with links to a unified first-year writing curriculum, courses like I taught while at Miami University, were not necessarily going to be the norm. And, I might have to undertake a long, hard climb before reaching a place where Studio could exist at my new home. It wasn't as if money was falling out of the sky for new program development. That's why, when I discovered space might indeed be available in our first-year curricula for Studio to start, I got creative.

Being a new WPA with the only composition and rhetoric degree on my campus has allowed me curious constraints and freedoms. In the case of Studio, the freedom came to the fore. Championing a failing course by shifting it to an approach my colleagues not only did not know how to do, but had never even heard of, could have been disastrous. Yet, thanks to everyone's good spirits, a firm focus on student development, a solid co-director, and willingness to compromise and adapt to current availabilities, Studio was able to emerge as a new, theoretically sound, life-affirming option for a population of students and faculty slowly being forgotten by the university. The change happened quietly, without fanfare, within the confines of a pre-existing budget. We just *shifted* the discourse.

Kairotic Intervention

I started by sitting in the part-time faculty meeting area and the English Department office, catching instructors on their way to their mailboxes and when they were in their office hours. I made sure to identify and engage the current TAs in "water-cooler" talk about their teaching experiences. I had these conversations in informal spaces—where my own power position was less, if at all, established. I never called anyone to my office, nor formally requested any meetings. I found that, overall, no one was happy with the current system, and many weren't interested in continuing to support or participate in the teaching of the course.

In my conversations with the new part-time faculty teaching ENGL 100, instructors and TAs stated they were not sure what to do with the extra time. Instructors felt their TAs, due to a lack of training and closeness in age with the students, could work as quiet-time monitors at worst, or grill-and-drill instructors at best. The TAs expressed feelings of anxiety and frustration during talks. Common themes of disinterested students, lack of attendance, and confusion regarding class rolls often emerged. In all, the teachers and TAs were looking for a way to make better use of the extended classroom time for sections; they knew they were losing their audience, and they didn't know what to do about it.

Not Talk

The main contention was a call for structure: to make the time and effort students put into the course as useful to them as possible. In fact, even though teaching ENGL 100 came with an extra unit of pay, two of the new instructors chose not to continue teaching the course. Here was what Nowacek (2013) identified as the "not talk" of bricolage. The instructors knew that what they were doing in ENGL 100 was *not* what they wanted for student engagement and interaction, was *not* serving the students well, and was *not* helping them develop into better teachers. The TAs also frequently engaged in "not talk" as they shared their experiences. The students were *not* interacting with them in ways they thought were positive, nor were the students respectful or open with the TAs, nor did the TAs feel like they understood how exactly to fix this situation. The "not talk" established that a pattern of behaviors was occurring that no one wanted and provided an opening for change. After the conversations, I asked the scheduling administrator to sign me up to teach the one, off-cycle course of ENGL 100 offered in the spring, and I asked the TA who seemed most interested in additional training, Kelsey, if she would like to try out studio pedagogy with me.

Resituating Available Materials for Uptake

In order to pilot the first Studio in spring 2013, Kelsey and I had to move quickly. Our initial conversations about curriculum plans began in October of 2012 with a projected class implementation of January 2013. In our conversations, Kelsey shared her experiences with me, and I shared my studio dreams with her. We took time to read studio texts together over winter break and crafted lesson plans to allow TA sessions to be governed by a mix of studio and workshop pedagogies. We took our knowledge of what was and wasn't working and shifted to a pattern of "uptake," asking, "What do we know about previous experiences that did work (assignments and activities the TA could remember were used to good effect)? What were we reading in studio texts that created positive results for others (hosting discussions about the purposes of the course in relation to larger university goals about whole-self education)? And, what were our local constraints that we could turn to our advantage (such as the highly diverse student body)?" Kelsey and I took time to talk and dream together before getting down to the brass tacks of course implementation, because I wanted to make sure ownership of Studio was happening from the ground up.

Once the course began, we debriefed after every class session, and we both kept teaching journals of our progress and understanding of the students. To plumb student understanding and experience, we held small group instructional diagnostics, or SGIDs, and we asked students to participate in anonymous surveys. The course—from the perspectives of Kelsey, the students, and me—was a success. Kelsey told others what a turnaround had occurred with the new curriculum, and other instructors saw students as they walked to and from my office and interacted with one another in the halls, noticing they had generally happy, upbeat expressions on their faces. These new watercooler moments resulted in one long-term adjunct offering to help teach ENGL 100, and a new adjunct excitedly volunteering to join in the project.

Seizing the Moment

We are now in the process of leading a team of three instructors and three TAs in the new studio courses. With a research study underway that includes interviews with students, portfolio evaluation and analysis of students' written reflections, we hope to demonstrate and validate the need for Writing Studio with mixed qualitative and quantitative data that should be persuasive to audiences outside of the department.

Although Kelsey and I are happy with our small successes, this is by no means a hero narrative. While student reflections and questionnaires from the pilot semester underscore how helpful and affirming students found the brico-lage take on studio pedagogy, as we move forward, I worry about sustainability and assessment. Resources, teacher-mentoring, and time are all already stretched too thin on a shoestring budget. My work as a bricoleur isn't finished; I must continue to engage in "not talk" and uptake, working to repurpose and honor the contributions of others who may not share my training or perspectives.

ON THE GROUND PREPARATION AT BIOLA—KELSEY'S STORY

I had received no training prior to walking into the classroom as a teacher's as-sistant for two courses. One day, on the walk to start class, my cooperating pro-fessor handed me article printouts she wanted me to go over with the students. I had no foundational understanding of the topic that I was teaching, and I did not understand how I was supposed to connect the materials to the overarching project the students were working on. Ten minutes painfully ticked by on the clock, as I tried to skim through the handout and still be social with the class. Once I officially began the session, we read through the piece together, before I asked the students to write about how they thought the article applied to their current essay assignment. When finished, the students discussed their answers in groups. It was a class of 12, and they were mostly English-Language Learner stu-dents, which led to a short discussion. By the time we completed my impromptu lesson, 30 minutes of class time remained. I had no idea what to do. We ended up talking about current football team statistics before grinding to a halt fifteen minutes early. This was not the only time a scenario like this played out.

Calling the class sessions ineffective is an understatement. I fumbled through the content because I was not confident in my own abilities, and there was no apparent structure to the class. Many days, most of the class would be wasted on conversation that had no apparent correlation with our scheduled topic. If I made it through a session alive, I considered it a success. However, my preparedness and the lack of understanding I had about my role weren't the only issues.

There was also a disconnect with students. Students were frequently disinterested in the content that I was trying to teach them and rarely asked for any type of assistance inside or outside the class setting. I was seen as a peer with no right to any kind of authority or, sometimes, respect. This only became more apparent as the semester progressed. Once, a student tried to sneak out by crawling across the floor. These hectic, first-semester snapshots of my experience highlight many different problems that I encountered on a daily basis: disrespect, lack of communication, lack of punctuality, and unpreparedness. The difficulties I describe here were not necessarily immediately solved through Studio, but studio pedagogy has definitely changed my experiences as a TA, and the experiences of the students, for the better.

Constantly Communicate

Every interaction with Aurora embodied what Studio is about—communication. Weeks before I began the studio course, she made sure that I was properly trained and that I clearly understood what my role in the classroom would be. I always felt like my opinion and teaching experiences were heard and validated. Because Aurora modeled what proper communication looked like, I was able to carry that model into my studio work.

Studio group is a time of trial and error: a place where students engage in not-talk and uptake without the fear of embarrassment. At the start of the semester, many students would preface a question with, "this may be a dumb or stupid question, but . . ." However, as the semester progressed, students slowly stopped prefacing their questions and began to allow the class to interact with their ideas, opinions, and queries at face value. In studio space, they were able to be raw and real human beings. They did not have to be successful, completely composed students. They could be frustrated or tired; these emotions were treated as suitable and normal feelings. Studio allows students to be upfront about their struggles, and it also presents a space where they can come alongside each other—either to find or give help to work through university requirements.

The most successful moments in Studio are when students practice uptake, when they realize how what we do connects back to the class' purpose. In the words of a current student, "Oh . . . so studio groups are supposed to help us be successful in whatever projects we are doing in this class?" To us, the educators, this seems obvious. But when students have breakthroughs like this, Studio is truly successful. When students learn to make connections and conclusions on their own, they have learned a skill they can apply to any class, job, problem, or situation they face in life.

REGIONAL, COMPREHENSIVE STATE UNIVERSITY—BRE'S STORY

Nestled on 1,600 acres in the northwest part of the state, University of West Florida (UWF) serves just over 13,000 undergraduate and graduate students. When I joined the Composition Program at UWF, one of my first anticipated actions was to implement Writing Studio. I aimed to increase the presence and visibility of writing intensive courses—a personal objective fueled by the university's charge to "reform writing." As a new community member and a brand new WPA, I knew I must couch any proposed changes in collaboration and research.

When I arrived, the Composition Program at UWF primarily consisted of two first-year Composition courses: ENC 1101 (Introduction to Academic Writing and Research) and ENC 1102 (Public Writing). I quickly discovered frustration and general discontent with student writing among my colleagues. This led me to wonder how I might start the process of transforming this culture of writing. How might I employ the bricolage methods of "uptake" and "not-talk" to switch the conversation from students' "lack" in writing skills to a "lack" of curricular writing support? One answer to these questions was to create a trial course, ENC 1990 (Writing Studio), a one-hour elective that functioned as an intensive, small group writing workshop.

Rather than spend time meticulously making a case for course implementation, planning course design, acquiring sustainable resources, and settling institutional logistics, I opted for learning through doing and action. In less than three months from my arrival at UWF, I offered the brand-new studio course as a three-semester pilot study. I used the pilot to accumulate the data I would use to propose an official course. Some may argue that more time was needed for advertising, securing stakeholder buy-in, and researching local needs. I do not disagree, yet I found extreme value in using a pilot study as a grassroots pedagogical exploration.

Uptake, Examining What Is at Hand

To explore possibilities for offering writing studio courses in spring 2013, I began by conducting informal, localized research that would determine *who* constituted studio audience(s) and *what* model or course design would most benefit UWF students. I spent weeks listening, observing, and socializing to identify available material, physical, and discursive resources. I attended open faculty forums and workshops sponsored by groups like The Center for Teaching, Learning, and Assessment; focus group discussions about the university's Quality Enhancement Plan and about university assessment demands; and "faculty happy hours" and Friday "Faculty Social Hour" sessions.

Through these communal engagements, I pieced together important facts about my campus: high power stakeholders prefer to be in the know about significant curricular changes; university advisors must be fully informed, as they are the sounding-boards between students and course endorsements; composition faculty need to feel included in the decision-making process; scholarship and aide students at UWF cannot always find space for *elective* hours in already tight schedules; classes with "low enrollments" are at-risk of getting cut; and university initiatives often involve student retention concerns.

Uptake Translates into Not-talk

In my fall 2012 conversations, colleagues across campus expressed disparate expectations regarding "good writing." I needed to set the program apart from any sort of "remediation" space. UWF, as part of the State University System of Florida, does not offer any remediation courses. While Studio, in general, has a history of helping writers marked as "basic" (in whatever way that term is used), Studio is not a stand-alone basic writing class. Part of my administrative approach included defining and positioning Studio as an elective curricular space, a workshop space, in which students investigate writing processes and rhetorical knowledges. I next reached out to the Committee on Retention Efforts (CORE), a task force offering financial support for curriculum designed to increase student retention. Listing the course was easy, yet sustainable curricular and pedagogical development evolved at a more gradual pace and less linear trajectory.

Seizing the Uptake Opportunity

Studio emerged at a kairotic campus moment, when the university shifted attention from increased enrollment to retention. Similar to the argument Ritola et al. make in this collection, timing is very much a part of studio curricular design, the launching and implementation and the sustained support. The administrative environment was particularly financially supportive of curricular ideas framed around "high impact learning" for first-year students. I attended meetings in which speakers discussed national data that links student success to the grades they earn in first-year composition. Students who pass first-year core courses in math and writing are more likely to return to the institution their second year. Therefore, I cast the class as a curriculum that would increase "first-to-second year retention rates." The class is small and the offerings few. Here arose a tension between theory and practice that I would consistently encounter.

Building Relationships through Course Design

With retention in the spotlight, I returned to my department to identify a teacher-collaborator and secure a cross-community partnership to attain university buy-in and, if possible, funding. A veteran adjunct faculty member, Justin

McCoy, expressed interest in teaching the course. Justin and I partnered with the Director of Student Success Programs (SSP) to offer a section of Writing Studio designated for TRIO students.[1] We worked closely with SSP to organize what would become a non-traditional studio model. The SSP Dean graciously provided us a teaching space and funded our initiative by offering to pay the instructor. However, to use TRIO grant money, the course instruction had to be characterized as "supplemental," meaning the class could not run as an official course. We feared, as a result, the course would carry connotations of a tutoring space rather than a space of robust production and revision. We would have to offer the course as a true "third space."

During spring 2013, we ran a pilot study of two sections of ENC 1990 Writing Studio. One section was listed on the course registration and granted students one credit hour and a letter grade; the second section was off-the-books and reserved for TRIO students. For the catalog section, students officially enrolled in the course and therefore had a personal incentive to arrive and participate. However, because we offered the TRIO section without any credit hours or grade affiliation, students lacked motivation to participate. In this volume, Santana et al. offer a compelling narrative regarding a studio that relies on Directed Self Placement. However, with an optional attendance policy, only two students attended the UWF Studio and attendance was not always consistent. Unfortunately, even though we believed as Santana et al., who contend, "optional studio classes therefore serve to allow greater scheduling flexibility for students and to demonstrate innovation and efficiency," we found, like them, that optional attendance and a lack of grades caused learning barriers for some students. In addition, because this section was not officially listed, we could not include these two students in our quantitative assessment data.

While the second section was open enrollment, advisors did not receive enough notice to properly advertise the course to students. When the semester began, only three students had registered, but within the first two weeks, two more students began to attend, making a total enrollment of five. Three of the students were first-years co-enrolled in ENC 1101 or 1102; two students were beyond their first year. In addition, two students were ELL learners from Brazil. Despite enrollment issues, the courses assisted the students. The once-a-week class session gave students repeated and consistent opportunities for deep reflection; collaborative, small group learning and sharing; and across the curriculum writing instruction.

---

1   TRIO is a federal outreach program often housed within Student Success Programs. Its mission centers around retention and graduation of program participants and offers financial and tutorial assistance to students identified as at-risk of leaving the university.

Uptake and Outcomes

To assess our pilot sections, we conducted mixed methods research. In the courses, each student identified a corresponding course for which he or she hoped Studio would assist with learning success. In review, no student in either Studio earned lower than a B- in that course. One student's composition instructor observed an explicit development of the student's writing, a growth both parties attributed to Studio. We also used anonymous surveys and focus groups to solicit student feedback. All students celebrated the courses, said they would take the course again, and would recommend the course to friends. One student remarked that she had never considered herself a writer, and she highly valued a collaborative space in which "peers listen and take her advice seriously." Both students in the TRIO section stressed a desire for a grade connected to participation, attendance, and arriving with required materials. We agreed and decided to only offer Studio as an officially registered course section, even if this meant losing funding from community partners. We also refused to offer required sections, much like Santana, Rose and LaBarge's work (this volume), opting for a self-placement model that would maximize student agency and ensure the open access nature of the curriculum.

In fall 2013, the semester following our pilot study, we offered two additional sections of Studio. We changed the location of the course and broadened our audience to writers across campus. And while the courses were not solely populated by first-year students, this became an unforeseen strength. For example, placing a first-year composition student working on a rhetorical analysis for ENC 1102 in conversation with a senior Environmental Science major writing a Capstone project allowed each writer to discuss genre conventions, audience, and disciplinary style in ways they would not otherwise have had.

As a bricoleur, curricular design taught me that I must arrange materials to invent new instructional spaces and constantly rearrange those materials to adapt and keep alive the language and bodies associated with such spaces. As we move forward, our main concern revolves around sustainability. Even now, as we enter the fall 2014 semester, Studio continues to evolve, adapting to fit the curricular demands and students' needs at hand.

On-the-Ground Preparation at UWF—Justin's Story

The idea for a Writing Studio Program emerged from Bre's training with Dr. John Tassoni and her dialogue with writing teachers about the region-specific needs of UWF students. In a collaborative, low-stakes workshop environment, students interpret assignment sheets and teacher feedback on assignments; generate and research ideas; invent topics; write, evaluate, revise, and edit drafts; and present works-in-progress as well as final writing projects. Studio teaches these activities as recursive, in that writers engage and re-engage in them throughout completing assignments. Through the experience of sharing both process materials and final productions, students learn to ask critical questions about their own writing, prompting broader, more nuanced conversations about academic conventions. My studio teaching can be characterized in terms of three divergent experiences: 1) the TRIO-funded pilot study in spring 2013, 2) my open enrollment section in fall 2013, and 3) my fall 2013 English Composition I section of TRIO students that included a studio day added to the regular course curriculum.

Uptake and Outcomes

The function of UWF's Writing Studio is to "re-enable" both the student and the curriculum, to re-embody students as authorities and the classroom as a site of possibility. My role as facilitator in this uptake process is one that I am constantly considering. Unlike other courses, Studio demands that instructors facilitate the learning of rhetorical strategies through students' initial studio-session discussions. In this way, student uptake determines the foci of classes. The instructor practices uptake by making spur-of-the-moment decisions that impact daily goals. This process can be exciting and engaging, because many opportunities for learning arise. Studio pedagogy affords students a type of spontaneous learning through which each student exercises his or her own agency and practices engaging me and his or her peers in writing workshops.

CONCLUSION: FORWARD MOVEMENTS

A few years later, we understand even more fully how studio implementation necessitates bricolage. Creators must acquire disparate resources, build new relationships, practice uptake and "not talk," identify gaps in curricula, and provide opportunities for institutional growth. As we move forward, we must establish stable funding, training, and more standard curricula.

Currently, unlike the work of Tonya Ritola et al. in Chapter Four, Biola and UWF do not have funding dedicated to training studio facilitators. We are exploring our collaborations with on-campus writing centers, and we are in negotiations to create teacher-training courses. While new approaches and additional pay create an impetus to teach studio courses, the contingent nature of both groups require methods of continual teaching and development. For example, in one small focus group at UWF, a student reflected, "Studio moments don't necessarily come from group work and collaboration, but from spontaneous discussions and conversations." Her insight captures the entire essence of studio pedagogy. Teachers of any course often gauge their success from assignment design, course organization, and content delivery. However, in Studio, the teacher must literally re-embody herself or himself as collaborative learner, guide, or facilitator—a process that requires training.

We are also applying for internal "course development" grant monies to formalize the results of our research. Through formalizing the results, we will make our case to upper administration regarding studio's value for retention, writing, critical thinking, and information literacy. The overwhelmingly positive student and teacher voices tell us we are on the right track. Yet, as also indicated by the work of Ritola, Minardi Power et al., we need "hard data" regarding increases in pass rates to back up our qualitative truths.

The other ongoing decision we face with studio design is about who will actually populate the courses. At UWF, the course was originally marketed as driving positive first-to-second year retention, and we ended up with a diverse accumulation of students from across the curriculum. At Biola, the course was already a "catch all" and requires that we work backwards to untangle whom, exactly, is in the course and for what reasons. And while these are not the best approaches from a program administrator or studio teacher standpoint, there are two benefits: 1) We fill seats, which ensure that the section(s) make, and 2) The students in the spaces find value in the experience.

Throughout our pilots, we have encountered a handful of challenges. The difficulties seem to center around misunderstandings about what exactly Writing Studio *is*: What purpose does it serve and for whom? Often, we must continue to cater to administrative audiences over student audiences, even though focusing on students and teachers at this stage helps more effectively with enrollment issues. In addition, teacher/facilitator training is an ongoing struggle. With the fast turn-around and mobility of TAs and adjunct faculty, we cannot assume we will have the same teachers for more than a few semesters at most. Teacher training and curricular revision require sustainable finances, which returns us to the continued arguments made for Studio—a circular dilemma to say the least. Last, we continue to work at increasing student motivation. Kelsey and Justin's stories point toward the need for extrinsic motivation: grades attached to the courses. Yet, we continue to seek more complex means of intrinsic motivation. How might we make the courses more personally worthwhile for students?

Despite nuances and bypasses, we value the grounded research approach that has thus far resulted in a revisionary pedagogy that truly places students and the teaching of writing first. In a bricolage fashion, our invention and delivery of different writing studio approaches has patched together a fine-tuned arrangement of disparate materials and resources. We have forged relationships in unlikely places and have recruited former studio students to help us market the class. The result is a model of extemporaneous instruction and embodied learning for students and teachers. We hope that our work helps others, both teachers and administrators, to identify or reconceptualize studio approaches and policies that will prove successful in their context.

REFERENCES

Council of Writing Program Administrators. (1998). *Evaluating the intellectual work of writing administration.* Retrieved from http://wpacouncil.org/positions/intellectual work.html.

Deleuze, G. & Guattari F. (1983). *Anti-Oedipus: Capitalism and schizophrenia.* Minneapolis, MN: University of Minnesota Press.

Derrida, J. (1978). *Writing and difference.* Chicago, IL: University of Chicago Press.

Grego, R. C. & Thompson, N. S. (2008). *Teaching/writing in thirdspaces: The studio approach.* Carbondale, IL: Southern Illinois University Press.

Grego, R. C. & Thompson, N. S. (1995). The writing studio program: Reconfiguring basic writing/freshman composition. *Writing Program Administration, 19*(1/2), 66–79.

Levi-Strauss, C. (1972). *The savage mind.* London, UK: Weidenfield and Nicholson.

Nowacek, R. (2013, March). *Transfer as bricolage: Assembling genre knowledge across contexts.* Paper presented at a meeting of the Conference on College Composition and Communication. Las Vegas, Nevada.

Selfe, C. L. & Selfe, R. J. (1994). The politics of the interface: Power and its exercise in electronic contact zones. *College Composition and Communication, 45*(4), 480–504.

Wibberley, C. (2012). Getting to grips with bricolage: A personal account. *The Qualitative Report, 17*(50), 1–8.

CHAPTER 4.

THE POLITICS OF BASIC WRITING REFORM: USING COLLECTIVE AGENCY TO CHALLENGE THE POWER DYNAMICS OF A FLAT ADMINISTRATION

Tonya Ritola, Cara Minardi Power, Christine W. Heilman, Suzanne Biedenbach, and Amanda F. Sepulveda

University of California Santa Cruz, Florida Southwestern State College, Miami University of Ohio, and Georgia Gwinnett College (Biendenbach and Sepulveda)

INTRODUCTION: THE IMPORTANCE OF DETERMINING ONE'S "COMPOSITIONAL SITUATION"

For more than twenty years, the Writing Studio model has provided compositionists with a theoretical framework for redefining basic writing instruction in the United States. Studio models move basic writing programs from skills-based remediation to process-driven pedagogy that "improve[s] both a student's skill at and attitude toward writing" (Sutton, 2010, p. 32). In many studio approaches, basic writers are mainstreamed in traditional first-year writing courses but are encouraged to participate in additional courses or writing workshops that enable students to interrogate the expectations of college-level writing, discuss openly their affective stances toward writing, and challenge the traditional displacement most basic writers experience before college.

Of course, implementing such an approach is not always an easy feat, in part because a one-size-fits-all approach has never been appropriate for creating studio programs. To this end, Grego and Thompson (2008) urged compositionists to interrogate their own "compositional situations" by examining how one's institutional location interacts with extra-institutional forces such as state legislatures, national accrediting bodies, and policymakers (p. 220). Such moves enable studio administrators to reconstitute basic writing instruction at the local level appropriately and, thus, to contextualize programmatic success.

Studio scholars' attention to localized contexts as a necessary first step in studio design should come as no surprise to readers of this collection (Grego & Thompson, 1995; Grego & Thompson, 2008; Sutton, 2010; Tassoni & Lewiecki-Wilson 2005). A key element, however, of fully comprehending one's compositional situation—an element that runs tangential to space/place in the landmark studio texts—is that of timing. Not only must compositionists reflect on their own place/space, they must also reflect on how kairotic, or opportune, timing influences what is possible in their place/space, as well as whether or not Studio is the right approach (See Matzke and Garrett, this volume, for another example of how kairos informs studio development).

At our institution, Georgia Gwinnett College (GGC), we considered Grego and Thompson's (1995; 2008) advice carefully as we implemented the Segue Program: a concurrent, mainstream model that blends pedagogical strategies of Writing Studio with the structural design of the Accelerated Learning Program (ALP) developed by Peter Adams at the Community College of Baltimore County. We had a distinct advantage in developing our program: In 2011, Georgia received a $1 million grant from the Bill Gates Foundation through the Complete College America Initiative to transform developmental education. GGC received $150,000 to transform developmental math, reading, and English courses.

As we created the Segue Program, we recognized the degree to which our program's success hinged upon the negotiation of several time-related factors: the national "crisis" of developmental education, Georgia's adoption of the Complete College America Initiative, GGC's mandate to transform developmental education, GGC's administrative structure, and problems associated with developing a writing program without an administrator. This confluence of national, state, and institutional demands presented us with kairotic political moments that, when combined with a determined faculty team, enabled the successful design and implementation of the Segue Program. In this volume, Cardinal's and Keown's chapter, "Story Changing Work for Studio Activists: Finding Points of Convergence," discusses the need to find places of convergence to "appropriate institutional arguments [in order to] redirect the argument by reframing the interests of the institution in ways that reflect Studio values." In other words, Cardinal and Keown argued that we must find multiple points of convergence among stakeholders as the basis of arguments supporting studio approaches, which we did in the creation of the Segue Program.

This chapter chronicles how we developed collective agency to appropriately negotiate various stakeholder demands in order to create a program that increased students' pass rates from an average of 55% to an average of 86%. Throughout the program's development, collective agency yielded positive institutional change, enabling us to produce a model program for our state. For readers who are in the process of creating a studio program, particularly those participating in Complete College America Initiatives, or for those who are interested in learning more about the political dynamics of building a studio model, this chapter offers useful advice for balancing extra-institutional, institutional, and disciplinary agendas, as well as advice for anticipating potential political struggles faculty may face during studio implementation.

The first half of this chapter outlines, in detail, how GGC responded to national and state demands, how we implemented the Segue Program, and how collective agency authorized us to produce a successful program. The second half of the chapter specifically addresses the political struggles we faced during the process, serving as an instructional tale for faculty at similar institutions who are in the beginning stages of creating a studio program. Finally, we offer the lessons we've learned at GGC and demonstrate the importance of recognizing how place, space, and timing can both constrain and open up possibilities for studio development.

NATIONAL AND STATE INFLUENCES: THE IMPETUS BEHIND THE SEGUE PROGRAM

The largest factor influencing our compositional situation at GGC began at the national level and filtered down to the state and local levels. In a February 24, 2009, address to a joint session of Congress, President Barack Obama called for a nationwide reinvestment in education and revealed his educational goal to "have the highest proportion of college graduates in the world" by 2020.

Alongside President Obama's call for increased participation in higher education, organizations such as Complete College America (CCA) began to study retention problems in post-secondary education. They found that educators have to effectively address the number of entering students in need of developmental courses in order to reach the nation's college graduation goals. According to a joint report written by the Charles A. Dana Center, Complete College America, Education Commission of the States, and Jobs for the Future (2012), "half of all students in postsecondary education tak[e] one or more developmental education courses" (p. ii). More problematic, students who are required to take developmental classes fail to graduate with degrees more often than those students who are not required to take such courses (Charles A. Dana Center, 2012, p. 2). Given the large number of students in need of developmental education nationally, educators cannot reach Obama's 2020 benchmark unless we effectively build programs that empower developmental students to graduate.

As noted by Jason Delaney and Pascael Beaudette (2013), half of all students admitted into four-year colleges and universities in the United States require developmental education, while 26% of students entering technical and two-year schools need developmental courses. The state of Georgia is congruent with these percentages. Further, the writers have claimed that the longer students spend in developmental classes, the less likely they are to graduate; in fact, only 24% of students entering four-year colleges and universities in Georgia will earn degrees within six years. Finally, Delaney and Beaudette recommended that Georgia improve college completion rates by accelerating and tailoring developmental programs to specific student needs. As a result of these findings, Georgia applied for and was awarded a $1 million grant from CCA to transform developmental education in the state. The grant required that participating institutions pilot new models and report their findings to the Georgia Board of Regents (BOR). The BOR would then evaluate the results of pilot programs so that successful models could be implemented statewide.

Participating two-year schools were Athens Technical College and Piedmont Technical College. The two participating four-year colleges were the College of Coastal Georgia and GGC. At GGC, we were awarded $150,000 to transform our developmental education initiatives in math, reading, and English. The CCA grant required a specific set of criteria: (1) the implementation of technology-based diagnostic assessments to determine the level of remediation needed for each student; (2) the development of modularized content remediation coursework appropriate to the level of the students as determined by diagnostic testing; (3) the option for the students to work at an accelerated rate using a mastery approach; (4) opportunities for the students who fall below the cut scores on the placement exam to concurrently enroll in a college-level course and to receive diagnostic-based learning support; and (5) student success skills offerings/support.

GGC administrators charged us to implement a developmental writing program that would fulfill these criteria. Even though we were given this charge, we did not actually author the grant, which was completed before our arrival. The call for modularized instruction and early exit opportunities for an at-risk population challenged our understandings of effective basic writing instruction. At the same time, we were given a unique opportunity to build a program with national funding and state-level support. During this process, it was imperative for us to consider how to meet President Obama's demand for increased college attendance and the governor's expectation for increased college completion. Further, we had to do so while upholding our pedagogical principles within an institution dedicated to serving the underprivileged population of Gwinnett County.

We had five months (from mid-August 2011 to early January 2012) to plan and implement a pilot program. After numerous discussions, the group settled on a modified version of the Accelerated Learning Program (ALP) developed in 2007 by the Community College of Baltimore County (CCBC), Maryland. CCBC had conducted considerable research on the success of its ALP program by 2011, so we felt confident that we could adapt the model and integrate features of the studio model that would support our institutional context.

Both the ALP and studio models focus on completion of English composition by students who need more support for their writing and for affective issues than they would receive without them. One important difference between Studio and ALP is that ALP teachers take on the role of both the studio teacher and the teacher of English composition. Another is that the focus of the collaboration is somewhat different. The Studio model is described as "outside but alongside" (Grego & Thompson, 2008, p. 65) a composition course, while ALP may be described as "*inside* and alongside"—a different model that gives more power to individual teachers to shape a complementary experience for developmental students.

Taking both models into account, we developed a concurrent enrollment sequence, in which each of us would teach two sections of first-year writing and one section of developmental writing. Within each instructor's first-year writing classes (ENGL 1101), eight developmental students were enrolled; later in the day, the same two groups of eight students met with the same instructor in a basic writing class (ENGL 099) (Davis et al., 2014). We also integrated the following Studio and ALP pedagogical methods: (1) individuated instruction with faculty conferences; (2) scaffolded assignments that top-load assignment instructions and divide them into manageable chunks or tasks; (3) student-driven instruction that practices inquiry-based learning; (4) activities and discussions that address community building and affective issues; and (5) a process-oriented approach that includes multiple draft sequences.

This approach matched well with GGC's mission of providing education to a broad range of students with a broad range of needs. The studio component of our adapted ALP model provides one-on-one instruction with the instructor, and it is a big part of why our students and the program succeed. However, we recognize the extent to which the national call for college completion and the timing of the grant itself served as productive catalysts for developing the Segue Program.

INSTITUTIONAL CONTEXT: GGC'S FLAT STRUCTURE

Located outside of Atlanta, GGC is a new open access, non-tenure institution in the University System of Georgia. GGC opened in 2006 with 118 students and grew to 8,000 in the fall of 2011. The institution's ethnically and economically diverse student population includes a high percentage of first-generation college students. Based on student data, nearly 50% of incoming students place into at least one developmental course (basic writing, math, and/or reading), making GGC an ideal place to transform developmental education. Our exponential growth alone, from 4,000 to 8,000 students in AY 2011–2012, enables GGC to function more like an organization than an institution, the latter of which is typically characterized by its sense of timelessness. In contrast to the adage that institutional change is "glacial," new programs at GGC are created every day, and faculty—often junior faculty—are responsible for their development.

While good, our "newness" presents challenges, compounded by the "flat structure" adapted by GGC's Inaugural president Daniel Kaufman. By definition, a flat structure limits the number of middle management positions; translated to an academic institution, this structure displaces the traditional departmental structure and omits the position of department chair altogether. Faculty report to the dean of the schools to which they are assigned and coordinate information and workload through their discipline's "Point of Contact" (POC), who serves without the authority of a chair. The only administrator with power to mitigate faculty grievances is a dean who may have limited knowledge of a given faculty's discipline. Further, this structure provides very real hindrances to faculty governance and programmatic development because no single academic unit on campus has power to institute changes without the "permission" of a dean, which in turn requires the permission of the Vice-President for Academic and Student Affairs, which requires the permission of the President.

The omission of middle management at GGC also means that the institution has no official writing program or writing program administrator. Further, GGC's writing courses occupy an interesting institutional location: First-Year Writing (English 1101 and 1102) is housed in the School of Liberal Arts (SLA), and English faculty are responsible for the design and assessment of those courses. Developmental English (English 099), however, is taught and assessed by English Discipline faculty, but is housed in the School of Transitional Studies (STS), which also oversees developmental math and reading. Structurally speaking, English 099 is subject to the policies and procedures of the STS, not the English Discipline. In this way, the politics of transforming developmental English become complicated because faculty in "charge" of overseeing the courses must report to two deans who sometimes have competing interests.

Despite these challenges, the "flat structure" at GGC gave us the opportunity to engage in what Michelle Miley (this volume) refers to as countermonumentalism, which in a sense denies the ideals of an authority and creates a situation that is counter to tradition. Even though GGC is a fairly new institution and had not had the time to develop its own traditions, those in authoritative positions had brought with them from their previous institutions traditions, constraints, and ideals about what programs should be and should look like. We had to work within these sometimes competing ideals to develop our own countermonument, which Miley describes as a "metaphor for the structural risks necessary for innovation." She explains that self-assessment, self-reflection, and a commitment to sharing and combining expertise are key for the "construction of identity," and that once created, "countermonuments provide new angles of vision necessary for creating innovative environments."

In order to circumvent hierarchical problems associated with a "flat structure," the English Discipline created its own internal governance system by establishing a traditional committee structure. As the Segue Six, we had to create our own countermonument to this structure, as even with committees in place, the English Discipline operated according to a consensus-building model, which meant that all faculty—regardless of concentration within English Studies—created, revised, and voted on curricular design related to writing program instruction. Also, all faculty taught developmental and first-year composition. However, the degree to which faculty in this program are afforded professional development and/or direct training in the teaching of writing is somewhat limited. There is no guarantee that all English faculty at GGC have had exposure to the theoretical foundations that support writing instruction; however, as Miley (this collection) demonstrates, collaborating with someone who may not have the same pedagogical training and recognizing one's own limits in communicating can open up new ways of communicating.

Oddly enough, the complexity of our institutional structure appears congruent with other open admission institutions. As Cynthia Lewiecki-Wilson and Jeff Sommers (1999) explain in "Professing at the Fault Lines: Composition at Open Admissions Institutions," the difference between open-admission institutions and traditional comprehensive research institutions is "the impact of local histories and conditions" (p. 443). More importantly, Lewiecki-Wilson and Sommers (1999) note that faculty in open-admission institutions "often conduct [their] professional work outside of an English department buffer zone, in an interdisciplinary department perhaps, which can very often put [them] in the middle of the political fray—whether campus-wide or community-wide" (p. 443). Reporting to two different deans of two different schools at GGC put us in such political fray, as the number of stakeholders invested in developmental education is, at best, challenging to navigate and, at worst, impossible to predict. Further, GGC's short history and lack of programmatic structure for writing affected the range of influence we could have as compositionists, both across the curriculum and at the state level.

THE NEED FOR THEORY: CREATING COLLECTIVE AGENCY

We had a seemingly insurmountable task: to carry out a large grant written before we were hired but which we were asked to implement, to accept a state-mandated charge to transform developmental education within an institutional structure lacking a writing program and writing program administrator, and to roll out this model to over forty faculty from various subfields within English Studies. In addition, while the other participating colleges in Georgia learned of the grant requirements in the spring of 2011 and were able to secure outside support, no one in the English Discipline was informed about the grant until the following semester. Luckily, we had over 70 years of combined pedagogical experience to guide us. In addition, five of us have Ph.D.s in rhetoric and composition, and one of us earned an MA in rhetoric and composition and a Ph.D. in educational psychology. We realized immediately that, in order to make this transformation successful, we had to harness our individual strengths and equitably divide our workloads.

The kind of collective agency we formed for the Segue Program is well documented in our field, specifically through the work of Marc Bousquet (2002) and Carmen Werder (2000), both of whom claim that collective action is the most successful approach to administering writing programs. As Bousquet (2002) argues in "Composition as Management Science," an ideal writing program does not make use of traditional hierarchical structures; instead, Bousquet advocates for "a *labor* theory of agency and a rhetoric of solidarity, aimed at constituting, nurturing, and empowering collective action by persons in groups" (p. 494).

While Bousquet has received criticism for his oversimplification of rhetoric and composition's disciplinary history, he makes a valid point: The work of a writing program, and the power distributions within it, should not be designated to a figurehead. Instead, all members working within a writing program should be invited to participate in the development of the program, with the expectation that shared governance will lead to a more ethical approach to program administration.

Though not entirely concerned with ethics, Bousquet's WPA-less writing program is precisely the kind of program we created at GGC for our studio initiative. We enacted, as best we could, what Carmen Werder (2000) terms "rhetorical agency," an approach to administration that reorients traditional concepts of power, authority, and influence to a collective shared ethos and thus a "shared agency" (p. 19). For Werder (2000), WPA work is "not about controlling others; it's about understanding our common needs. It's not about forcing others; it's about choosing with them from an array of perspectives available. It's not about managing others; it's about analyzing a situation and figuring it out—together" (p. 12). As a result, our institutional limitations—no WPA, no writing program, courses "owned" by different schools—actually enabled us to be ethical collaborators who developed "shared agency" in order to offer GGC students a first-rate educational experience.

We banded together collectively because we realized the power we could wield as a solidified team. Each of us spearheaded projects most closely aligned with her expertise. We designated a point person to communicate with our deans and to organize meetings; a tutor facilitator who hired and trained part-time faculty tutors; a resource facilitator who investigated content management systems, textbooks, and classroom materials; a grant compliance and budget representative who completed our purchasing requests and represented us to the BOR; a liaison who guided us through the IRB approval process and interfaced with Admissions and Testing; and, finally, a researcher who reviewed disciplinary models, including Studio, stretch, mainstreaming, and bridge courses. Yet these roles were flexible, and we filled in for each other when needed. We met weekly—sometimes twice a week—to report on our progress, to discuss new developments, and to troubleshoot. We quickly became a collective with one focus.

Even though we did not author the CCA grant proposal, we had the rhetorical positioning and pedagogical expertise to leverage the grant and to create an innovative program; however, like most institutions engaging in such transformation and/or redesign efforts, we faced specific challenges that were, at times, political. In our efforts to negotiate with various stakeholders, we learned valuable lessons about the hindrances one may face while developing a program and how collective agency can serve as a panacea to potential setbacks.

POLITICS AND CHALLENGES OF THE SEGUE PROGRAM

Studio scholarship is rife with stories of success *and* failure. At GGC, we consider Segue a measurable success, but we cannot pretend that the implementation process was seamless. Often, transformation efforts are met with resistance: sometimes from faculty, sometimes from administrators, sometimes from students. Most often, such resistance is motivated by personal and political conflicts preceding the moment of transformation. When new initiatives filter through institutional pipelines, they enter into a complex web of relationships, practices, and policies, and it is often faculty who must mitigate these complexities as they respond to administrative charges to change curricula. In fact, even Werder's (2000) sincere optimism in "Rhetorical Agency: The Ethics of It All" is calculated, as she notes:

> [T]here will always be some people who choose to perceive
> us exclusively as threats to their own power. . . . Not only are
> they sometimes unable to conceptualize relationships based on

> mutual agency, they are unwilling to do so because it means
> that they would have to give up control of others. (p. 20)

Such obstacles are unavoidable when campus-wide curricular change is afoot. For us, negotiating the complexities of our stakeholders, the grant criteria, testing practices, flat structure, and disciplinary communication presented us with challenges that we could only allay through collective agency and consistent messaging. Our work on the Segue Program demonstrates the importance of finding points of convergence among stakeholders, particularly a large variety of stakeholders with differing ideas and levels of power (Cardinal & Keown, this volume).

Challenge 1: Multiple Stakeholders

Georgia's participation in the CCA Initiative immediately positioned GGC's transformation effort as a top-down initiative, filtering from the Georgia BOR to four colleges in the state. We had to negotiate relationships and convince our stakeholders that the Segue model would work—that it could lower attrition rates and be adapted in other institutional contexts across the state. Luckily for us, Peter Adams' ALP model yielded impressive quantitative data demonstrating that students moved through the program faster and were retained at higher rates than students in traditional basic writing classes. Attrition rates, retention, and accelerated progress were all major concerns for CCA and the State of Georgia. As our team was becoming convinced that a modified version of the ALP would best serve GGC, the Dean of the STS attended a conference where Adams presented, and afterwards, supported our recommendation and invited Adams to our campus. With the support of the Dean of the STS, we were better able to convince campus-wide stakeholders to endorse the model. The timing of these events—our Dean's attendance at Adams' talk coupled with the national conversations about developmental education—was instrumental in our transformation efforts.

Additionally, we gained support for Segue because we created credit-bearing courses. Our stakeholders—CCA, Georgia's BOR, and GGC's deans—wanted a model that helped developmental students enroll in credit-bearing courses as quickly as possible. Because the Segue model allows students to enroll in developmental English and first-year composition during the same semester, it did just that. Our collective messaging about Segue focused on this aspect and has since won us advocates all over campus. In fact, when discussing GGC's mission to not only grant students access to higher education but also to support student success, GGC's President has mentioned the Segue Program in particular as an example.

CHALLENGE 2: THE COMPLETE COLLEGE AMERICA GRANT

One of our major concerns about the CCA grant was its imperative to modularize instruction. We agreed that a purely modularized approach was not pedagogically sound for diverse students from the working class or those from impoverished homes because these students generally have less access to and experience with technology. None of us wanted technology to become a new stumbling block for student success. The question became: How could we satisfy the dictates of the grant while providing pedagogically sound courses?

We came up with a creative solution: We included a series of exercises and quizzes for grammar instruction, in which students completed modularized instruction on their own time and at their own pace. Doing so allowed us to meet this grant requirement while enabling us to spend class time on global writing issues. Our decision to offload grammar instruction and to use in-class time for global issues was an easy, collective choice to make. We will also add that our common training helped us build collectivity; it was not difficult to agree on enacting similar pedagogical practices and to share our approaches with others.

CHALLENGE 3: DISRUPTING TESTING PRACTICES

One of our goals was to modify how standardized tests were used at GGC to assess student writing. Prior to our program implementation, the ACT Compass exam determined students' placement in English, reading, and math. If students were placed in developmental English, reading, or math, they were also required to pass the Compass exam at the end of each course. This added hurdle meant students could pass the basic writing course, but if they did not satisfy the Compass exit requirement, they would be required to repeat the entire course.

We wanted two changes to testing that were supported by the grant: to include multiple measures for writing placement and to dispose of the Compass exam as an exit measure. For placement, we chose the E-Write exam, in combination with the Compass, to gain a better sense of students' writing abilities and to create a more accurate placement system. Disposing of the Compass an as exit requirement was a more difficult matter, in part because of communication difficulties among the SLA, the STS, and the Office of Testing Services, all of which interpreted the grant differently.

To manage the uncertainty over the Compass exit, we presented our stakeholders with a non-punitive exit measure that would more accurately assess students' exit abilities, and we were granted permission to implement it. We created a standard in-class writing prompt for students to complete during the last week of classes, and we all administered the prompt in the same manner, with the same time limit. In order to assure objectivity when evaluating the essays, we conducted a holistic blind scoring, a practice we have continued. In this instance, our common training in best practices for writing instruction provided us with the support we needed to revise a punitive exit measure, a success we are proud of.

CHALLENGE 4: GGC'S FLAT STRUCTURE

Within a flat structure, an uncommon hierarchy exists, one that omits traditional means of transmitting information. Without the administrative support of either a WPA or a writing program, our efforts to implement the Segue Program were sometimes stymied by institutional idiosyncrasies. Part of the struggle lay with identifying the key administrators and staff to assist us during Segue's implementation; we were new to the institution and unfamiliar with the offices and people needed to make the pilot a success. In addition, before our contracts started, a number of returning personnel moved into different positions within the institution, further complicating our progress. Often, we realized we had neglected to inform someone important of our activities only when a new problem came to light.

In addition, a flat structure requires faculty to absorb much of the administrative workload, most of which is conducted within work groups, committees, and other taskforces throughout campus. One of the difficulties in working within "GGC time" is that two very different decisions about one issue may be simultaneously made by two different committees, or one committee's decision can unknowingly impact or even contradict the choices made by another. In order to minimize miscommunication, each member of the group re-appropriated all her non-teaching time to implementing the program and worked diligently to identify and contact committees or administration needed to make the program work. Each member acquired multiple assignments to relevant work groups, taskforces, and committees to support the program.

In essence, placement in various groups became key to the success of the Segue Program because, within a flat structure, connections were, in some ways, more possible than they would have been in a more traditional structure. For example, one of us served on a college-wide committee called First-Year Matters. This committee was comprised of administrators, including the Vice-President of Academics and Student Affairs, the Associate Provost for Academic Affairs, Associate Vice-President for Quality Enhancement Programs and Institutional Policy, the Dean of the STS, and the Associate Vice-President of Public Affairs. Our colleague's membership on the committee helped the group stay abreast of changes to tutoring on campus, the college's orientation process, and issues of public relations, all relevant to Segue.

Further, these connections helped the group ameliorate political questions regarding where the Segue Program and its faculty should reside. At the same time, the STS and the English Discipline wanted to protect their interests and investments in the courses taught, and we were often put in the midst of the political foray when power and authority were uncertain. For example, classroom assignments became difficult because the STS claims control of several small rooms appropriate for Segue classes. From an outside perspective, it appeared that Segue faculty obtained better teaching assignments. We, however, made connections to the key people and groups on campus, effectively establishing Segue as belonging to both the STS and the SLA and allowing classroom assignments appropriate to class size, which also helped to dispel concerns in the English Discipline. We have kept appointments in English but continue to work closely alongside the STS, including faculty involved with the newly developmental basic math program, Access Math. We also forged a program with reading faculty in AY 2014–2015.

Importantly, we found that GGC's institutional structure may actually help reinforce the notion that developmental education is the work of the entire college, not just one discipline or group. In a sense, then, the Segue Program allowed us to make structural vulnerabilities that impede GGC's mission more visible and paved the way for more open collaborations among faculty and schools within the institution.

CHALLENGE 5: DISCIPLINARY CONFLICT AND PROTOCOL

The structural peculiarities of GGC created conflicts within the English Discipline primarily with regard to communication and protocol. First, because GGC essentially doubled its student population (from 4,000 to 8,000 students) in the fall of 2011, a change which forced personnel positions to shift the previous summer, it was initially unclear who had the authority to enact the curricular changes required for the Segue Program. Since its inception, the English Discipline managed its own curricular changes, but because Georgia's BOR awarded GGC the grant, its purview extended beyond the discipline. As a result, neither the SLA nor the English Discipline had an established protocol for delegating tasks assigned by the BOR because neither unit understood the extent to which the BOR could intervene in curricular matters.

In fact, the process revealed that the BOR absolutely has the power to dictate curricular matters, but the lack of established protocol led some English Discipline faculty to question whether the grant violated GGC's accreditation since it was a top-down administrative directive, as opposed to a faculty-driven initiative. The unorthodox curricular process surrounding the creation of the Segue Program provided many opportunities to review institutional practices and to develop stronger protocol to protect new faculty and maintain curricular integrity.

Further complicating matters was the fact that the grant award was announced in August, before most faculty returned to campus. The Dean of the SLA approached us during orientation, before we became acquainted with our English colleagues, the Discipline's structure, and the curricular processes the discipline created. Our agreement to participate in a major curricular revision outside of the discipline's processes created obstacles for achieving immediate buy-in from our English colleagues. Ultimately, these obstacles were significant enough to place us in a vulnerable position between the Dean's Office and the English Discipline. Because the Dean had broken English Discipline communication protocol by approaching us directly, Segue became a "Dean's Taskforce" and worked outside of the discipline's committee structure. Hence, we were under no obligation to communicate the purpose and work of the taskforce to the Discipline. The Dean's approach to delegating the grant responsibilities led to conflicts over communication, power, and decision-making, conflicts that called into question the very structure of the discipline, as well as the relationship between the English Discipline and the Dean's Office. One of the results was our inability to cast the Segue Program as discipline-specific work in keeping with the English Discipline Constitution.

Moreover, some English faculty members had limited knowledge of Segue's existence, even one year after the program began, and/or were unsure about how the model worked. Finally, the implementation of Segue highlighted an additional tension concerning the location of Segue courses as part of the SLA or the STS, which led us to question whether English faculty believed that developmental education should be the work of the English Discipline at all.

Understandably, tension mounted. The English Discipline felt alienated from the Segue Program and was afraid that the Dean's breach of discipline protocol would set an unfavorable precedent for future faculty. For us, this tension created obstacles for productive communication. It was also difficult to communicate the nuance of the Segue Program in the limited time allotted in discipline meetings. Leach et al. (this volume) notes that their conversations too were also brief and in hallways, but they did have the shared space of department workrooms that a flat structure like GGC's cannot provide. Without a departmental structure in place, and having little face-to- face time for communication, English faculty members were expected to use a discipline-only Google Group to have more in-depth discussions about Segue. Sometimes, these discussions were fruitful, but other times, misunderstandings occurred. Despite these challenges, the Segue Program is one example of a program on GGC's campus that, while messy, navigated the flat structure for the benefit of students.

THE FUTURE OF SEGUE

The political challenges faced by the group all led directly to the need for collective agency. As a result of our efforts, faculty and administrators have also learned from the experience of Segue, and several new initiatives are now in place to ensure that our transformation of developmental education continues to prosper. First, one year after Segue's implementation, GGC created The Council to Advise Transitional Studies, a collaborative unit that brings faculty from across campus together to discuss issues related to developmental education. Second, GGC's next project was to develop a new course that combines developmental reading and writing, typically offered as two classes, into one course. The course, English 0989, was created by a collaborative committee of English and reading faculty, in conjunction with the Dean of the STS. In other words, faculty from the SLA, the School of Education (where reading is housed), and the STS developed the curriculum for the course during the 2014–2015 AY. The collaboration and ensuing course suffered from far fewer difficulties during its creation and implementation than did the Segue Program. The course will be available in the fall of 2015 when the new guidelines for developmental courses in the State of Georgia take effect.

LESSONS LEARNED

Developing the Segue Program taught us valuable lessons about studio implementation, and while many of GGC's institutional features are non-traditional, we have some generalizable takeaways applicable to range of institutions. As faculty, administrators, and staff begin the planning phases of studio implementation, they should work collaboratively to

1. Characterize their compositional situation, with attention to the extra-institutional, institutional, and disciplinary stakeholders that will invest in the model.
2. Take advantage of timing and recognizing potential opportunities afforded by campus strategic priorities, statewide initiatives, and internal and external grants.
3. Identify allies across disciplines through committee or taskforce work.
4. Leverage collective agency wisely so that studio implementation is a concerted effort.
5. Structure productive communication opportunities by providing campus-wide workshops and events to educate faculty and administrators about the benefits of Studio.

6. Develop clear communication protocols among academic units and understand the channels required for programmatic development.

7. Recognize that studio implementation will generate institutional critique.

While not exhaustive, these lessons serve as first steps in considering who will be served by Studio, what resources are required for implementation, and what institutional pieces must collaborate. We invite—and welcome—other novice studio designers to contribute to our discussion by sharing their compositional situations and revealing other factors that lead to successful studio design and implementation. Such stories are helpful and can provide immeasurable guidance; we need to hear them.

REFERENCES

Bousquet, M. (2002). Composition as management science: Toward a university without a WPA. *Journal of Advanced Composition, 22*(3), 493–527.

Charles A. Dana Center, Complete College America, Education Commission of the States & Jobs for the Future. (2012). *Core principles for transforming remedial education: A joint statement.* Retrieved from https://jfforg-prod-prime.s3.amazonaws.com /media/documents/RemediationJointStatement-121312update.pdf.

Davis, K., Biedenbach, S., Minardi, C., Myers, A. & Ritola, T. (2014). Affective matters: Effective measures for transforming basic writing programs and instruction. *Open Words: Access and English Studies, 8*(1). Retrieved from https://www.pearsoned .com/wp-content/uploads/Kim-Davis.pdf.

Delaney, J. & Beaudette, P. (2013). *Complete college Georgia: Transforming remediation.* Retrieved from http://gosa.georgia.gov/complete-college-georgia-transforming -remediation.

Grego, R. C. & Thompson, N. S. (1995). The writing studio program: Reconfiguring basic writing/freshman composition. *Writing Program Administration, 19*(1/2), 66–79.

Grego, R. C. & Thompson, N. S. (1996). Repositioning remediation: Renegotiating composition's work in the academy. *College Composition and Communication, 47*(1), 62–84. https://dx.doi.org/10.2307/358274.

Grego, R. C. & Thompson, N. S. (2008). *Teaching/writing in thirdspaces: The studio approach.* Carbondale, IL: Southern Illinois University Press.

Lewiecki-Wilson, C. & Sommers, J. (1999). Professing at the fault lines: Composition at open admissions institutions. *College Composition and Communication, 50*(3), 438–462.

Obama, B. (2009). Remarks of President Barack Obama—As prepared for delivery address to joint session of Congress. Retrieved from http://www.whitehouse.gov /the_press_office/Remarks-of-President-Barack-Obama-Address-to-Joint-Session -of-Congress.

Sutton, M. (2010). Messages to and from third space: Communication between the writing studio and classroom teachers. *Open Words: Access and English Studies, 4*(1). Retrieved from https://www.pearsoned.com/wp-content/uploads/Sutton-Open _Words-Spring_2010-5.pdf.

Tassoni, J. P. & Lewiecki-Wilson, C. (2005). Not just anywhere, anywhen: Mapping change through studio work. *Journal of Basic Writing, 24(*1), 68–92.

Werder, C. (2000). Rhetorical agency: Seeing the ethics of it all. *Writing Program Administration, 24*(1/2), 7–26.

CHAPTER 5.

NAVIGATING OUTSIDE THE MAINSTREAM: OUR JOURNEY SUSTAINING WRITING STUDIO

Dan Fraizer

Springfield College

Today, mainstreaming those labeled as basic writers into regular First-Year Composition (FYC) courses seems a mainstream practice itself. Increasingly, the question is not whether to mainstream but how. With its emphasis on "third spaces," Writing Studio differs from other mainstreaming forms as it encourages student learning to take place outside, not only alongside, the regular FYC classroom. But we can also think of studios as opportunities for teachers and administrators to work out how to sustain and enrich all writing spaces, not live apart from them. In this chapter, I draw on one institution's twenty year history of administering and teaching in a writing studio program to describe the dynamics of our process. Two key areas of engagement emerge. The first area is placement and enrollment. In our experience, placement strategies should take into consideration two realities. The first is the way students and their families make decisions about first-year schedules. The second is the management of studio enrollment over time. In our experience, test scores should be a tool to initiate placement, not define it. The second area is how teachers engage productively with studio students and each other. Studio teachers and students benefit most from clear lines of communication that lead to mutual respect and trust, and studio and FYC teachers should work together to identify and meet the needs of students as individuals. Productive collaboration may seem like a buzzword, but when a non-traditional "third space" becomes part of the curriculum, the quality of that collaboration may make or break a new studio program. My insights are based on my personal experience as a studio teacher and coordinator, and on survey data on placement, course content, and teaching strategies collected from FYC teachers, studio teachers, and studio students in 2007 and again in 2012.

WHO WE ARE AND WHAT OUR STUDIOS LOOK LIKE

Springfield College is a small private college in Western Massachusetts with an undergraduate residential enrollment of about 2,000 plus students. The average size of the incoming student population is about 500. First-Year Composition is a two-course sequence, each course worth three credits, and each course is taken in the first year. The courses are called College Writing 1 and 2, and they are part of the general education requirements. Each semester, approximately 25 sections of College Writing are offered with about 20 students in each. College Writing classes are taught by faculty in the Humanities Department. Approximately one-half to two-thirds of the sections are taught by full-time faculty, most of whom specialize in literature or writing.

When I arrived at Springfield College in 1995, I was aware of the criticism of traditional remedial/basic writing classes through my reading of Mike Rose's *Lives on the Boundary* and Mina Shaughnessy's *Errors and Expectations,* and my head was still full of Paulo Freire and Ira Shor and others from my graduate school days in the early 90s. I'd started teaching in the early 80s in basic literacy and GED programs because literacy education seemed like a lasting way to empower people to improve their lives. My story is not that unusual.

What may be unusual is that Rhonda Grego and Nancy Thompson's work fell into my hands at an opportune moment. I knew little of the nascent mainstreaming debate/movement in basic writing. I was familiar with the emerging criticism of basic writing (Adams, 1993; Bartholomae, 1993), but I didn't know that criticism was being translated into new writing program initiatives. I knew nothing of the Stretch Program at Arizona State University, the enrichment program at Quinnipiac University, or the Accelerated Learning Program at Community College of Baltimore (all cited in Adams, Gearhart, Miller & Roberts, 2009). I also didn't know about the enrichment course at CUNY or the mainstreaming program at Cal State Chico (Fox & Rodby, 2000).

Grego and Thompson's Studio approach seemed to be a model for doing two things I thought would be feasible and beneficial for students and faculty at Springfield College. First, since no remedial writing courses then existed at the college, I could quickly create a course for struggling writers that wouldn't disrupt existing FYC courses. Second, Studio would create opportunities for me to talk about teaching writing with the teachers who taught FYC, some of whom I thought might benefit from re-thinking the way they had been teaching writing for many years.

Our students come from mostly middle-class backgrounds and often come to the college because of its reputation as a school for Division 3 athletes who want to prepare for athletic and health-related professional careers. Some students come well-prepared for college work, while others struggle to adapt to these demands. Although the college is not an open-access institution, it is also not a highly selective one. Students can be admitted with relatively low SAT scores. The college depends on those tuition dollars. When the administration embraced writing studios, it knew writing support was necessary for some. Studio was a good fit for the kind of student who needed extra attention but in a small group setting.

From the beginning, we believed Studio would focus student attention and create opportunities for learning activities in small group settings. Many students at the college identify as experiential or kinesthetic learners (a trait perhaps common in student athletes), and Studio was perceived to be more conducive to this type of learning than traditional remedial classes. As a support system, Studio might also contribute to increased retention rates, an important factor in maintaining enrollments and revenue. Students might be more likely to remain at the college because they were successful from the beginning.[1] They might also be more likely to graduate in four years, a concern that has increased as the certification requirements in professional programs have become more demanding. These demographic and institutional realities laid the groundwork for establishing our studio program and helped to achieve "buy-in" from vital stakeholders. These structural considerations are very much aligned with the "efficiency" narratives described by Cardinal and Keown in this volume. Studio first needed to be perceived as a program that would both enhance the success of students and contribute to the financial stability of the institution. Studio also needed to help facilitate the goals of the established FYC courses. Many stakeholders needed to "buy in" to Studio, and key leaders needed to enable a collective satisfaction with Studio. All of this needed to happen in line with what Cardinal and Keown call "convergence theory." Studio may be seen in different ways by parents, by administrators, by FYC faculty, by students, and finally by the faculty who teach Studio. All of these groups' interests needed to "converge" in order to achieve agreement that Studio was beneficial. It is worth noting that what studio instructors might value most, namely interactional inquiry, was enabled but not necessarily endorsed by other stakeholders.

When Warnick, Cooney, and Lackey described their struggles beginning a studio program, the obstacles they encountered were named the "enemies of sustainable Studio programs everywhere: a lack of buy-in from undergraduates, a lack of support from faculty, and an inadequate administrative support structure" (2010, p. 82). We were also concerned about achieving faculty support and an adequate administrative support structure. Two key players that helped smooth the way were the chair of the Humanities Department, who oversaw all writing faculty appointments and curricular decisions, and the Director of Academic Advising,

---

1   According to data collected by the Director of Academic Advising over the last twenty years, students enrolled in Writing Studio are more likely to remain enrolled at the college than those who did not enroll in Studio.

who supervised the enrollments of all new incoming students. We wouldn't get students enrolled in Studio without help from Academic Advising, and the right people wouldn't teach it unless the Humanities chair took on the task of building it into the right faculty work plans. Our small size also helped us do this more quickly and efficiently than if many programs were impacted by Studio.

My job at the beginning was to help the Humanities chair understand what Studio was about and what shape it might take at our college. My first concern was that course sizes for Studios remained as small as possible. Since the three-credit FYC course cap was 22, the administration settled on a studio enrollment cap of 15 students for the equivalent of one three-credit course. It was also important that Studio be an "add-on" to FYC, not another full course in addition to it. Also, in order to expedite enrollment, we shrunk the footprint of Studio, making it worth only one academic credit. The smaller the commitment, the more likely students would enroll and the more easily the department could adapt to it. Studio thus became a one-credit, recommended option. For workload purposes, full-time and adjunct instructors, who also teach FYC, would teach three one-credit studio courses that would count as one three- credit course. Each one-credit course would be capped at five, since three sections of five each would total 15. Making Studio worth only one credit also made it easier to schedule many sections at many different times and dates, which in turn made it easier to work into both student and instructor schedules. Students from any FYC class might be placed in any studio section that met their scheduling needs. While this met an institutional need for flexible enrollment, it also invited interactional inquiry among FYC and Studio faculty over assignments and student needs, and among first-year students generally about what college writing means.

Although we've made some small adjustments to studio enrollment based on the survey responses, the existing course caps and teaching load requirements remain the same. Approximately 100 students are enrolled in Studio every fall, with a reduction of about 20 to 25 during the spring semester as some choose not to re-enroll. However, about ten new students add Studio in the spring.

PLACEMENT

OUR INITIAL POLICY

From the beginning, we sought to establish a reliable referral and placement process for Studio. We recognized Studio not as an "optional" program that students could choose to participate in once they enrolled in other courses (as described in this volume by Santana, Rose, and LaBarge at Arizona State), but as a separate, credit-bearing course that would be recommended to students based on a referral process. To do that, we made use of an existing program. New students come to the campus every June to participate in a process called "SOAR" or "Student Orientation and Enrollment." They get to know the campus and other new students, and work with advisors to determine their course schedules. We initially administered a required writing sample during the day's visit that took about 45 minutes to complete. I collected the samples and brought them to a waiting group of FYC faculty, and together we evaluated them holistically on a six-point scale. Students who scored a one or two were recommended to Studio. These assessments were made while students were doing other pre-enrollment activities. I and another FYC faculty member would then take the studio recommendations to the location where advisors were working with students to determine their fall schedules. Students would generally, but not always, follow our writing-sample-based recommendation and enroll in Studio. I used the time during the administration of the writing sample to explain to students what Studio was and to encourage them to enroll if they thought they would benefit from it. In this way, I was re-telling the "story" of studio work, defining a utopian narrative to new students that emphasized benefits over punishment (as described in this volume by Cardinal and Keown). I never used the language of deficiency, but as Cardinal and Keown would say, created a climate emphasizing "novice" writers over deficient ones. This referral process filled most of the roughly 100 studio seats available each fall semester, but during the first week of class, FYC instructors also explained what Writing Studio was and referred students to Studio based on their own preliminary assessment of students' writing.

For roughly ten years this was our referral process, and it usually worked to maintain enrollments. Participants understood their role, and the process of how students were recommended was clear to students. Without a clear referral process, the novelty of Studio could have led to confusion about who should take it and why. Tassoni and Lewiecki-Wilson described this difficulty when a standardized referral process was not implemented and their Studios were "populated by overlapping and knotted social, cultural, and institutional contexts and constraints. Students had been referred to the Studio through various diagnostic devices (writing placement recommendations, scores from a computer editing skills test, advising recommendations, and self-sponsorship" (Tassoni & Lewiecki-Wilson, 2005, p. 81).

Our studio enrollment was consistent because placement and purpose were clear to students. Studios were not required of all students. They were not used as a means of increasing the efficient use of time and FYC classroom space (like at a large institution like Arizona State). They were separate, third-space *courses* with their own credit-bearing weight and evaluation criteria based on clearly articulated goals, not drop-in opportunities similar to writing center visits.

This doesn't mean our referral system was without flaws. Despite my efforts to impact the narrative of novice writers, first-year students were sometimes embarrassed when told they should enroll in Studio. Since Studio was always recommended, not required, some students might not enroll, using the excuse of schedule conflicts or athletic commitments. Advisors, parents, and FYC faculty would work during the space of a single day to convince students that Studio was a good idea and would not be an extra burden. But data from surveys showed that instructors felt the neediest students were sometimes not enrolling, even though both instructors and students believed that a writing sample and instructor referrals were the best methods for placement. Although efficient, over time we began to appreciate the flaws in this system from the perspective of how students and their families make decisions about the first semester of college. We moved to a different referral process that enabled another element of Cardinal and Keown's "efficiency narrative" by locating placement out of the public eye and into the private decision-making realm of the family.

PLACEMENT POLICY CHANGES

Writing samples sent an early message to students that writing was important at the college, and allowed writing teachers to get a general sense of new students' writing abilities long before the first day of classes. But the samples were underutilized. I had imagined other uses of them, such as benchmarks in student portfolios or as faculty development tools. For many reasons, this didn't happen, and the rating system seemed unnecessary since we were only using them to determine who would be recommended to Studio. The criticism of using writing samples as one-time assessments was increasing, and our referral system seemed too dependent on filling as many seats as possible in a single day.

So the decision was made by the Director of Academic Advising to use SAT scores to initiate studio placement recommendations. This decision was based largely on expediency in enrollment management. The scores would be known long before SOAR began, giving Academic Advising an opportunity to do two mailings to new students.

The first letter went out to students who scored in the bottom third of SAT scores. These students were pre-enrolled in a yet-to-be-determined section of Studio. The letter explained what Studio is and why the student was being referred to it (SAT scores). It was then up to students to respond by email if they did not want to be enrolled. Out of the approximately 50 students who usually received this initial letter, typically two-thirds would not reject enrollment. The Director of Academic Advising attributed this to two factors: the perceived credibility of SAT scores among parents, and the extent to which these scores reinforced students' perceptions of their writing abilities. Students may have already felt they were poor writers. The SAT scores probably confirmed this for many. Roughly half of the 100 studio seats were usually filled after the first letter went out.

Once the first 50 seats were filled, a second letter went out (still before SOAR) to students from the middle third of SAT scorers. This letter was called a "priority enrollment letter" and also explained what Studio was but did not inform students they were "auto-enrolled." Instead, these students were asked to email the Office of Academic Advising if they DID want to be enrolled. The course was described as a "bonus" (again, implementing the story-changing goal described by Cardinal and Keown in this volume) that would help students succeed. Two-thirds of this group typically responded by requesting enrollment.

At this point, most studio seats were filled. If seats were still available, a second letter went out before classes started to the second group that did not respond by requesting Studio, giving them one more chance to respond. After that effort, the few remaining seats (usually no more than ten) were filled at the beginning of the semester through referrals from FYC instructors who requested writing samples from FYC students and/or gave students an opportunity to self-identify as someone who would like to enroll in Studio. Although it could be more difficult to enroll students at this point due to schedule conflicts, fewer students seemed to slip through the cracks with this system, no one was embarrassed during student orientation, and families could discuss the recommendation privately in a timely manner.

Along with these placement changes, students enrolled in Studio during fall semester are now auto-enrolled in Studio for spring semester. If they have a schedule conflict due to their new spring schedule, they are temporarily held in studio sections that have not yet been assigned a time or date until all student schedules and studio enrollments have been determined. Studio enrollment does typically drop off between fall and spring semesters. On average, 22 out of 100 students don't continue in Studio after fall semester because they drop the class, but approximately 10 new students do enroll, leading to a net loss between fall and spring semesters of about 12 students, or three sections of Studio. Students may not enroll in spring semester for a range of reasons, including problems with the instructor, the sense they don't need it, or because they are leaving the college. Each year, the past year's enrollments are reviewed to determine how many sections to offer in the coming year.

In survey data, a majority of both FYC and studio instructors, as well as students, indicated they felt like a writing sample (done by our faculty) was the best way to place students. But with SAT placement, there were few complaints that students were wrongly recommended to Studio or that students were slipping through the cracks. Instructors could continue to recommend students through a writing sample, and some still do, but there are advantages to placing students as early as possible in order to establish faculty and student schedules early on in the process.

As of this writing, we continue to leave open options that will balance administrative concerns (for example, having a writing sample done before student registration) with the need for adequate placement information. Directed Self-Placement (DSP) might be considered (Royer & Gilles, 1998), but at least one study indicates DSP is no better at predicting success than standardized test scores (Balay & Nelson, 2012) and would negate what many studio participants believe is the best way to place students: writing samples. Arguably, we already offer students a DSP-like choice through the letters inviting students to enroll in Studio. We might choose Accuplacer, a College Board product that would return us to using writing samples, but these assessments could be no more useful for our purposes than SAT scores. We could also invest in a more meaningful assessment, such as iMOAT, an on-line placement system created by MIT that enables local faculty assessments of writing done by students at home in response to a meaningful reading assignment. But again, for what purpose?

Whatever the next phase entails, we will probably keep in mind Elbow's (2012) reflections on when and how evaluation should be done; in an essay in honor of Edward M. White, Elbow recommends evaluations that are pragmatic, no-nonsense, and what he calls "good enough." In good enough evaluations, educators move beyond dualistic, polarized arguments over the value of different forms of evaluation and towards assessments which are feasible and do no harm. Although Elbow (and White) tend to see single score assessments as more harmful than useful, Elbow believes placing students in a one-credit supplement to their regular FYC course could be done by FYC instructors during the first week of classes (2012, p. 317). In the past, we have opted not to wait that long, even if it means relying on standardized scores. Although we would not use such scores for high stakes assessments, the use of these scores to initiate placement recommendations for a one-credit course has seemed reasonable. We agree with Elbow that during the first week of classes FYC instructors can and should make recommendations to Studio. But we also need a pragmatic approach to determining first-year student schedules before they come to campus. We have yet to determine how to do that pragmatically and intentionally with local placement tools.

WORKING WITH STUDENTS IN STUDIO

When we talk about Studio at Springfield College, we start with the goal of helping students make the transition to college life in general and college writing in particular. This is difficult because, as one studio teacher said in a survey response, if they are in Studio, "writing is a mystery to them. They may have good ideas, but not know what to do with them for a college class." Writing can be a hit or miss activity done "their way" successfully or not at all. In a FYC class with 20 or more students, this hit or miss approach may be enabled when the student fades into the background of a class lesson plan. Students can feel safe in their anonymity, but may not be. The collision of teacher and student expectations for their writing may just be postponed. Writing instruction and expectations are also different in college compared to high school for developmental and pedagogical reasons. These differences can lead to conflicts when students use old methods to solve new problems. Reiff and Bawarshi (2011) showed that new college students will cling to genres learned in high school regardless of the new tasks requiring new genres for college. For example, students who were taught to write using five-paragraph themes in high school in order to learn structure and organization in their writing may struggle to move beyond that in college assignments.

Writing Studio can be a space to take on this transition. Students reported in survey responses that Studio is a safer and more relaxed place for them than FYC. Because of the smaller class size, and because the studio instructor may be less of an authority figure than the FYC instructor, students may get to know and trust studio teachers sooner. Studio is a place where they may feel safer asking questions or making comments than if they were in a larger classroom, so their anxiety levels may be lowered. More one-on-one discussions take place with the studio instructor, who may need to understand the expectations of several different FYC classes. The studio teacher's interactions with students needs to be positive, since, as one instructor observed, "these students need gold stars." The smaller class size also encourages students to witness and imitate the positive writing behaviors of their peers. They may then feel more confident about trying new approaches rather than fall back on old strategies that are no longer effective, especially when the instructor draws attention to more successful strategies.

All of this might be possible in any remedial/basic writing classroom. But in our Writing Studios, teachers may not always define the agenda. As one studio instructor said, "It's what they [students] bring to you, not what you bring to them." And even though what they may be "bringing to you" is usually coming from an FYC class, students must own and accurately represent the problem, issue, and agenda in Studio. As a result, pre-determined lessons for studio work only to the extent that the instructor is able to anticipate student needs related to FYC requirements. Teachers used to being the center of attention find they must shift from a teacher-centered approach to a student-centered one in Studio. When the curriculum is student-centered, intervention into individual student problems can happen sooner. FYC instructors noted this as a benefit in survey data, suggesting that the content of the traditional basic writing class may not lead to appropriate interventions that address problems the student faces in real FYC classes, while the focus on FYC assignments in Studio enables students to respond to actual course-related writing problems. This approach is consistent with what researchers are discovering about knowledge transfer. Wardle (2007) tracked the knowledge students transfer from FYC to other courses, and found that an awareness of what strategies "work" for them is what "sticks," not particular "skills" taught by teachers. She also found that as students completed new and different writing tasks, they needed context-specific support to complete those tasks. Studio can enable both of these outcomes.

However, FYC instructors also noted that success within this student-agenda focus depends to a great extent on the individual studio instructor. As years passed, it became clear to us that some instructors were not meant to teach Studio. Some have misunderstood their role, taking advantage of Studio's intimacy to have discussions that had little to do with writing. Others have seen Studio as an opportunity to teach the same content as in a traditional basic writing class, only in a small group. And some have not communicated with FYC instructors or each other in productive ways.

Studio teachers also come to recognize a range of challenges to teaching what can seem like an "easy" course. Logistical challenges can be difficult, including keeping track of the different assignments students are working on, managing the amount of time they spend individually with students, dealing with student pessimism and adjustments to their first year of college, and navigating unclear assignments from FYC instructors. Studio instructors must also make decisions on the fly for each student in Studio: whether and how they should be working on intervention strategies, editing drafts, reorganizing material, or rethinking their purpose in writing. Studio instructors have to know what intervention, activity, or discussion is appropriate for each student in Studio, and they often have to make that determination quickly in order to keep everyone on task. All of this is usually done as students are mulling over an assignment. The best studio instructors tend to be veteran teachers who also understand larger global concerns such as departmental expectations and dynamics as well as the institutional climate.

THE VALUE OF TEACHER DIALOGUE

In our program, it's been essential that faculty who teach Studio also teach FYC classes. This ensures that studio discussions are between colleagues who know and respect the challenges of teaching FYC. As I mentioned at the onset, this opportunity for collegial dialogue drew me to Studio from the outset because of the potential for constructive pedagogical exchange.

From my perspective, and at its best, interactional inquiry has meant not only redefining "dominant stories about writers and writing" through student dialogue about writing (Cardinal and Keown, this volume) but creating a new form of dialogue among faculty members talking to each other about student issues and sharing strategies for addressing those issues. This discussion usually starts by talking about what's going on with students. Often it doesn't get much beyond the personal information the student allows to be shared: how the student has been sick or had family problems or is struggling with one issue or another. When the talk is about writing, the best place to start is often with what feels like shared values—how the student can't seem to get started, doesn't know how to organize her thoughts, or seemingly can't write a thesis sentence—and especially what's happened in Studio to address those goals. This sort of discussion establishes common ground and encourages further follow-up discussions. This sort of talk is embraced by Leach and Kuhne (this volume) who recognize the unique collegial needs of studio instructors. Instructors can benefit from on-going communication, reflecting on both the mundane, like attendance, and the major, like curriculum and assignments.

But these discussions can sometimes be more an ideal than a reality. Del Principe (2004) described the conflicts between basic writing teachers who believe in a process of linear development that requires students to work from the "simple," usually sentence-level, work before they can take on more "complex" research or other activities, and those who work beyond "the ground level." The gap between teachers grounded in "lore" and their own experience (but usually not research) and those grounded in a more complex view can be huge. One particular studio instructor in our program became unable to work with any other FYC instructor's students in Studio because of the distance between his reductive vision of what was necessary in both FYC and Studio compared to what other faculty members valued. He was appeased for several years by allowing only his FYC students to enroll in his Studios. Eventually, he was reassigned so he no longer taught Studio. Fortunately, he has been the exception. Most studio instructors have been eager to work with FYC instructors in order to help students succeed. At the same time, surveys from both in 2007 and 2013 show that both FYC and studio instructors were frustrated when communication did break down or when there was disagreement about what should be going on in either the FYC class or Studio. Studio instructors have, on occasion, questioned the value of an FYC assignment or activity; and FYC instructors have occasionally felt that studio work wasn't addressing student needs.

Some form of regular communication between faculty members about course content can sometimes head off these conflicts, especially since students can inaccurately report FYC class activities, poorly explain the purpose of an assignment, or even misremember assignment due dates. Teachers who may disagree about how or what students should be taught can nevertheless agree on the common goal of helping a student to succeed, and when departments define their goals for FYC, those goals can be agreed upon. But even when there is buy-in on goals, attention to communication issues can make a big difference in program success. Seemingly small adjustments, such as enabling all parties to have easy access to assignments, can lead to less confusion about expectations and reduce potential conflicts. Online access to all FYC course materials means less dependence on forgetful students, and regular communication means faculty members can quickly relate basic information about whether a student is showing up or what is or is not going on in Studio or FYC. In this volume, Leach and Kuhne describe the way their blog became the place where follow-up conversations that might be initiated on the way to class can continue in more depth later.

Although technology can be indispensable, the best way to have the most important discussions, in my experience, has been face to face. Questions are more easily answered, confusion more easily clarified, and a bond between colleagues more readily made, even if the interaction is relatively brief. When our Studios began, email was new, and many faculty members didn't yet use it. Going to faculty offices and chatting in doorways for five minutes before a class was often the best way to find out what was going on in both FYC and Studio. Grego and Thompson's dialogue sheets never really took off for our program. We tried them briefly, and FYC faculty lost or ignored them. However, one of our studio instructors used a form of a dialogue sheet. At the end of a studio class, each student wrote on a 4 x 6 card what they had done in Studio that day. The student then brought the card to their FYC class and placed it on the instructor desk or table at the beginning of class. At some point during the class, the FYC instructor read the card and wrote a brief response before returning the card to the student, who then brought the card back to the next studio class. The student enabled communication between the two instructors, but could also add their own comments or questions to the card. This worked as long as the FYC instructor didn't have too many studio students in the class and didn't have to write the same thing repeatedly on many cards. But even at their best, dialogue sheets don't provide FYC and studio instructors with an opportunity to bond as a team working to serve the needs of a particular student the way face-to-face communication does.

Are there other ways to achieve face to face dialogue? Regularly scheduled meetings might be the answer for some programs, but like most schools, we rely on adjuncts to teach both Studio and FYC. Their schedules often prevent them from attending regular meetings. Those of us fortunate enough to be full-time faculty members need to take on the responsibility to communicate with those who can't stay on campus all day. Our program has also benefitted from a full-time faculty member whose duties include coordinating the concerns, observations, and insights of all studio instructors. This person can organize meetings at different times, provide support materials, and serve as a liaison between the department and administration. Electronic tools can help with this process, but they are only a part of the solution.

Email is now a typical way for FYC and studio teachers to communicate about their students, and electronic classroom management systems have enabled everyone to have the same information. Our campus currently uses Moodle 2.3 (soon moving towards D2L). Studio teachers can be added as guests, making access to everyone's course materials easily done.

Even with the benefit of electronic resources, communication between faculty members does not necessarily go smoothly. A small number of faculty members who teach FYC are reluctant to share syllabi, allow access to Moodle, or generally correspond with studio teachers because of perceived threats to academic freedom. They may assume that a conversation about what goes on in their classroom is not appropriate unless initiated by an authority figure. Much depends on the level of trust that develops between studio and FYC teachers. Cooperation, not confrontation, most often leads to trust. But sometimes achieving that sense of cooperation is more a goal than a reality. Some faculty may be well-meaning, but hard to track down or slow to respond. Although a more standardized communication system might help, we haven't yet figured out how to do it in a way that formalizes consistent communication between faculty members. There are real limits to the extent to which technology can help, because real people are always the ones making the technology work.

NEGOTIATING CONFLICTS AND FINDING COMMON GROUND

Students are usually evaluated in Studio on the basis of attendance, preparation, and participation, as well as the quality of the one-on-one interactions outside of Studio. In other words, they are mostly evaluated in terms of the extent to which they model successful student behaviors in general rather than the quality of their writing. Evaluations take into consideration the answers to questions such as: Did they bring their most recent FYC assignment or draft to Studio? Do they demonstrate an understanding of what the assignment requires? Have they started to work on the assignment? Did they bring a draft in progress to Studio? Do they move forward and make progress on that work during Studio? Do they have an understanding of the genre expectations, purpose, and audience for an assignment? And do they follow up by meeting with the studio instructor outside of Studio when necessary to discuss their progress? It is ultimately up to FYC teachers to formally evaluate the quality of a student's writing. But what if there's a conflict between FYC and studio instructors over that quality?

One of Grego and Thompson's goals for Studio was to challenge the overly prescriptive curricula of some writing classes. In order for any of us to be open to change, we need a safe space where that can happen. Studio can be a space where students initiate discussions with teachers. According to Tassoni and Lewiecki-Wilson:

> Students and instructor work together in the workshop to
> examine individual, diverse writing curricula in order to
> uncover the rhetorical situation, including the contextual con-
> straints and determinants, of particular writing assignments;
> teacher expectations; and social issues in students' lives at
> home, work, and in the university. All these form the "place"
> from which students must write. . . . In short, understanding
> "place" requires a "space" from which to view it that is both
> inside and outside its boundaries. (2005, p. 70)

It's possible to imagine the studio instructor as limited to the role of "outside" service-provider or at best a framer of rhetorical constraints, as someone who has no territory to maintain but is negotiating the expectations of others. Tassoni and Lewiecki-Wilson recognized this in their discussion of third space as a contested zone, an "intersection of emplaced interests and concerns constitutive of our campus" (2005, p. 75). In order to negotiate this contested zone and maintain an on-going dialogue with FYC teachers and students, studio teachers must sometimes subordinate their own agendas to those of others. Tassoni and Lewiecki-Wilson recognized that sometimes Studios can become "complicit with the values and approaches to writing external to it" (2005, p. 87) when teacher dialogue breaks down and the values of those outside the Studio creep into it. How do we balance what the FYC teacher wants with what studio teachers or students believe to be important? How do studio teachers teach both "outside" and "alongside" the FYC teacher?

This question would be familiar to most faculty who have taught Studio, and may lead some to see Studio as a flawed agent of empowerment. Studios may challenge hegemonic models of teaching writing, but they might also reinforce those same models if the studio instructor does not respond to them. Still, the same instructor might both challenge certain FYC practices and reinforce them in the space of a single session, ideally choosing carefully when and how to engage with others based on an understanding of classroom circumstances and student needs. From this perspective, Studio's third space can be a malleable and selective tool for affecting change, perhaps more so than other mainstreaming models which tend to contain the "extra assistance" within established course boundaries and maintain established classroom "silos" that preserve the pedagogical status quo by discouraging dialogue across boundaries. In this sense, studio instructors must negotiate Cardinal and Keown's "interest-converging arguments" that sometimes focus on student success over conflict about the curriculum (this volume).

Since we began using Studios, not only has our placement strategy evolved, but the purpose and tone of the dialogue between FYC and studio teachers has become more predictable and purposeful. We are more likely to find common ground over what a student needs most, not disagree about whether the assignment is worthy. We are more likely to learn from each other's assignments when we acknowledge common student needs. But the core principals of Studio remain: mainstreaming students while creating and maintaining a third space to work and talk about writing, not necessarily settle conflicts over what's going on in FYC. Studio faculty members can "see" and "be seen" by others as we work together to understand each other's goals and meet student needs.

WHAT STUDENTS GET OUT OF STUDIO

Studio instructors are usually grateful for the opportunity to work both one-on-one and in groups with students in an environment that feels "out of class." They see meaningful benefits in having the time to review assignments from FYC, but they especially appreciate the relationships they form with students. Studio instructors see themselves as friendly supportive advisors providing guided assistance and helping students to enter the academic mainstream. But what do students value?

A student-centered approach focused on attendance, preparation, and participation means if students don't bring something meaningful to Studio—whether it be questions about an assignment, a rough draft of a paper, or some other starting place—they demonstrate a lack of personal responsibility, one cause of student failure in college. If they do come prepared, they have taken the first step in beginning a dialogue about their writing, and when the Studio becomes the place where the dialogue begins, they see their own writing process in action over time in a different location than FYC. This is where student perceptions of the benefits of Studio begin.

More than 75% of students reported in survey data that Studio helped them start essays earlier and learn to self-correct errors, both indicators of becoming more independent learners. Studio allows a space for these habits to be nurtured, most importantly by the studio teacher. But because students listen to not only the studio teacher but also each other in Studio, they get a sense of how others think about and approach various writing tasks. Students may sometimes be from other FYC classrooms with different assignments. Studio students explain to each other what their assignments are about and how they've responded to them. Students may read each other's drafts from different assignments with fresh eyes and see problems the writer hadn't seen or considered. Writers can also defend a rhetorical choice based on the nature of the differing assignments, and studio instructors can model rhetorical thinking about different assignments. As students begin to write more about what they read, Studio can also be a place where diverse reading strategies are discussed from a wide range of reading assignments.

Studio student survey responses indicated that students see working with peers as being an important benefit of Studio. Over the years, we've experimented with different combinations of students in a studio section in order to understand the benefits of various configurations. We wondered what the benefits would be if students in one studio section all came from the same FYC class compared to a section with students from different FYC classes, or even half from one FYC class and half from another. When students are all from the same FYC class, the Studio is typically easier to manage, and students are more likely to talk about shared reading and writing assignments. Students are also more likely to see how their peers approached the same writing assignment in different ways. When students are from different FYC sections and instructors, they see peers working with a wider range of writing assignments, but are less likely to see what their peers are doing as helpful to them since they may be doing something very different. Our experience suggests that quality peer relationships start with shared experiences in the FYC classroom, but can also be nurtured in Studio. We are currently moving towards studio groups in which students are all from the same FYC class, but the studio teacher is different than the FYC teacher. Our goal using this iteration is to enhance peer cohesion while maintaining Studio/ FYC teacher dialogue.

A WORK IN PROGRESS

Writing Studio at Springfield College continues to be a work in progress, but one with a past anchored in pragmatically meeting the needs of new students as they adjust to the demands and expectations of college writing. As illustrated in this discussion, Studio cannot succeed without a keen understanding of who your students are and how they learn. Studio also cannot succeed unless the goals and "efficiency narratives" of the institution are taken into consideration. In our case, that especially means retaining and graduating students on time. Placement needs to be done responsibly and consistently, but also efficiently and with flexibility so that no student who needs what Studio offers will be left out. The identities students bring with them to college must also be taken into consideration. We may not have a perfect referral process, but we will continue to explore a range of consistently reliable methods that respond to the ways students and their families make decisions about their class schedules. In the process, Studio needs to be framed in a positive way to students and their families so that it is always seen as a course that will enhance students' self-confidence as writers and improve their chances of success in FYC and at the college generally.

Teaching Studio will always be a student-centered enterprise. Studio teachers will always work both alongside and outside the regular FYC classroom for the reasons reviewed in this chapter. That work depends on successful communication between studio and FYC instructors. Although this communication may never be perfect, when done well and consistently, students who struggle in FYC are less likely to be forgotten. If student writing and academic struggles are neglected early on, students are more likely to drop out, transfer to another institution, or face academic challenges later that they are not prepared to meet. Studio teachers improve the likelihood that students will succeed and also sustain the value of the studio program by engaging in this dialogue with FYC teachers in a way that is not threatening but purposeful and constructive, with students at the center of the discussion. Studio teachers must be both patient and helpful, because Studio success depends on success in FYC.

This sort of faculty-led interactional inquiry may be one of the most noteworthy distinctions between Studio and a more generic stretch course. Among stretch programs, Studio is uniquely situated as both a student support system and a faculty development initiative. Faculty dialogue can enhance the potential for faculty development, but it can also model the sort of space where students experience writing as a rhetorical process. Studio students should listen to how their peers address writing challenges, and they should talk about their own writing on a regular basis outside the FYC classroom. Studio works best when writing teachers and students are talking to each other in order to work together to solve real writing challenges. Under the best of circumstances, faculty and students grow and develop both individually and as a community in order to help students adjust to the demands of college writing. That's what student writers and teachers of writing should want.

REFERENCES

Adams, P. (1993). Basic writing reconsidered. *Journal of Basic Writing, 12*(1), 22–36.
Adams, P., Gearhart, S, Miller, R. & Roberts, A. (2009). The accelerated learning program: Throwing open the gates. *Journal of Basic Writing, 28*(2), 50–70.

Balay, A. & Nelson, K. (2012). Placing students in writing classes: One university's experience with a modified version of directed self-placement. *Composition Forum, 25*. Retrieved from http://compositionforum.com/issue/25/placing-students-modified-dsp.php.

Bartholomae, D. (1993). The tidy house: Basic writing in the American curriculum. *Journal of Basic Writing, 12*(1), 4–21.

Cooney, E. & Lackey, S. (2010). Beyond the budget: Sustainability and writing studios. *Journal of Basic Writing, 29*(2), 74–96.

Del Principe, A. (2004). Paradigm clashes among basic writing teachers: Sources of conflict and a call for change. *Journal of Basic Writing, 23*(1), 64–81.

Elbow, P. (2012). Good enough evaluation: When is it feasible and when is evaluation not worth having? In N. Elliot & L. Perelman (Eds.), *Writing assessment in the 21st century: Essays in honor of Edward M. White.* (pp. 303–325) New York, NY: Hampton Press.

Grego, R. & Thompson, N. (1996). Repositioning remediation: Negotiating composition's work in the academy. *College Composition and Communication, 47*(1), 68–84.

Grego R. & Thompson, N. (2008). *Teaching/writing in thirdspaces.* Edwardsville, IL: Southern Illinois University Press.

Reiff, M. & Bawarshi, A. (2011). Tracing discursive practices: How students use prior genre knowledge to negotiate new writing contexts in first-year composition. *Written Communication, 28*(3), 312–337.

Rodby, J. & Fox, T. (2000). Basic work and material acts: The ironies, discrepancies, and disjunctures of basic writing and mainstreaming. *Journal of Basic Writing, 19*(1), 84–99.

Royer, D. & Giles, R. (1998). Directed self-placement: An attitude of orientation. *College Composition and Communication, 50*(1), 54–70.

Tassoni, J. & Lewiecki-Wilson, C. (2005). Not just anywhere, anywhen: Mapping change through studio work. *Journal of Basic Writing, 24*(1), 68–92.

Wardle, E. (2007). Understanding transfer from FYC: Preliminary results of a longitudinal study. *Writing Program Administrator, 31*(1/2), 65–85.

CHAPTER 6

A HYBRID MEGA-COURSE WITH OPTIONAL STUDIO: RESPONDING RESPONSIBLY TO AN ADMINISTRATIVE MANDATE

Christina Santana, Shirley K. Rose, and Robert LaBarge

Worcester State University, Arizona State University, and Piñon High School

What can ethically-minded writing instructors do when their administration mandates innovation at the level of delivery mode? This essay offers a responsible response to this question. It provides data and observations from the study of a two-semester, small-scale first-year composition (FYC) studio pilot program at the Tempe campus of Arizona State University (ASU). Studio courses for the pilot were populated by approximately 50 students per section. These mega-courses were both hybrid, requiring students to complete weekly asynchronous online assignments, and attached to optional Studios that students could choose to attend. This chapter details the design of this ASU program; investigates how problems with large composition class sizes can be mitigated by smaller, optional Studios taught by the same team of instructors who shared a curriculum; and explores the consequences of giving students the choice to attend Studios in the face of the truism that "academically optional" can mean "not important" in the minds of first-year students. Although our pilot program did not continue beyond two semesters, it did succeed in shedding light on the intersection of self-placement and required attendance in the context of studio courses and FYC.

PROGRAM DESCRIPTION

When institutional pressures compelled Arizona State University Writing Programs on the Tempe campus to explore innovative ways to make instruction in FYC more "efficient," several studio projects involving online instruction were initiated on multiple ASU campuses ("Downtown," "West," and "Tempe/ Main") around the same time. Each studio program had a unique design and program-specific goals, yet they shared student learning outcomes with FYC courses taught on all ASU campuses, which were aligned with the 2014 version of the Council of Writing Program Administrator's Outcomes Statement. Regardless of campus, most students enroll in a two-course required sequence— English 101 and English 102 with a writing-as-inquiry approach. The first course is "stretched" across two semesters for developmental writers; more advanced student writers take English 105, a one-semester "accelerated" version of FYC that combines the two courses into a single semester. Non-native speakers of English can enroll in dedicated FYC sections if they wish. Our provost asked the Tempe campus' Writing Programs Director, Professor Shirley Rose, and then Chair of the English Department, Professor Maureen Daly Goggin, to try out a studio design that asserted a new kind of efficiency within the composition classroom with the understanding that if successful, the design would be instituted program-wide, possibly affecting up to 13,000–15,000 students in FYC courses every year. Although "efficiency" in academic contexts is often a shorthand term for spending a smaller percentage of tuition dollars on instruction, in our case, "efficiency" efforts were directed at changing the way students experienced the FYC classroom (see the *Design Interpretations and Constraints* section).

In effect, and as Paul Butler explains, our studio pilot became a countermonument to our traditional writing program in that instead of "run[ning] the risk of becoming monolithic or static in [it]s evolution," we entered into a process of reinvention "as a kind of self-destruction" to revise and change our program structures (2006, p. 11). This revisioning meant that both students and instructors experienced composition instruction differently. Students who enrolled in our FYC studio pilot program were minimally required to 1) attend class once a week for 75 minutes with approximately 50 other students and 2) complete weekly asynchronous online course assignments. Readers may recognize the requirement to complete online assignments as typical of courses from a "hybrid" or "blended" model, which allows students to cut their in-class time in half. Unlike other hybrid models, including those already in place at ASU, our studio pilot program offered students the opportunity to attend *optional* 75 minute Studios on one or more days, up to five times a week with their own or another studio program instructor. Even though students' attendance at studio sessions was optional, attendance at the weekly whole-class meetings was not, as the Writing Program's policy of allowing no more absences than the equivalent of two weeks' worth of class meetings was in force for the pilot sections. As instructors, we individually led one weekly face-to-face class, supervised the concordant hybrid work, pair-taught two Studios per week, attended weekly or bi-weekly planning meetings, and shared a curriculum—all the while doing our best to maintain a critical stance (Adler-Kassner) in the interest of helping students succeed within these novel constraints.

THEORETICAL BASIS FOR PROGRAM DESIGN

Studios and their practices change from setting to setting. Traditionally, Studio is "[a] small group . . . [which] provides a place where students, concurrently enrolled in different writing classes, meet once a week to discuss and question the demands of their various writing assignments" (Tassoni & Lewiecki-Wilson, 2005, p. 69). Studios typically require attendance (Grego & Thompson, 2008, p. 8), are taught by a separate instructor (p. 10), and are informed by "interactional inquiry" (p. 12–13), in which

> [s]tudents and instructor . . . examine individual, diverse
> writing curricula in order to uncover the rhetorical situation,
> including the contextual constraints and determinants, of par-
> ticular writing assignments; teacher expectations; and social
> issues in students' lives at home, work, and in the university.
> (Tassoni & Lewiecki-Wilson, 2005, p. 70)

The use of interactional inquiry combined with a studio that is separate from students' "regular" writing classes is thought to create a thirdspace—a space/place outside of traditional writing classrooms and the institutions/disciplines that inform them.

The combination of interactional inquiry and thirdspace creation are hallmarks of Studios that reach well beyond the students and composition classrooms, meaning that studios can show up in institutional, economic, political, and faculty contexts. Studios can even spring up in digital spaces, as one does in Leach and Kuhne's work (this volume), where faculty sort out issues regarding shared students or curricula. Owing in part to their modularity, studios' contextual variances offer affordances and constraints that are not always, as Matzke and Garrett (this volume) point out, "easily aligned with studio best practices." This is true especially given the unique challenges studio practitioners face in borrowing from successful studios and/or their theoretical foundations to find space and enable interactional inquiry.

For us, our studio pilot program faced two clear challenges: large class size and optional attendance to Studio. These features of the program affected both instructors and students. Large writing classes can compromise both student-teacher and student-student interactions, and supplemental studio classes can be a long shot at mitigating negative effects. In addition, academically optional programs are a tough sell, especially at the freshmen level. Our students were asked to attend Studios out of their own volition. Composition theorists' ongoing discussions about Writing Studios, class size, required attendance at writing centers, and the efficacy of directed self-placement provided a basis for inquiry into the design of our studio program.

CLASS SIZE AND STUDIO THEORY

We expected that valuable teacher-student interactions were unlikely to occur in our large, 50-person, face-to-face sessions. In her discussion of "why small writing classes are better," Alice Horning (2007), shows "smaller class size in writing courses improves student success" because small classes are more likely to require writing, which improves students' engagement and motivation, and because teachers are better able to assess and target students' varying learning styles (p. 11). The ideal writing class size, according to the CCCC's "Statement of Principles and Standards for the Postsecondary Teaching of Writing" is 15 with preferably no more than 20 students.

Being highly aware of issues pertaining to the negative effects of large class sizes, we recognized that the success of our pilot program relied on Writing Studios' potential to provide supplementary support to "at-risk students" who would benefit from a smaller class (Tassoni & Lewiecki-Wilson, 2005, p. 69). Unfortunately for us, the constraints of our program design did not allow us to require studio attendance, staff with separate studio instructors, or consistently perform the usual style of interactional inquiry in a thirdspace setting, points we return to throughout this chapter. For these reasons, our study is also informed by two other strands of scholarship that are not typically found in studio theory: research on required attendance and directed self-placement.

REQUIRED ATTENDANCE AND DIRECTED SELF-PLACEMENT

We expected that students might sometimes choose to attend Studios even though they were optional. As such, our studio design was informed by scholarship that explores students' abilities to make choices with regard to their writing instruction, in particular, research on the efficacy of required attendance at writing center tutorials and on directed self-placement.

While acknowledging that Studios and writing centers create different student experiences, we shared writing center researchers' questions about the effects of mandating student engagement with supplementary writing instruction. That is, writing centers sometimes discourage teachers from requiring attendance at writing center tutorials for two main reasons: 1) negative student attitudes could influence the effectiveness of tutorial sessions, and 2) required tutorial conferences could create a demand for services that the writing center could not meet. Student attitudes mattered in our pilot program because the effectiveness of changed teacher-student roles presupposed positive student engagement and interaction. Students who chose to attend would encounter their teachers in a light that was much more casual, personal, and anecdotal; these differences might not have been valued or sustained without student buy-in.

Secondly, our studio design was informed, albeit indirectly, by discussions of directed self-placement. These discussions have mainly been limited to the level of course students may choose in a multi-level or sequenced FYC curriculum (Gere et al., 2010) or whether second language writers make informed choices about enrolling in special sections of FYC for multilingual writers or in "mainstream" sections (Costino & Hyon, 2007). Although the question of self-placement is of increasing interest, as more and more undergraduate writing programs experiment with other instructional formats, little formal study has been done about students' success in making good choices about the instructional format or delivery method of writing instruction. Dan Fraizer's article (this volume), is an exception, however, as his work argues that our systems of placement must be responsive to time and relational decision-making dynamics. For our study, questions about the effects of self-placement arose not only in students' initial choice of a hybrid class offering with elective face-to-face Studios, but also when students were asked to make a choice whether or not to self-place in studio sessions every week (or up to five times a week).

These research threads informed our inquiry as we sought to answer two key questions: 1) What was the nature of the support that instructors provided across the three pilot program modalities (lecture, hybrid, and Studio)? and 2) What was the nature of the choices that students made with respect to attending Studio? These questions lead us back into studio theory to consider the ways attending or not attending studios provided opportunities for students and instructors to rethink what it means to do school effectively.

DESIGN INTERPRETATIONS AND CONSTRAINTS

As Ritola et al. and Matzke and Garrett demonstrate (this volume), getting a studio off the ground and functioning can be a tricky, uphill battle. As we developed and implemented our Tempe Studio pilot program, we worked to respond to key mandates outlined by our administration, which we interpreted and experienced as design constraints (detailed in Figure 6.1 and discussed following the figure).

Administrative Mandates	Design Interpretations and Constraints
Innovate curriculum to more efficiently use instructional time and classroom space	Offer instruction in several delivery formats: • in-person whole-class meetings ("lectures") • asynchronous online activities ("hybrid") • in-person, optional workshops ("Studios")
Develop flexible delivery options within current contractual definitions of instructional workloads	Respect/maintain current instructor workloads: • no heavier overall student load • no additional contact hours with students
Create and teach a standard curriculum without undermining individual teachers' agency	Teach a shared curriculum: • developed collaboratively (before and during semester) • managed in weekly/bi-weekly meetings
Offer alternative instructional delivery options without additional capital expenditures and without disruption to class scheduling practices	Maintain classroom configurations: • no extensive classroom architectural renovations or refurnishing • no new classroom scheduling configurations

Figure 6.1. Administrative mandates vs. design interpretations and constraints in our studio pilot.

OFFER INSTRUCTION IN SEVERAL DELIVERY FORMATS

The enrollment process for our studio pilot program was similar to signing up for a physical science course with a corresponding lab. For example, if a student registered for a "lecture" (whole-class meeting) that met on Wednesday, he or she would be prompted to register for a corresponding "lab" (Studio) session on either Friday or Monday. The teacher of Wednesday's class, likewise, would co-lead Studios on Friday and Monday. Figure 6.2 shows the weekly schedule of all the "lecture" classes and their corresponding Studios. However, even if a student from Wednesday's "lecture" class was officially registered for Friday's (or Monday's) Studio, she or he had the realistic option of attending *any* Studio during the week.

	Monday	Tuesday	Wednesday	Thursday	Friday
9–10:15	Class A	Class B	Class C	Class D	Class E
10–11:45	Studio C, D	Studio D, E	Studio E, A	Studio A, B	Studio B, C

Figure 6.2. Schedule for Tempe studio pilot ENG 101 and 102.

As mentioned, forging new areas of innovation and efficiency were goals charged to our department by our provost. Earlier hybrid models had paved the way in this regard by giving students format options regarding how much time they spent in face-to-face portions of the class. Studios took this a step further by allowing students to make choices about how much and what kind of face-to-face supplementary instruction they felt they needed. We assumed that high-performing students would choose to go to Studio sparingly, while students who needed extra help could attend Studio as needed. Theoretically, a student could spend as little as 75 minutes per week in their FYC class (75 minutes of required whole-class, in person "lecture" time and zero minutes of optional studio time) or as much as 450 minutes in class if they chose to attend Studio every day! If students decided to attend studio sessions, they would have been very likely to encounter students from other classes, engage with students from their own class on a personal level, and see their own teacher interact with a co-teacher, or even avoid their own teacher entirely by choosing to attend completely different studio sessions. All of these options would be either impossible or simply not available to students in more traditional two- or three-day-a-week classes, or even in more contemporary hybrid or online formats. The optional studio classes therefore serve to allow greater scheduling flexibility for students and to demonstrate innovation and efficiency.

Respect/Maintain Current Instructor Workloads

Teaching in the Tempe studio pilot program did not mean that instructors worked harder for less pay. Instead, they actually spent less time in front of a class than teachers teaching traditional two- or three-day-a-week classes. Ordinarily, for example, a fall schedule would require a graduate teaching associate to teach two classes of approximately 25 students each.[1] A typical two- or three-day-a-week teaching schedule would then place teachers in front of students for 300 (150 x 2) minutes every week. Our studio model, on the other hand, allowed instructors to teach the same number of students in one "double"-sized section (50 = 25 x 2) while being in front of the classroom only 225 minutes per week (75 minutes of "lecture" and 150 minutes of Studio). This reduced not only teacher workload, but number of classrooms being filled per week.

---

1   In fall 2012, the enrollment caps for first-year composition courses were maintained at 25 students per section, so the corresponding caps for these pilot sections were 50 students per section.

TEACH A SHARED CURRICULUM

Team-teaching the Studios motivated the five pilot teachers to develop a shared curriculum in which basic content and concepts were the same, and variability was limited to presentation styles and classroom activities. We spent time discussing the limits and possibilities of major writing assignments, and we mapped out daily plans the summer before the fall semester and during the winter break before the spring semester. To streamline the process, teacher pairs were formed in the spring and given the responsibility of providing the group with optional materials corresponding to their vision of one entire assignment sequence (approximately five weeks of plans). During the semesters, instructors met weekly or bi-weekly to negotiate their own and their students' interpretations of shared assignments and to develop shared grading rubrics.

MAINTAIN CLASSROOM CONFIGURATIONS

The "pilot" nature of our program required us to work with existing classroom space. So, much like Matzke and Garrett's (this volume) bricolage approach, which utilized "uptake" and "not talk" as tools for recognizing and assessing available resources for program design, we made use of existing computer-mediated, mid-sized classrooms. These rooms accommodate approximately 50 students at a time and are located in the Engineering Center Complex. Each student had access to a desktop computer but limited space for actual pen-and-paper writing. The presence of computer monitors made interaction among students, as well as between instructors and students, difficult. In fact, students were seated facing computer monitors and had to turn or move their chairs to follow lectures or to work with other students, which might have provided less incentive to engage or interact.

PROGRAM ASSESSMENT METHODS AND DATA COLLECTION

INSTRUCTORS

Ten FYC sections—five English 101s in the fall of 2012 and five English 102s in the spring of 2013—were enrolled in this study. Eight different instructors (three of the original five stayed in the spring) taught 377 students (approximately 47 students per section in the fall and a range of nine to 44 students per section in the spring). Graduate Teaching Associates, full-time Lecturers and Instructors, and part-time Faculty Associates were recruited in the new TA training seminar or through direct invitation from ASU Writing Programs Director Shirley Rose. Instructors in the study had a range of FYC teaching experience (between 25 years and one year); the TAs were less experienced, though each had taught at least one section of English 101 and 102 prior to the start of the study.

Data Sets

In all, five separate data sets are included in this study. The first and second sets include optional student surveys collected at the midterm of the fall 2012 semester and at the end of the spring 2013 semester. These Likert-style surveys focused on self-reports of attendance patterns, attitudes toward discrete components (in-person whole-class meetings, asynchronous online hybrid activities, and in-person studios), perceived value of discrete components in achieving course objectives, and students' self-anticipated final grade. Participation in the optional student surveys across semesters resulted in a 21% and 63% sample of students, respectively, in the fall 2012 and spring 2013 semesters. The third data set comprised instructors' reflections on student attendance at studio sessions. Since program policy did not require students to sign-in and restricted teachers from counting studio attendance toward students' overall grades or participation, we depended upon instructors' recollections of individual student attendance in the optional Studios, which they recorded in three categories: "never attended," "occasionally attended," and "often attended." The fourth data set is made up of students' final grades, which, along with the survey data (Sets 1 and 2) and teachers' reports of students' studio attendance (Set 3), were subject to statistical analysis in consultation with the Arizona State University Statistical Consulting Center in the College of Liberal Arts and Sciences. The fifth data set is comprised of transcribed recordings of five focus groups conducted with approximately 50 students (five groups of ten) during a week of studios around the midterm of the fall semester. Students responded to a series of questions regarding the value of studios and their own attendance patterns. These live group interviews lasted between 15 and 30 minutes. Grounded theory was used to code, discover patterns and analyze these qualitative data.

DATA

Much like Grego and Thompson's Studio model, instructors used the studio space, in both the fall and the spring, as a way to engage in interactional inquiry with students. However, one difference between their model and ours loomed large: while Grego and Thompson used Studio to give students a break from their teachers (in order to draw students from different writing courses into discussions about the demands of their assignments and the expectations of their teachers), we provided supplemental instruction for our own students in our program when they chose to attend Studios co-led by their instructor. In this section, we draw from survey and focus group data to evaluate what happened in our Studios.

During both semesters, the shared curricula informed the kinds of supplemental instruction teachers provided to mitigate the effects of the large lectures. In the fall, for example, the multi-modal curriculum carried over to Studios to help students develop the digital literacies required to do well in the course and adjust to the technological aspects of the projects, which for this particular class included using Google Maps, Blogger, and Audacity. Similarly, in the spring, major curricular projects required more advanced traditional rhetorical critiques and arguments, which used citation formats (MLA, APA) and outside research. Unfortunately, content covered in the spring semester Studios lent itself to a different, somewhat stilted style. Students and teachers seemed to struggle to find ways to match the stride of their fall Studios. As Fred, a student who enrolled in both semesters of the pilot program, describes:

> In the fall [in Studio we would] work together, collaborate on projects, ask questions, and watch brief presentations to clarify information about the project. In spring, it was structured like a full on lecture. I much preferred the laid back environment that allowed me to freely work on my assignments and ask questions or work as a group.

Even though spring Studios did seem to put some students off in terms of pre-determining the paths of inquiry and somewhat scripting responses, interactional inquiry remained. Students who chose to attend Studios continued to interact with teachers in ways that the larger lecture classes did not allow. Students were able to observe co-teachers navigating the same content, getting in each other's way, and reconciling their different perspectives through intelligently productive conversations, as the following instructor says:

> [While in Studio] we share different answers to the same question, and discuss how our assignments differ . . . [or we] disagree. These are moments where [students] see that education is not simply about memorizing concrete facts but rather being able to justify your interpretations and observations— developing tools for knowing. (Instructor Donald)

In fact, the highly interpretable and often contentious nature of the content of English 102 combined with the varying disciplines of each instructor (three in literature, one in rhet/comp, and one in linguistics) often made for much more productive and institutionally-revealing co-teacher conversations than the fall Studios' focus on using new technology.

Gerald Graff's (1992) arguments for "teaching the conflicts" in *Beyond the Culture Wars* came to mind when we heard teachers discuss the benefits they saw in students being able to observe two teachers working together—disagreeing productively and respectfully as well as bringing complementary skills and expertise to the studio meetings. Such conflict further helped students "build experiences with and validate knowledges about writing, experiences and knowledges that . . . struggle with the institution's desire to turn [students and teachers] into its objects and instruments of power" (Grego and Thompson, 2008, p. 175). In many cases, these exchanges between studio teachers modeled the tone and rhetorical strategies of civil debate that teachers wanted their students to learn and adopt for their writing in the course and beyond. Moreover, whether instructors are modeling or students are engaging, these moments—or sites of interactional inquiry, as Leach and Kuhne's (this volume) explain—can create safe spaces where individual realities are affirmed and situated knowledge can be brought to bear to the service of creating community and better futures for all involved.

Ultimately, however, only 77 percent of students enrolled in the studio version of English 101 in fall 2012 completed the course with a passing grade of a "C" or better; 22 percent either dropped, failed or withdrew, a full 11 percent lower than the completion rate for non-studio English 101 hybrid courses. The spring 2013 numbers were no better: 78 percent of English 102 students passed with a "C" or better compared to the 91 percent pass rate for non-studio 102 hybrids (see Figure 6.3). These results led our provost to decide to cease the studio pilot program.

	Fall 2012: English 101	Spring 2013: English 102
In-person courses	89%	90%
Hybrid courses	88%	91%
Studio course	77%	78%

Figure 6.3. Delivery models and passing students (students who passed with a "C" or better).

COMPLICATED RELATIONSHIPS: INSTRUCTIONAL SUPPORT AND STUDIO ATTENDANCE

In line with our expectations but contrary to our hopes, students were to a great extent opting out of Studio. In both the spring and fall semesters, studio attendance was highest at the beginning of the semester, lowest toward the end, and peaked at 12 and sunk to zero; attendance averages were different depending on teacher pairings or particular days, but it was unusual to see more than three students at a time. And some students never attended. These "wild" fluctuations were both a blessing and a curse in the eyes of instructors who on particular days or weeks collectively celebrated opportunities to co-lead effective Studios only to experience empty classrooms the next time around.

These outcomes compelled us to consider ways that we as instructors might challenge the dominant script in the classroom, tap into student underlife, their counterscript, to merge our world views in moments of "unscripted improvisation" (Gutierrez, Rymes & Larson, 1995). We hoped to manage the tensions we felt as a result of maintaining dual commitments: 1) to the integrity of the program design (which we felt left students out to dry), and 2) to our responsibilities as writing teachers to closely structure and scaffold student success. We responded by working to help students think more—not just once or twice, but again and again—about the potential drawbacks of the openness of the program. Because students' success was in part riding on their willingness to make choices about attending studios, we wanted to cultivate a critical consciousness to encourage student discernment and ownership of their writing education again and again over the semester (See Dan Fraizer's article, this volume). More specifically, we went to work developing formative self-assessments to demonstrate what Studios were good for, and we reviewed the assessment questions with students in class and emailed them as reminders. See Figure 6.4 for an example self-assessment. On paper, the self-assessments identified essential components, concepts, and milestones of projects we developed by circulating questions among ourselves. We asked questions such as: "Is it critical for the assignment?" or "Do you think that *most* students know how to do that?" or "What should students have done by this point?"

Week 8 (10/15–19) Draft Workshop: Developing Blog Entries and Evaluative Criteria

Do You Need to Attend this Workshop?

Are your annotations focused by evaluative criteria?

Have you had someone navigate your links successfully?

Does your introduction prepare a reader for the project?

Do you have at least 500 words drafted?

Figure 6.4. Example self-assessment for students.

Furthermore, we made sure we framed the questions in ways that clearly signaled what were desirable outcomes and features of the project. Specifically, we focused on developing self-assessments in keeping with what Frank Pajares' (2003) research on self-efficacy of student writers has shown to be critical for the development of good judgments about one's own writing abilities. In retrospect, we noted that our self-assessment exercises were sometimes directed toward what students were interested in or felt they needed help on. This got them in the door with practical promises, and we could then work in interactional inquiry as integral to the larger process.

Another way the self-assessments affected Studios was that they helped us to plan what content would be covered or which questions would be attended to (at least), an effect which challenged the philosophy we had established at the start of the studio pilot. Within this initial orientation, instructors were encouraged to respond to issues students brought to Studio, rather than coming to the studio class with a set agenda. However, as we began to recognize the highly significant dependent relationships between grades and studio attendance, especially between semesters,[2] we were inclined to hybridize Grego and Thompson's (2008) guideline that Studios should be "orient[ed] toward responding to what students say, do and need" with our formative self-assessments in hopes that students might think again and again about attending Studios (p. 10).

While studio attendance did not markedly improve after the introduction of the self-assessments, neither did it slide, and some pilot instructors held steadfast by promoting the Studios anew, posting assessments to course online Blackboard shells, and asking the questions out loud in class. As Grant put it, "like in class, he'll put stuff on the board and say, 'these are things that we will be covering in the Studio, so if you need help with this stuff go ahead and come along.'" Despite the drifting of our Studios away from some of Grego and Thompson's (2008) general guidelines, the weekly student self-assessments gave instructors the chance to bring interactional inquiry into the lecture class itself because the assessments guided students through a process that allowed them to make their own informed choices.

COMPLICATED RELATIONSHIPS: STUDENTS' PERCEPTIONS AND STUDIO ATTENDANCE

We looked to the surveys and focus groups to take a pulse on students' perceptions of the relative importance of the Studios and see what more we could do to get

---

2   Students who were reported to have "occasionally" attended the workshops passed the course with higher grades than those who never attended workshops. The correlation between grades and attendance in the spring semester has a P-value of <0.001.

students to attend them. But questions concerning how conveniently scheduled the Studios were, the usefulness of studio topics, opportunities to improve their writing, or their confidence in making good choices about whether or not to attend a Studio yielded no significant data. Furthermore, their self-reported studio attendance and their assessments of how well they were learning to meet any of the course outcomes also failed to illuminate much. These results suggested that these factors were not the bases students used to make decisions. However, one key finding that surfaced from our data was students' use of a general rubric of feeling "completely confused" to determine whether they would attend a particular week's Studio. That is, when students were "sure of what [was] expected and clear about what [would] be covered" in Studio, they seemed to be less likely to attend (James). As Sam explains: "Studios are designed to aid you if you are not understanding, comprehending, or you just don't know what to do at all. . . . If I understand what is going on in class, or we were just going over something we've been over already, then I don't need to attend Studio." Since Sam does not mention the self-assessments as contributing to his decision-making process, his example stands in contrast to David's, which relies on the self-assessments, but is still based on degrees of feeling informed: "Every week [Professor Hardy] posts when Studios are and what's going to happen, so I feel very well informed on whether or not to go." Because studio attendance seemed to hinge on the information we provided, we may have encouraged students' to skip Studio by circulating self-assessments, which actually made them feel informed. In fact, no students reported that they attended Studio for personal or goal-oriented reasons.

Additionally, in understanding how and why students made their individual choices about studio attendance, we anticipated that even if students recognized they could benefit, they might not actually choose to attend or follow through due to unpredictable events and circumstances (as we all have no doubt experienced). Sonia's regret sheds light on our point: "I honestly wish I would have gone to more Studios." The importance of her reflection is intensified when coupled with another student's sense that his decision to attend Studio should not have been his decision at all: "Studios should be mandatory, but since they weren't, I busied myself with mandatory things out of priority" (Earl). Students like Earl often have more demands than they have time for, which realistically means that anything not required (like Studio) is low priority. These answers demonstrate that students' theoretical valuing of the Studios was not what drove decision-making. Instead, more pressing everyday events were larger factors, a consequence of a more pragmatic approach to education's role in their lives, as Elly explains: "What determines it for me is that I have a really early work schedule, and so I try to come because I know that it is beneficial, and it has helped me when I do come. . . . but it is a matter of if I need more sleep."

DETERMINING THE ACCURACY OF ASSESSMENT WITH PROGRAMMATIC GOALS

Despite students' perceptions of the significance of studio attendance to achieving several of the outcomes, from the analysis we did *not* find a statistically significant association between optional studio attendance and high student grades. Frequent studio attendance did not cause students to receive higher class scores, and infrequent studio attendance did not cause lower class scores. To investigate the relationship more deeply, we asked instructors to classify each student's studio attendance into one of three categories: "never attended," "occasionally attended," and "often attended." According to their reports using these criteria, everyone (with the exception of one student) who attended elective Studios *often* received a course grade of "A" or "B+." We also saw that some who received high grades had *never* attended Studio; yet no one who attended Studio *often* ended up failing the course. Simply stated, while studio attendance was not essential to receiving a high grade, frequent attendance appeared to assure a high grade.

There are a few caveats to mention. First, course grades are a crude indication of whether students could have benefitted from attending Studio because most students were earning "A's" and "Bs" anyway. Secondly, our analysis showed that student grades were statistically different from instructor to instructor, and patterns of student attendance at the optional studios varied with the instructor. Final grades and teacher's reports of students' studio attendance indicated highly significant dependent relationships between grades and studio attendance, and teachers and studio attendance. Individual instructor attributes and teaching styles that inspired high studio attendance, may have also tended to belong to instructors who awarded higher grades.[3]

CONCLUSION

Given the need for more research on understanding students' abilities to make efficacious and strategic choices regarding their supplemental writing instruction, this study described the results of a studio pilot that investigated the possibility that large composition class sizes could be mitigated by smaller, optional studios taught by the same team of instructors who shared a curriculum. We found that students had highly variable studio attendance patterns (which we count as evidence that choices were being made), and those who attended Studios at least *occasionally*—in the recollections of their instructors—had a higher

---

3   The correlation between teacher and grade for spring 2013 had a P-value of <0.001, and the correlation between teachers and student attendance patterns in spring 2013 had a P-value of 0.011.

success rate than those who did not, validating to an extent the usefulness of the Studio program. Our findings are in line with Writing Studio theory and recent class size research (Horning, 2007) that recognizes small class sizes as a vital part of student success. Additionally, our study draws an important distinction between self-placement (which allows students to determine the level of difficulty of the material they are required to master) and required attendance (which structures student choice regarding elements within a course) to show that though students may seek out extra attention when they need it, they may only do what is required for a number of pragmatic and very rational reasons.

Two key limitations of our study are important to note. First, the attendance requirements attached to the lectures and hybrid components may have implied a higher value compared to the optional Studios, a point that students who expected higher grades may have picked up on. They considered the hybrid component more important to their success than the Studios, but less important than the lectures. Second, while we felt that the self-assessments did much to characterize Studios as of substantive value, our studio design may have implied that Studios were only for writers who needed help. Although we believe that all writers have something more to learn about writing, we are not convinced that our model communicated that belief.

We have since pondered a number of possibilities to account for why students failed our hybrid mega-course with optional Studio at a higher rate than the traditional or hybrid FYC courses offered at ASU, possibilities that this study was not designed to answer. First, once students discovered the attendance policy, the offer to "cut in-class time in half" may have proved too tempting an offer for "weaker" (or simply busier and thus—in some ways—more at-risk) students, who may have recognized an opportunity to spend the least amount of time possible in class. And, as Dan Fraizer (this volume) points out, "without a clear referral process, the novelty of Studio could have led to confusion about who should take it and why." Second, additional research could shed light on ways that failing grades earned in the Studio might be seen *positively*, as representing important learning. After all, by allowing students to choose their own course of study, we were asking them to take responsibility, which entailed making mistakes as well as doing things correctly. However, it may very well be the case that more students felt like Sonia, who "wished she had attended more sessions," suggesting that our studio course may have prompted students to think more about the importance of going to class. Perhaps students who failed the FYC studio course might (in the long term) have a higher rate of finishing college because they were given a chance to make a relatively low-stakes mistake. It may also be that students felt empowered by the choices the course offered and were able to identify their own goals outside of those outlined by the course. In any case, we as instructors, had we had the goal of programmatic sustainability, might have borrowed more from Dan Fraizer's work (this volume) to further enable decision-making (in terms of exploring options for pre-enrollment and sending initial and follow up letters home that marketed the benefits of choosing the Studio). As Fraizer showed, these efforts may have benefited our students greatly, especially in terms of supporting decision-making strategies as transferable (Wardle).

Unfortunately, our studio design created significant barriers to achieving one or more implicit or explicit goals for our FYC curriculum. And even though improvements in student persistence in the second semester of the pilot suggest that perhaps those barriers can be overcome as teachers develop strategies for addressing them, our College of Liberal Arts and Sciences Deans' office reviewed our disappointing "DEW" (Drop, "E," and Withdraw) rates for our fall 2012 studio sections and petitioned the Provost for permission to discontinue the Studio. We did not object. There have been no subsequent plans to revisit this particular studio model.

Instead, for us, the experience of participating in the studio pilot has meant that we see the potential in countermonuments (Butler) and counterscripts (Gutierrez et al.) at the level of program or instructor as allowing for a reinvigorated commitment to ethical teaching practices, particularly those that invite, support, and encourage interactional inquiry regardless of context.

REFERENCES

Adler-Kassner, L. (2008). *The activist WPA: Changing stories about writing and writers.* Logan, UT: Utah State University Press.

Butler, P. (2006). Composition as countermonument: Toward a new space in writing classrooms and curricula. *WPA: Writing Program Administration, 29*(3), 11–25.

Costino, K. A. & Hyon, S. (2007). "'A class for students like me': Reconsidering relationships among identity labels, residency status, and students' preferences for mainstream or multilingual composition. *Journal of Second Language Writing, 16*(2), 63–81.

Council of Writing Program Administrators. (2014). The WPA outcomes statement for first-year composition (3.0). Council of Writing Program Administrators. Retrieved from http://wpacouncil.org/positions/outcomes.html.

Gere, A. R., Aull, L., Green, T. & Porter, A. (2010). Assessing the validity of directed self-placement at a large university. *Assessing Writing, 15*(3), 154–176.

Graff, G. (1992). *Beyond the culture wars: How teaching the conflicts can revitalize American education.* New York, NY: W. W. Norton & Co.

Grego, R. C. & Thompson, N. S. (2008). *Teaching/writing in thirdspaces: The studio approach.* Carbondale, IL: Southern Illinois University Press.

Gutierrez, K., Rymes, B. & Larson, J. (1995). Script, counterscript, and underlife in the classroom: James Brown versus Brown v. Board of Education. *Harvard Educational Review, 65*(3), 445–472.

Horning, A. (2007). The definitive article on class size. *WPA: Writing Program Administration, 31*(1/2), 11–34.

Pajares, F. (2003). Self-efficacy beliefs, motivation, and achievement in writing: A review of the literature. *Reading and Writing Quarterly, 19*, 130–168.

Tassoni, J. P. & Lewiecki-Wilson, C. (2005). Not just anywhere, anywhen: Mapping change through studio work. *Journal of Basic Writing, 24*(1), 68–92.

Wardle, E. (2007) Understanding "transfer" from FYC: Preliminary results of a longitudinal study. *Writing Program Administration, 31 (2)*, 65–85.

CHAPTER 7.

PROFESSIONAL DEVELOPMENT, INTERACTIONAL INQUIRY, AND WRITING INSTRUCTION: A BLOG CALLED "ACCELERATED ENGLISH @ MCTC"

Jane Leach and Michael Kuhne

with Kathleen Devore, Jenifer Fennell, Liz McLemore, and Darren Wieland

Minneapolis Community and Technical College

In 2013, a small group of composition instructors at Minneapolis Community and Technical College began teaching a new studio course, one designed to streamline students' transition from developmental writing to the successful completion of a college-level writing course. We based the course—Accelerated Developmental English—on the Accelerated Learning Program at the Community College of Baltimore County. An integral aspect of Accelerated Developmental English is the use of the Studio model. In fact, the Studio model functions in two different settings for us. First, the Accelerated Developmental English (ADE) course is a Studio model designed for students to workshop their writing with one another and their studio group facilitator. Second, we created a blog—Accelerated English @ MCTC—that provided us a place for interactional inquiry, a basic tenet of the Studio model.

In *Teaching/Writing in Thirdspaces: The Studio Approach,* Grego and Thompson (2008) coined the term "interactional inquiry" to refer to the process of "using small group collaboration for rounds of listening, talk, and writing to generate ideas; acting upon [those ideas]; and reflecting about them—a continual to-and-fro between action and reflection" (p. 72). Our blog, in particular, focused on the action aspect of this methodology, which involved "trying out approaches, actions or changes discussed within the inquiry group in their daily lives at the site" (p. 50). Although the Studio model's origins were in the classroom and focused on writing students, Grego and Thompson wisely recognized the value of interactional inquiry for composition instructors. They suggested that "Studio staff interactional inquiry helps us to formulate our own plans and proposals for local change" (2008, p. 159). This was evident throughout the exchanges on the blog, as writing instructors posed plans for the course, received feedback, and revised those plans. Grego and Thompson also suggested that "Studio communication . . . with teachers . . . helps us to resist the isolation from each other encouraged . . . by higher education institutional structures" (2008, p. 160). Teaching a 5:5 load while addressing the writing of over 100 students per semester made it difficult to find time to do anything other than attend to our students and their writing. Our use of a blog as a site for interactional inquiry mitigated some of that isolation by fostering professional development, collegiality, and support. In particular, the blog was useful in helping us create community, support one another, and affirm our reality, as well as celebrate success and plan for the future.[1] It is this blog and the faculty's interactional inquiry that serves as the focus for this chapter.

INSTITUTION AND INSTRUCTOR CONTEXT

Minneapolis Community and Technical College (MCTC) is a public, urban, two-year comprehensive college located in downtown Minneapolis.[2] According to the college's website, of 13,874 students enrolled in fall of 2013, 32.3% were Black, 8.5% were Hispanic, 5.5% were Asian or Pacific Islander, and 1.7% were American Indian. In addition, 54% were Pell grant recipients, and 27% were first-generation students. The average age of students was 28. It is not uncommon for many first-time students to be placed into courses at the developmental, pre-college level. For first-time students entering in the fall semesters of 2005, 2006, and 2007, 36% were placed in developmental writing (98% were placed in developmental mathematics, while 41% were placed in developmental reading courses). The percentage of students placed in *all three developmental courses* was 30% (Asmussen, 2012, p. 2). Like many community colleges nationwide, our department sought to streamline the experience for students who tested into developmental English, which led to the creation of the ADE course.

Faculty who initially taught ADE and participated on the blog had extensive experience teaching developmental writing, ranging from 13 to over 30 years at institutions throughout the county and, in some cases, outside of it. Kathleen Sheerin Devore, who initiated the accelerated curricular change with her guerilla acceleration (more on this later), taught composition for 27 years everywhere

---

1   For another discussion of this idea, see Fraizer in this volume.

2   "Comprehensive" here means that the college provides both liberal arts and career/technical education curriculum.

from south Boston to South Africa to south Minneapolis. With a Ph.D. in Composition, Rhetoric, and Literacy Studies from the University of Minnesota and a minor in Post-Colonial Studies, Kathleen taught developmental writing for 13 years. Jenifer Fennell earned a doctorate in English from the University of Minnesota and taught developmental writing for 13 years. Michael Kuhne taught for over 30 years in both secondary and higher education settings and taught developmental writing courses for 14 years. His Ph.D. (English) focused on composition studies and rhetoric. Jane Leach received her Ph.D. in English with an emphasis on American literature at the University of Minnesota in 1999, and she taught developmental writing at MCTC for 14 years. Liz McLemore received her master's in English with training in composition and rhetoric at the University of Oklahoma and taught composition, rhetoric, and cultural studies courses at the University of Minnesota before joining the English department at MCTC. She taught developmental writing off and on for over 20 years. Darren Wieland received an MFA in creative writing from Minnesota State University-Mankato and taught developmental writing for four years. A number of us have worked together on various initiatives throughout our time at the college, and the more veteran instructors worked closely with one another on an earlier developmental English curricular revision effort, which transitioned from exit examinations to portfolios. In addition, all developmental English instructors met three times a semester to discuss various curricular and evaluation issues. These past work experiences and the relationships we developed helped us work together more effectively in the curricular change to ADE.

ACCELERATED DEVELOPMENTAL ENGLISH AND STUDIO MODEL

In spring 2013, we piloted six sections of ADE, inspired and informed by the Community College of Baltimore's County's (CCBC) Accelerated Learning Program (ALP). Key to our interpretation of the ALP model, ten developmental writing students are embedded in a three-credit college-level writing course with fifteen college-level writing students. That instruction is supplemented for the developmental writing students with a two-credit ADE course which uses the Studio model. The ADE course meets for a 50-minute session immediately after the 75-minute college-level writing course, and this pattern repeats itself twice a week. Students enrolled in the supplementary course submit a final portfolio that is evaluated by a committee of developmental writing instructors. When we designed the curriculum for the ADE course, our focus was on retention. Our nod to course content was little more than a reiteration of and support for the college-level writing course.

Like our colleagues at CCBC, we see the Studio model as a fundamental concept for this course. At the same time, our pilot differs somewhat from the model created by Grego and Thompson. Echoing the idea of "bricolage" (or "what is at hand") raised by Matzke and Garrett in this volume, "shapeshifting" our curriculum meant that the lead faculty in the college level course also served in the role of studio leader. Our position as faculty in a two-year college means that we have no graduate students or teaching assistants "at hand" to step into that role. Nevertheless, we ask the same question asked by Grego and Thompson (1995) in "The Writing Studio Program: Reconfiguring Basic Writing/Freshman Composition": "What if we had no separate basic writing course?" (p. 77). In fact, ADE answered this question for us; there is no separate basic writing course. Developmental writing students are enrolled in the college-level writing course, and their experiences in the ADE course provide a time for additional writing, sharing, and reflection. This subtle shift away from a separate stand-alone developmental writing course and toward a supplemental studio course for college-level writing courses constructively blurs the boundaries between "developmental" and "college-level" writing. The version in place at MCTC is a college-level writing course with a studio model course attached to it.

PROFESSIONAL DEVELOPMENT, INTERACTIONAL INQUIRY AND THE COURSE BLOG

As we expanded the number of ADE course offerings, questions about professional development, not unlike those raised by Santana, Rose, and LaBarge, surfaced. The faculty-driven, curricular shift to ADE, although supported thus far by the administration, nevertheless had no structured faculty development. There was no time devoted to ADE training, and there were no stipends and no release time.

Many of us had done individual work in preparation for the creation and on-going development of the course. Kathleen presented on "Guerilla Basic Writing Acceleration" at the 2010 National Conference on Acceleration in Developmental Education and returned filled with visions of the national ALP model. Jane and Liz attended ALP director Peter Adams' one day visit and lecture at a local community college in May of 2012, and Liz and Darren attended the 2012 National Conference on Acceleration in Developmental Education. In February of 2014, Jane and Michael attended the Minnesota Developmental Education Faculty Institute at another local community college, where Peter Adams presented a morning session on ALP. At this time, we had the opportunity to continue our conversation with Adams and were gratified to hear him mention Grego and

Thompson's Studio model and acknowledge the connections we write about here. At the start of our pilot, we felt the strong advantage that all of our pilot faculty save one had either attended national conferences on acceleration or had had inspiring and productive conversations with Adams—which is echoed in the narrative of Ritola et al., who had the good fortune of an administrator who also was touched by the spirit of Adams' work. However, this was the extent of faculty training. We needed another mode of professional development to help sustain our efforts. Whereas Santana et al.'s, approach was to pair writing instructors to encourage dialog, we developed an approach that invited all studio model writing instructors to participate.

That mode was the blog where we engaged in interactional inquiry. Michael developed the blog using WordPress as the publishing platform. Each instructor would be able to question, chronicle, pose and solve problems, and reflect. We opened the blog only to MCTC ADE instructors and a few other colleagues who were interested in the course so that audience issues would be simplified. We wanted to be in conversation with one another, not an anonymous external audience. Through these conversations, we wrestled with many of the same issues that the Studio model addresses: student access, student anger and resentment at the idea of "remediation," student persistence, the need for college acculturation, the need for focused writing time—on computers—and the need for safe spaces to write. What emerged from the blog was a different iteration of interactional inquiry, one that expanded beyond the studio facilitator-to-student dynamic within the classroom and embraced interactional inquiry between ADE faculty. This approach, in many respects, aligns with Fraizer's assertion (this volume) that interactional inquiry has meant "faculty members talking to each other about student issues and sharing strategies for addressing those issues." Our blog became not only the site for this discussion but also a repository for the ideas and approaches raised in those discussions.

The first blog entry appeared on 14 January 2013. Not surprisingly, it was a sample syllabus. Through June 2014, there were 44 posts by six different instructors. In addition, there were 67 comments made in response to the postings. This may seem like a small sampling, but remember that this was a private blog with few participants. The greatest activity occurred between January 2013 and November 2013 (38 posts and 61 comments). This activity corresponded to the first two semesters that the ADE Studio course was offered.

A number of recurring themes appeared throughout the blog, and we tagged each posting with descriptive titles. Although the small number of postings overall precludes any indication of how our concerns changed over time, a quick review of the tag cloud (Figure 7.1) indicates what some of those recurring themes were.

Tags

academic progress

academic writing conventions

acceleration ALP

ALP facutly handbook assessment

assignments

attendance barriers

conferencing course changes

course description curriculum

D2L data developmental writing students

disabilities disability Discussion

ENGL1110 in ENGA0900 sessions

enrollment first week goals

grades handbook history of acceleration

homework

In-class Activities

in-class work pattern

instructor motivation

instructors' expectations

interactional
inquiry

Jessica Shyrack Leigh Cressman

mid-term motivation

moving to 1111 new faculty training

Paul Tough pedagogy

peer review persistence

placement placement scores

portfolio proposal

READ 0100 readings

reflection letter

resilience retention

retention strategies revision

scaling up small group work

STATWAY Student Behavior

student motivation

studio model things that work

traditional 900 week six

Why Children Succeed wiki

writing studio

Figure 7.1. Tag cloud from blog.

The physically largest words correspond to the most frequent issues addressed (and named) in the postings. Since retention was a main goal behind creating the course, "attendance" rose to the top of recurring issues, with a total of 14 postings (over one-third of all postings) addressing the issue. "Portfolio" was the second most frequent tag. The eight postings on portfolios (25% of all postings) addressed the student outcome that students created by the end of the semester. "Interactional inquiry" tied with "portfolio" yielded eight postings. We concede that, once we knew we would be writing this article, interactional inquiry became more of a focus than it might have been without the looming responsibility of writing this chapter. As we began to analyze our use of this space for development, for questions, for concerns and for support, we began to see it as a mode of interactional inquiry for us, the studio facilitators.

BLOGGING COURSE HISTORY

One of the ways in which the blog helped us was by providing a space where we could establish the course's history for instructors who would teach the course for the first time. Chronicling the course's history provided all instructors with a common narrative. It also served to energize people: We developed a collective story, purposes, and goals. Developing this narrative, together, on the blog, worked as interactional inquiry, and that process created and nurtured community. In a key post, Kathleen described the course's evolution, and even here, one can see the germs of both the Studio model in general and interactional inquiry in particular:

> I explained that my approach to Accelerated [Developmental] English grows out of my history of creating a "guerilla acceleration" model in my own [Developmental English] sections about 5 years ago. Some other [Developmental English] instructors and I would whisper in hallways about how maybe a third of our [Developmental English] students could complete the portfolio work weeks before the term ended, and so some of us had encouraged those students to work faster and allowed them to end the class sooner than their peers. As we were not strictly sure this was institutionally approved, we whispered about this practice in the hallways!

We hungered for conversation amongst ourselves so that we might learn from each other. These conversations were usually rushed and frequently occurred in our department's workroom or as we briskly walked with each other to teach our classes. Although these talks were sandwiched into odd moments, they were important because they planted the seeds for future curricular changes. Kathleen's description of these whispered conversations showed us already engaging in a surreptitious form of interactional inquiry as we "formulate[d] our own plans and proposals for local change" (Grego and Thompson, 2008, p. 159). Kathleen then wrote:

> It felt important to share this history to show how very new this approach was at the college, as [faculty new to the course] wondered what the department's stand was on use of texts and assignments in the [ADE] section—I told [them] we are too new and marginal to have a "stand," but I could tell what

> led me to my choices and invite [them] to talk with others
> about theirs!

Kathleen's post was, in one way, interactional inquiry because she shared the history and her own enthusiasm with others. However, she went one step further and encouraged the post's readers to "talk with others." This was key. Kathleen's post embodies what Grego and Thompson (1995) described as a "continual to and fro between action and reflection," and Kathleen actually encouraged others to do the same (p. 72). When Kathleen suggested that she "could tell what led me to my choices," she actively reflected on her actions; she also provided a blueprint for others to participate in their own action and reflection.

Kathleen concluded the post with phrasing that captured the flurry of conversation and writing that we experienced through teaching the ADE course collaboratively:

> This discussion actually energized me—as do the blog posts—
> because both give me the opportunity to theorize and articu-
> late my practice, and hear others theorize and articulate theirs
> as well. This is especially exciting with innovative curriculum
> as there is no precedent—we are creating this as we go: excit-
> ing! Michael stopped me in the workroom during our pilot
> semester and said he hadn't felt this much energy around cur-
> ricular development since we shifted to portfolio assessment
> ten years earlier. (Blog post, October 4, 2013)

Kathleen's post spoke to the instructors' need for interaction, just as Ritola et al. chronicle the dearth of opportunities for faculty for "fruitful" discussions in the creation of their studio model. The most important part of this passage was that the discussion "energized" her (and, by extension, many of the other instructors). The blog became our airport plug-in station, the site where we went to get energy to power our future efforts.

CREATING COMMUNITIES: SUPPORTING ONE ANOTHER

One of the main issues to which the instructors frequently returned was the effective use of classroom time. This was both liberating and disconcerting. We could use the time with our ADE students as we saw fit; however, we did not have much of a sense of where to begin. We, though seasoned full time, tenured Basic Writing faculty, were in something of the same position as the "new part time instructors and teaching assistants" that Matzke and Garrett (this volume) describe: we were "not sure what to do with the extra time." Early blog entries and comments necessarily focused on what students would be doing in the class. These exchanges not only helped us understand what to do during the studio support hour, they also allowed us to engage in the kind of questions and comparisons about discourse and form that take place in student-centered Studios.

For example, Darren posted with enthusiasm about his first weeks of teaching the course: "Through the past two weeks I've managed to maintain full or near-capacity with the ADE students." Darren went on to share with the other instructors how he and his students had been working together during studio time. He compared an activity done in the ADE class with the same activity in his traditional developmental writing course: "The first week we went over the 'Why Do I Miss Class?' activity, and the lessons seem to have stuck with them." Later on, Darren wrote about his design process for peer review:

> Both the [college-level writing] students and the ADE
> students seemed very eager to debate how to structure peer
> review, and we came up with a great, concise list of by-laws
> for workshop. I've done this activity in my other classes with
> mixed results, so I am quite pleased as to how this group is
> jelling. Discussions are robust and thought-provoking, with
> nearly every student contributing, and even the one shy stu-
> dent is now starting to come out of his shell and speak up in
> class. (blog post, February 1, 2013)

He ended with a post-script: "If this sounds like a love-fest, it kinda is" (blog post, February 1, 2013). Using the comment feature of the blog, Jane replied, "Darren: I would love to see the list of 'by-laws for workshop.' What a great idea. And yes to the love-fest!" (blog post, February 3, 2013). Darren responded that he would post the "by-laws" later in the semester. In these exchanges, Darren and Jane were able to take situations specific to one course and generalize actions in ways that could be applied to other courses, all while supporting each other's efforts.

In another series of postings and comments during the fall 2013 semester, instructors began to share the changes they began to see with the ADE students. These postings and responses made public to us what could have easily remained private. Michael wrote that he had exhorted his students "to be my stars" in the college-level writing class. He explained

> I told this to my [ADE] students during the first couple of
> weeks of class. I thought that they would be my stars in some
> very specific ways. One, because I use D2L (Desire to Learn)
> discussions and my [college-level writing] sections don't meet

in computer classrooms, I knew that if they used their [ADE] support] time wisely that they would be the first students to post. I knew, too, that they would know the readings that we did in class more intimately than the other students because we would have more time to unpack them. I suspected that they would have fewer challenges navigating the course wiki, again because we were in computer classrooms for [ADE]. (Blog post, September 25, 2013)

One month later, Jane built upon this idea in greater detail. Jane described a particular assignment and how students volunteered to have their drafts shared with the large group. She then continued,

What transpired in the workshop seemed to occur (in my eyes, at first, before I sat down to reflect here) as a matter of chance: Out of the 8 students who volunteered to be work-shopped for this essay, six are [ADE] students. No [ADE] students volunteered for the first whole class workshop on our first essay. And here's the thing: All their drafts of essay two were completed, on time, full drafts (this is an early date for completion; those who are not workshopped get an extra week to compose the first draft). And not only did the first workshops show the ability of the [ADE] students to fulfill the academic requirements, the discussion of their papers that ensued during the oral part of the workshop was energizing, and was driven by the comments of the [ADE] students who spoke up, a lot, about their peers' work. (Blog post, October 25, 2013)

Jane highlighted a transformation that occurred among many of her ADE students, students who might otherwise be reticent to share their writing in large group settings. More importantly, Jane articulated these observations only after she had had time to reflect, to recognize, and to chronicle—activities for which the blog proved an invaluable interactional inquiry tool.

In the comment feature, Kathleen responded:

Your comments about how the [ADE] students become leaders in the [college-level writing] class mirror my experience, and have me thinking about how community and confidence function in classrooms. Because we have more time with them, and they with each other, the 10 [ADE] folks become kind of a team in the [college-level writing] class modeling strong student involvement and engagement that surpasses some of the students [who are placed into college-level writing]. I feel the [ADE students] see this in class and gain even more confidence as they see their own skills surpass those of some who tested "above" them. This is of course not true of all [ADE] students—but I'd argue it is most of them. For me this is another reason to expand the program as it raises the level of engagement and therefore raises levels of critical thinking and writing in the [college-level writing] class as well. It's like the ADE classes provide a small, well-supported model of what the whole class can be; then, those students bring that engagement into the larger class and show the others what the class could be. (Blog entry, October 28, 2013)

Michael, Jane, and Kathleen collectively acknowledged an outcome that none of them might have been able to predict prior to teaching the course or on their own: that the developmental writing students would, with additional support and practice, become effective classroom leaders in the college-level writing course. This kind of interactional inquiry, where the three instructors "[tried] out approaches, actions or change," served a number of purposes (Grego and Thompson, 2008, p. 50). First, it made more public what can be an intensely private activity between instructors and their students. Second, it affirmed observations that allowed for specific experiences to become more generalized to a larger group. Finally, it built a network of powerful support among those participating in the exchange. This shift permeated much of what transpired afterward in the ADE sessions. Our shift in perspective and behavior was critical to the instructor's role in ADE classes, and the interactional inquiry of the blog entries helped us to name a different way of seeing, acknowledging, and acting upon a new understanding of the students in the room.

STUDENTS' LIVES AND AFFIRMING REALITY

Faculty members also wrote frequent posts to explore issues associated with student persistence. Our campus, like many community colleges, is the first step to post-secondary education for many students of color, as well as low-income and first-generation students. Students who test into developmental writing at MCTC require extra academic support, but without support for life circumstances affected by poverty, housing, childcare, and similar issues, such academic support is often insufficient. Kathleen named the issue in one posting: "What are the struggles or biggest issues [for ADE students]? The work, home, family, health issues that plague underclass Americans" (blog post, October 4, 2013). These are not the types of issues that could easily be set aside. If we were to help students succeed, we had to find ways to acknowledge and address these issues.

In this light, one of the biggest challenges to ADE instructors, especially those new to the ADE classroom, was how to address student attrition. When the very reason for the course's existence is to expedite ten (or fewer) students' academic progress through both developmental writing and college-level writing in one semester, it was remarkable how fixated we became about the numbers, both for those in the room and those missing. With no support provided by the college, the blog became our professional development site for exploring causes and developing strategies to aid in retention. Issues such as homelessness, mental health, the health of loved ones, and child care arose time and time again. Almost obsessively, we checked with one another about whether or not our students were attending and why. The following excerpts create a montage that spoke to this obsession:

> Kathleen: Here in week 12 my [Developmental English] numbers are not what they were. 6–7 fairly consistently come and have work turned in and of those I have 2 Cs, 3 Bs, 2 As. An A student got a job and moved her kids out of a shelter 2 weeks ago and I haven't been able to reach her since, . . . (Blog entry, October 20, 2013)

> Jenifer: One is likely to drop; she moved here to Minneapolis to live with her father, her only relative in the region, and he's suddenly dying of cancer.. . . The other lost her childcare; she, too, wanted to keep going. (Blog entry, April 10, 2013)

> Michael: I started with nine, but one dropped before the end of the first week (so that doesn't count, right?).. . . I have one student who is a very good writer but who possesses [a] paralyzing anxiety disorder—she has missed over 50% of the class meetings. I have another student who is a single mother of three children under the age of seven. Two of her children have been sick consistently since the start of the semester, so she has missed over 50% of the class meetings. (Blog entry, February 22, 2013)

> Jane: [B]ecause I had the extra hour, a few weeks past, to read what this [ADE] student wrote [in an essay in which] the student disclosed urgent feelings of depression, I was able to take him aside during that support hour, query him for a few minutes regarding interventions, and get him both

to an MCTC counselor and in touch with his father. What I'm saying here is without that time to look at the [ADE] writing, I may not have seen this essay for at least a few more days (which is when I could get to the [college-level] essays). (October 25, 2013)

Jane: I have one ADE student who has missed a number of sessions of both the 1110 and the support hour who has been dealing with an infant daughter who has been hospitalized. (September 18, 2013)

In this exchange, we used interactional inquiry as a way to reaffirm reality. In these five postings, we see the real-life issues—child care, health, homelessness—that students confront every day. Through interactional inquiry, individual instructors tested his or her own sense of reality. Through interactional inquiry, we saw not only our students' individual barriers but also, in aggregate, that these barriers were systemic. Additional postings corroborated this understanding. The instructors used the blog in this case not so much for problem-posing and -solving (though there is some of that happening in these postings). Instead, the blog served as a reality check for all of us. When things happened in the classroom that seemed extraordinary or exceedingly difficult, writing about them to a sympathetic audience reaffirmed the students and our humanity. It also reminded us that our students' lives exist within systems and structures that often do not serve them well; in fact, some of those very systems work against their success.

SUCCESS AND NEW QUESTIONS

At the end of spring 2014 semester—the third semester of offering ADE—our college's Institutional Research reported back the solidly successful numbers. We found that we had more reasons to celebrate our success with ADE, beyond the shared, in-class moments already described in the previous posts. The completion rate of those students who submitted the ADE portfolio for evaluation was 71%, compared to 61% in the college's traditional developmental writing course. Those who completed passed at 93%, which is comparable to the traditional development writing course pass rate of 91%. The ADE students also did quite well in the college-level writing course, with 59% of them earning a grade of C or higher (Cressman, 2014). The support hour and its use of the Studio model for the students worked: More students were completing the developmental writing course while also achieving success in the college-level writing course. This was welcome news for the department as we began to think about the future of developmental writing at MCTC.

Yet, there are still questions, concerns, and doubts. In the spring 2014 semester, we convened our first-ever face-to-face meeting of ADE faculty, where we discussed these future concerns and what it would mean to "go to scale" with ADE, particularly in light of our successful assessment numbers. In a follow-up blog entry, Jane listed the ADE faculty's discussion points regarding those doubts:

1. About problems with placement: Can we just blow up the whole model? Get rid of Accuplacer? Demand that writing samples be used to assess student placement in developmental? And what to do about Reading? [Developmental students are assessed into developmental writing courses through their Accuplacer Reading score.]

2. Current faculty issues: What does it mean to teach ADE for a semester or two, change your approach to the developmental curriculum, and then go back to teaching that traditional course? What does it mean for the ADE instructor who is currently teaching **both**? How does teaching in ADE change our traditional developmental teaching? **Does** it change? Can we go back to it in the same way? What is different about the two courses?

3. On future ADE faculty: More folks want to teach ADE—how do we maintain a fair system and assure effective ADE teaching?

4. On future assessment: What questions do we now need to ask for assessment? We need research on persistence and start times, on completion rates in [the second semester college English research writing course], on computer literacy skills coming in, etc. (Blog entry, March 2, 2014)

In many ways, this list was the direct product of the interactional inquiry made possible through the course blog. We did not get to this point of raising questions without first articulating them in the blog. The blog became our site for collaborative knowledge making. Along the way, the blog created a magnetic form of consensus, one that new and prospective faculty members found attractive.

CONCLUSION

As the previous section shows, this group of faculty members has continued to question the course's curriculum, the college's context for the course, and our pedagogy, even with the success of the course. In many ways, the blog, and the interactional inquiry process that we embraced, provided a space which allowed the classroom and the Studio course to become sites for reflection and action research, sites increasingly rare in community college settings.

That said, it was interesting to the primary authors that the use of the blog diminished considerably after the initial flush of activity during the first two semesters the course was offered. On one level, this decreased activity made sense. When the group was teaching a new course for the first time, it was logical that the urge to communicate would be at its greatest. During that time we used the blog in an ontological sense: We were looking for ways of being together in the process of starting this new course. It felt good to have this shared space where we could read and respond to one another's postings.

On another level, however, we have become less sanguine about the decreased activity, especially as the college and the English department expand the offerings of the course. This means that new instructors will be teaching the course, supposedly with some of the same concerns, doubts, and needs as the original instructors. In the future, too, there will be new challenges that all ADE instructors must confront. As we write, the department has made revisions to professional development for developmental writing: One of the three meetings is devoted entirely to ADE. Over time, we imagine even more of the professional development time being committed to ADE, as the number of offerings increase. Indeed, ADE is becoming an "institutional fixture."

Along those lines, Grego and Thompson posited, "Whenever a course becomes an institutional fixture, as [developmental] writing courses have, we run the risk of allowing institutional labels to render invisible the richness and complexity of the backgrounds that all students bring into the academy" (1995, p. 76). Other program parts—pedagogy, daily lessons, instructors' anxiety, to name but a few—run just as much risk as becoming as invisible as students' backgrounds. Our developmental writing course represented 25% of all of the sections offered within the department, and yet discussions about its context, curriculum, and pedagogy were often "render[ed] invisible"—until, that is, we co-created a blog where we wrote about these issues. In the same article, Grego and Thompson (1995) suggested that the Studio approach provided a "process of slipping outside the traditional slough of familiarity [that] can enlighten and enliven the theories and practices which inform our writing programs, and can move us to integrate research on and learning about writing within those programs." In this regard, the Studio model has certainly helped us "enlighten and enliven" our "theories and practices" (p. 77).

Interactional inquiry provided a process for us as we started teaching the course, and the blog became the vehicle for the interactional inquiry. In truth, the course and the blog brought the instructors together to discuss matters that too frequently are left unwritten or unspoken in our work environment. And these types of exchanges deeply enriched the work lives of the participants.

REFERENCES

About us: MCTC 2013–2014 fact sheet. (2014). Retrieved from http://www.minneapo lis.edu/About-Us/Fact-Sheet.

Accelerated English @ MCTC. (2013–2014) [Web log posts]. Retrieved from http:// acceleratedenglishatmctc.wordpress.com/.

Asmussen Research & Consulting LLC. (2012). *Minneapolis Community & Technical College Charting Student Success II: Developmental Education, Final Report Summary.*

The Community College of Baltimore County (2014). What is ALP? ALP: *Accelerated learning program.* Retrieved from http://alp-deved.org/what-is-alp-exactly/.

Cressman, L. (2014). *ENGA student outcomes. Internal report to English Division.* Minneapolis Community and Technical College, Minneapolis, MN.

Grego, R. & Thompson, N. (1995). The Writing studio program: Reconfiguring basic writing and freshman composition. *Writing Program Administrators, 19*(1/2), 66–79.

Grego, R. & Thompson, N. (2008). *Teaching/writing in thirdspaces: The studio approach.* Carbondale, IL: Southern Illinois University Press.

CHAPTER 8.

GTAS AND THE WRITING STUDIO: AN EXPERIMENTAL SPACE FOR INCREASED LEARNING AND PEDAGOGICAL GROWTH

Kylie Korsnack

Vanderbilt University

> Writing, like every other performance, requires space to practice: a space where students can be supported and critiqued by a semiprofessional that has done what they're doing before them. This is the overarching philosophy of our Studio—to provide this space.
>
> —Dr. Alanna Frost, Director of Composition
> at the University of Alabama-Huntsville

> Studio was a safe space for me to discover my interest and ability in teaching with fewer dire consequences.
>
> —Lee Hibbard, former Graduate Student Teacher
> at the University of Alabama-Huntsville

Historically, universities with graduate programs have enlisted English graduate students as primary instructors for freshman composition and developmental writing courses. Although this practice continues to be an economically smart investment and, in some cases, a financial necessity for university budgets, it also creates significant challenges. More than half a century ago, Joseph Schwartz (1955) was already lamenting that: "For more years that I can remember, English departments have carelessly assumed that anyone can teach Freshman English," and moreover, "for too many years we have delegated the teaching of Freshman English to people who have been unprepared for such teaching" (p. 200). Schwartz convincingly argues for the necessity of a training course for graduate students, and since his original argument, many universities have implemented training of one variety or another. In fact, according to Sally Barr Ebest's (1999) study of over 137 WPA member universities, "77.4% of the WPAs observe their TAs teaching, 61.3% provide students with a mentor, and 57.5% hold summer workshops" (pp. 67–68).

Despite these positive figures, one wonders if this design is providing enough training for incoming graduate teaching assistants (GTAs), given that studies continue to suggest that many of these students feel ill-prepared for the task of teaching first-year composition. Indeed, Ebest's (1999) own work reveals that one-third of the respondents admitted to feeling as though their graduate students were only "somewhat" or "not very well prepared" to teach freshman composition, and this apprehension comes even with the organized teacher training programs offered at most universities (p. 70). Clearly, there is still room to strengthen and develop these programs, especially given the May 2014 Modern Language Association report on the state of doctoral study in modern language and literature, which contains an entire section recommending doctoral programs be "modified . . . [to place] greater emphasis on the development of skills in teaching" (p. 6).

One possible alternative to the instruction-based classes first championed by Schwartz, and the focus of my research here, is to adopt a mentorship practice where new GTAs function as facilitators in a writing studio environment. Research into the Studio model has made clear how this approach might be beneficial to both the students and to the structural framework of composition programs, but these accounts do not consider how this space can also be utilized as a training ground for new GTAs. In fact, while many of the other essays within this collection focus on alterations that can be made to the studio format itself, this chapter instead explores the Writing Studio as an ideal space for pedagogical exploration and growth. In what follows, I offer findings from a study which examined the experiences of GTAs who taught in the writing studio environment at the University of Alabama-Huntsville (UAH), a small, public, tier-one research institution in Northern Alabama. My findings suggest that the integration of GTAs as studio leaders first, and composition teachers second, offers a transitional method of GTA training that not only works to more adequately prepare GTAs to teach composition classes but also benefits the students enrolled in the writing studio sections at UAH. Elsewhere in this collection, Cardinal and Keown discuss the impact of transforming the narrative of writing development by emphasizing the importance of reframing the story of basic writing students from deficient to novice writers. In a similar vein, my study suggests that positioning novice GTAs in the role of studio facilitator also reframes the story how of pedagogical development takes place. Rather than assume that "just anyone can teach Freshman composition," scaffolding GTAs from studio facilitator to course instructor promotes an understanding of writing pedagogy as that which develops over time and through the process of practical teaching experiences. Moreover, such an approach gives GTAs the chance to learn from a more experienced expert *and* the opportunity to practice methods of teaching *before* stepping out on their own. In this way, the Studio serves as a sort of support practicum experience to help ease GTAs into their role as composition teachers. I offer this method of training GTAs as a model which can both decrease the anxiety experienced by many GTAs, and help provide more confident and effective writing teachers in our field.

TEACHING ANXIETIES AND STUDIO AS A TRAINING SPACE

The prevalence of graduate student teachers in the academy has given rise to a fair amount of scholarship seeking to address how best to prepare these young professionals for teaching undergraduate courses. Ebest (1999) cites studies conducted by James Slevin, Leo Lambert, and Stacey Tice, among others, to justify the claim that "Whether graduate students are majoring or minoring in composition/rhetoric, or merely fulfilling the requirements of a teaching assistantship, they are being prepared to teach" (p. 67). Ebest's (1999) conclusions stem from the perspective of program instructors and WPAs—not from the graduate student teachers themselves. More recent studies, which derive their data directly from past and current graduate student teachers, offer findings of a different nature. These studies reveal that despite participation in a variety of teacher training programs, many graduate students still feel underprepared to teach first-year composition courses.

For example, Tina Lavonne Good and Leanne B. Warshauer (2000) describe their experiences as GTAs at the State University of New York at Stony Brook, and their perspective fails to align with the data collected from the program instructors and WPAs in Ebest's study. Writing from a context familiar to English GTAs across the country, they state:

> Everyone in the room shared the same nervous anticipation.
> We were all beginning Ph.D. students, which meant in a
> week, many of us would be walking into our own classrooms
> for the first time. Although [our] professors . . . did their best
> to build our confidence while offering suggestions for the first
> few weeks of class, they could not appease our anxiety. (Good
> & Warshauer, 2000, p. ix)

Good and Warshauer (2000) stress that despite receiving direct mentoring by professors, informal peer support, and a solid grounding in theoretical pedagogy from their enrollment in a formal practicum, "we often found ourselves having coffee in each other's offices, desperately struggling to create in-class activities and writing assignments that would prompt our students to produce portfolios that would meet university requirements" (p. ix). More importantly, their own research led them to discover how many graduate students across the country find themselves in a similar situation. The persistent anxieties and struggles to teach first-year composition faced by graduate students, as documented in this study, call us to reexamine the way in which graduate students are traditionally trained in teacher preparation.

In a more recent account, *First Semester: Graduate Students, Teaching Writing, and the Challenge of Middle Ground*, Jessica Restaino (2012) follows four graduate students at a large U.S. public university as they navigate the demands of teaching undergraduate composition courses while also beginning their own academic endeavors. Even after being put through a new teacher orientation and required to enroll in a writing pedagogy class during their first semester of graduate school, all of the study's participants were still dissatisfied with the preparation they were given prior to teaching college composition. One of the teaching assistants felt that "those of us with no teaching experience ha[d] been tossed into the deep end" and resented "the FYWP's [First-Year Writing Program's] failure to better prepare new teachers for the first day" (Restaino, 2012, p. 8). Even those with prior teaching practice expressed anxieties; one student who defined herself as an experienced teacher remained reluctant about grading: "We received handouts on grading, but we didn't really talk about it as a group. . . . I don't feel . . . that I would know the difference between an A and a B paper" (Restaino, 2012, p. 10). Although Restaino's study is limited to a handful of graduate students in an isolated university setting, the implications of her discussion register with many graduate students at other institutions.

Whether it is a crash course in teaching at the university level or concurrent enrollment in a writing pedagogy course or some other form of pedagogical instruction, the teacher preparation programs implemented by the institutions in these studies do not seem to be providing enough training to make graduate students feel adequately equipped for the task at hand. Given this problem, might graduate programs, in addition to maintaining the programs already in place, also consider giving their GTAs some practical experience teaching *before* allocating them with the responsibility of their own composition class? At first glance, this sort of modification may seem difficult to manage; however, an increasing number of universities already have a space conducive to the experimental learning that incoming GTAs need built directly into the framework of their existing composition programs—that is, the Writing Studio.

Since the early work of Rhonda C. Grego and Nancy S. Thompson on the Studio approach (1996) and especially since the culmination of that work was published in *Teaching/Writing in Thirdspaces: The Studio Approach* (2008), many studio programs have been implemented within first-year writing programs across the country. While studio programs are often designed with developmental writing students in mind, the studio space itself contains many features that make it an exceptional training ground for new GTAs. One of the most important of these features is the fact that the GTA in charge of each studio section acts as a facilitator as opposed to an instructor of record. This distinction helps to alleviate the common anxieties graduate students often bring into the program in regards to assessing student writing and establishing themselves as legitimate, authoritative figures in the eyes of their students. In addition, because the graduate students who are group facilitators are often required to sit in on their students' main course session, these GTAs are able to learn from more seasoned instructors and see pedagogy in action. These classroom observations further enable graduate students to begin to understand the external and institutional factors that can affect the interactions taking place between students and teachers. Finally, the intimate and student-driven nature of the studio class offers GTAs countless opportunities to begin developing their own unique pedagogical practices. Through an analysis of the Writing Studio program at the institution where I was an MA student, I will show how the studio space can function as an exceptional training ground for first-year GTAs; indeed, at the most basic level, by positioning GTAs as writing studio instructors, graduate programs can facilitate the development of writing and instructional pedagogies by their GTAs prior to assigning them a freshman composition class of their own.

METHODS

In order to offer a comprehensive analysis of what GTAs learned about teaching writing from their studio experiences, I reviewed program documents, from the initial proposals for the studio course to current syllabi. I also observed weekly meetings between the GTAs and the instructors of the main composition course. These meetings often served as a forum for graduate students to share ideas, ask questions, and get help from their peers and the more seasoned instructors.

In addition to analyzing course documents and observing meetings, I conducted interviews—in person and/or through email—of 10 graduate teaching assistants who taught within UAH's composition program between the fall of 2011 and the spring of 2014; the bulk of my data for this analysis came out of these interviews. Interview participants came from a variety of educational, socio-economical, and racial backgrounds, and they entered the program with varying levels of prior teaching experience. The goal of each interview was twofold: to establish the interviewee's approach to pedagogy prior to teaching Studio, and to determine if and how their studio teaching experiences may have influenced or changed that pedagogy. Along with these primary goals, my interviews with the GTAs also provide an account of the studio class as it is taught at

135

UAH, with particular attention paid to the opportunities and/or limitations to pedagogical practice inherent to the Studio classroom.

Finally, I conducted interviews with the Director of Composition, Professor Alanna Frost, and two other faculty members involved with the initial development and implementation of the Studio model at UAH—Professor Laurel Bollinger, who was Acting Director of Composition at the time of Studio's creation, and Professor Andrea Word, the Director of the Intensive Language Center at UAH. These interviews helped to construct an accurate picture of the studio class from its conception through its present context.

UAH'S STUDIO APPROACH

Like many of the Writing Studio approaches discussed within this collection, our course was originally designed to replace a remedial, noncredit-bearing developmental writing class preceding the EH 101, 102 composition course sequence; however, the UAH Studio was also created with the development and training of GTAs in mind. Bollinger turned to the Studio approach out of frustration with the fact that the developmental class was burdening students by putting them a semester behind from the start of their academic career. Moreover, many of the students who did take the original developmental class were still not passing EH 101 and 102. The new Studio eliminated the developmental course and placed students directly into a credit bearing class—EH 101S. Students enrolled in EH 101S receive extra support through concurrent enrollment in the writing studio class (EH 100)—a lab-like writing course, limited to no more than 10 students, which provides supplemental instruction and one-on-one writing assistance from a more experienced writing expert. Upon successful completion of both courses, students earn credit for the first course in the composition sequence and move on to EH 102.

Although the writing studio philosophy at UAH is very similar to Grego and Thompson's model and to many of the studio formats discussed within this collection, several variations in our approach make it an exceptional space for teacher training. Bollinger founded the Studio program because she "felt the need to do something to improve the experience of our GTAs, to give them better training at some level, and to improve the outcome for those [developmental] students." She therefore designed studio sections so that first-semester graduate teaching assistants would be "the experienced writing experts." This decision to have GTAs as opposed to veteran instructors facilitate the studio sections is significant. Whereas Fraizer (this volume) suggests that the challenges of teaching Studio are best tackled by veteran teachers, these same challenges are what make Studio an ideal space for pedagogical training. Just as in Grego and

Thompson's (2008) model, studio leaders serve as "facilitating experts" who "listen to what students say about their work, their class, or their assignments and, where appropriate, provide contextualizing information about the genre or the kind of assignment being asked for" (p. 10). Thus, in their role as studio leaders, new GTAs must learn to adapt to student needs, which in some cases means they have to come up with lesson plans on the fly, develop a variety of methods for teaching complex writing concepts, and find ways to help individual students overcome emotional, intellectual, and institutional boundaries to success. All the while, these pedagogical techniques are being honed in a space that exists outside but alongside the main course. Indeed, in its status as a thirdspace, the Studio offers a space for both students and the studio leader to take risks, make mistakes, and foster genuine learning experiences. In this case, studio leaders and student participants learn side-by-side, each benefiting from the unique space that the Studio provides.

However, this does not mean that hierarchy is completely eliminated within our version of the Studio approach. As facilitators, GTA are not directly responsible for evaluating student work, but they do assign students with a pass or fail grade based largely on class participation and attendance. Studio leaders are placed in control over the class and content, with their main objective being to supplement the instruction students receive in their regular composition course by designing mini-lessons, conducting writing work-shops, facilitating peer reviews, and providing other types of instructional activities to augment student learning. While our approach could be feasible in an online environment, our approach would look less like the minimally structured asynchronous meetings highlighted within this collection by Miley and by Santana, Rose and LaBarge; and more like Gray's model that emphasizes instructor-directed online activities. Whether in-person or online, it is through the development of individual lessons and writing activities that the GTA is able to foster a unique studio section and begin developing their own approach to teaching. This control over content is imperative for facilitating pedagogical development, but so is the collaborative nature of our studio model. Whereas Gray's studio facilitators are kept separate from the main course and are supervised by a senior Writing Center staff member, our instructors maintain a close collaboration with the course instructors. By attending the main course and meeting regularly with the course instructors, our GTAs are given a chance to learn from a more seasoned instructor while still maintaining their role as studio facilitator as opposed to instructor of record. This flexible course design coupled with the on-going collaboration with FYC instructors enables each facilitator to individualize his or her approach to teaching and begin developing and enacting their own instructional and writing pedagogies.

FINDINGS: PEDAGOGICAL IMPLICATIONS OF USING STUDIO AS A SPACE FOR GTA TRAINING

1. Using GTAs as Facilitators, as Opposed to Instructors of Record, Helps to Alleviate Anxieties Related to the Establishment of Authority and to the Assessment of Student Writing

Many graduate students at our institution enter the program expressing doubts and anxieties about their ability to teach writing; more specifically, they are apprehensive about assessing student writing and developing adequate classroom management techniques. In "Uneasy Transitions: The Graduate Teaching Assistant in the Composition Program," Brian K. Bly (2000) asserts that among the difficulties faced by teaching assistants is their responsibility to "evaluate student writing from a tenuous position of authority" (p. 2). Whereas graduate students in Bly's (2000) study complained about the difficulties they faced trying to teach regular classes while still being seen as less legitimate than fulltime faculty, GTAs in the UAH Writing Studio serve in a capacity that is conducive to their level of experience. If, as Bly (2000) asserts, GTAs will be seen as less legitimate and less authoritative than traditional instructors, one of the greatest strengths of UAH's Writing Studio is that GTAs are not required to assume the place of authority at the front of a regular classroom.

In fact, the idea of authority in the Writing Studio is fundamentally different. In the spirit of Leanne B. Warshauer's collaborative approach (2000), the UAH Writing Studio includes the GTA in the process of learning, widening the "locus of authority" (p. 87). This collaboration is made clear in one GTA's assertions that "Studio gave me a more personal relationship with my students. While I still make clear that I am the instructor, I also remind them that I'm a student much like they are. I exist in a sort of middle-ground, making me feel like I'm more accessible to them and their concerns." This GTA's recognition of the possibilities offered to them as both student *and* instructor is an example of the potential affordances of placing GTAs as studio facilitators. GTAs are themselves positioned both inside and outside of the institutional structure and the main course setting, which makes them an ideal choice for the cultivation of what Grego and Thompson define as Studio's greatest asset—its ability to exist as a sort of thirdspace. Whereas often this dual positionality can create difficulties and anxieties for GTAs, our studio approach recognizes the unique potential of their place within the institutional structure and encourages them to embrace their status in that "middle-ground." The result is a thirdspace that is not only more conducive to student learning, but also one where the GTAs and students can meaningfully learn from one another. As one of the other GTAs recalled:

"My students saw me as a big sister who was there to help them in any way possible. I liked this a lot because we developed personal relationships as well as professional ones when it was time to work." In the Writing Studio, the leaders and students learn together, and the leader develops the skills that he or she will need to teach effectively in the regular classroom.

Anxieties over the legitimacy of "classroom authority" are largely avoided in UAH's Writing Studio by making the studio leaders function as student mentors whose goal is to support instruction rather than assess performance. This positioning of the GTA as studio leader has the potential to combat some of the challenges contributors to this collection have experienced when trying to maintain a distinction between the FYC and individual studio sections. For example, while Fraizer insists on the importance of having faculty who teach Studio also teach FYC classes so that studio discussion can arise from shared experiences teaching FYC, such dialogue can pose challenges when instructors' beliefs about writing expectations and student learning fail to align. However, placing GTAs as studio facilitators might help to both preserve the Studio's status as a third-space and also eliminate some of the possible barriers to constructive dialogue among FYC instructors. In our model, because the studio leader is *not* an FYC instructor, the GTA, along with the Studio itself, can exist outside but alongside the main course. The result is that GTA becomes a neutral resource for student support. Such a position empowers students to be responsible for the expectations of their own FYC instructor, but they can use studio and the GTA-facilitator to help them navigate the challenges of those expectations. Moreover, this positioning helps to alleviate the apprehension that many GTAs have about grading student work and allows them time to hone their assessment skills. As one of our GTAs put it, "If I would have had to teach a regular composition class right away, I would have been especially apprehensive about the grading component; you know, how do you set your standards for grading? What do you use as your base?" By teaching Studio first, graduate students are given a space to discover the answers to these questions. Free from the responsibility of grading, they are able to effectively embody the role of writing guide while they develop the skills necessary to become better teachers and more confident writing assessors. Embedded in this structure is time for more experienced instructors to introduce graduate students to different assessment strategies. Of this aspect of the program, one of the GTAs explained: "We [both the studio leaders and the main course instructors] did a group grading of student portfolios at the end of the semester, and this really helped me learn how to grade. . . . Now I feel much more comfortable with the grading aspect of teaching a composition class in the future." In this way, graduate students become more comfortable with assessing student writing before they are tasked with the responsibility of evaluating an entire composition class. By placing a GTA in the role of studio instructor instead of a veteran teacher, Studio becomes both a space for students to take control over their own learning and one for GTAs to develop their facility as new teachers in a low-stakes environment.

2. Using GTAs as Studio Leaders Allows Them the Opportunity to be Students of Teaching and Writing Pedagogy by Observing and Learning from Veteran Instructors and Colleagues

Through required observations of the main composition class, studio leaders are able to see pedagogy in action and learn from the more experienced instructors in charge of the main composition course. Professor Word (personal communication, spring 2014) emphasized this benefit as one of the foundational principles of UAH's transition into the studio approach: "In this model of the GTA running Studio and attending [the class], [the graduate students] can actually be really conscious about what is going on pedagogically." They "can learn to see what works and what doesn't work for [the teacher they are observing]" on the way to developing their own personal pedagogy.

Studio leaders themselves often commented on this advantage to their pedagogical growth. For example, of their experience, one GTA recalled: "I was able to see how different approaches to writing worked and how I might incorporate them into my own teaching." A former GTA, who now holds a full-time lecturer position at a small, southern liberal arts college, admitted: "Honestly, I feel like I would not feel [prepared] if I had not had the experience within the Writing Studio at UAH because I would not have gotten the opportunity to engage with all the different pedagogical choices that go into teaching these writers who are at a most vulnerable position in their college career." Similarly, another studio leader found herself learning not just from the seasoned instructors, but also from her graduate student colleagues: "If I had a question about an assignment we were teaching, I would hop in on another GTA's Studio and see how she approached it. . . . For me, overcoming and learning was more about peer education and being able to observe other teachers teaching, seeing how different teachers and styles of teaching came together."

Along with regular observations of the main composition course, studio leaders were also tasked with planning for and teaching that main course at least one time in the semester's second half. This experience allowed the graduate students to get a feel for a full-length composition class and practice interacting with a group of 25 students prior to taking on a section of their own. One studio leader commented specifically on this experience, saying that "having taught the main course on a few occasions in front of these same students helped me feel more at ease with a larger classroom." She admitted, "The first two weeks [of the semester] were overwhelming simply because I felt unprepared and unqualified, but as things progressed, it became easier for me, and I developed a little more confidence." Most significantly, she attributed this confidence to her time observing and teaching the main course section: "The observations helped me tremendously; [now,] if I were placed in a classroom of 25 students, I'd be prepared because of the guidance and teaching methods I received from [the main course instructor]."

Besides experiencing an increased understanding of the complexities surrounding writing instruction, the graduate students became attuned to the effect that external and institutional factors can have on the interactions between students and teachers. Just as in Grego and Thompson's (2008) Studio approach, which encourages "studio communication both with teachers and with other group leaders," the Writing Studio model at UAH also incorporates regular meetings between the composition instructors and studio leaders, and these meetings often reveal the communicative and institutional barriers that can affect the way students understand or misunderstand classroom expectations (p. 160). Much like the instructor blog discussed by Leach and Kuhne in this collection, these meetings provided space for the process of interactional inquiry. In these weekly meetings instructors and GTAs could share lesson plans, get feedback on different approaches to teaching, and raise concerns about individual students. For example, one of our studio leaders explained how the weekly meetings helped her formulate different approaches to teaching unfamiliar concepts: "I think collaboration helped us come up with strategies for teaching subjects that we were a little bit afraid of approaching." Another agreed, suggesting that one of the strengths of the weekly meetings was "being able, when you weren't sure how to approach a paper or a specific aspect of writing, to talk it through with the instructors and the GTAs who had taught it before." These meetings helped the studio leaders solve problems but also informed the main course instructors of areas where their students were struggling. Indeed, like the constructive pedagogical exchange that Fraizer identifies as a by-product of the studio environment, in our model, these meetings also promoted collegial dialogue in a slightly different way. Because they are weekly attendees of the main FYC, the GTAs are able to be part of a dialogue between FYC instructors and FYC students. The composition students often felt more comfortable admitting to the studio leaders when they were having trouble, so by keeping regular lines of communication between studio leaders and course instructors, the course instructor could alter their lessons to address these troublesome areas. Thus, the GTAs in our model function as mediators between FYC students and instructors, carrying to the weekly meetings the voice of their students. According to one of the GTAs, this communication "could really inform the main section, the instructor's section" so "we [the studio leaders] were able to catch a lot of problems before students turned in a pile of drafts and, you know, nobody had a thesis statement." Through these interactions, the graduate students learned a lesson in evaluation and transparency, becoming aware of how much they must assess student understanding as part of their own pedagogy, and why it is important to make both their course expectations and assignment instructions as straight-forward as possible. Moreover the dialogue that takes place within these weekly meetings fosters collegiality between graduate students and faculty, offering graduate students an important role and voice within the institutional framework of the department.

3. The Intimate and Student-Driven Nature of the Studio Class Provides New Graduate Students with an Exceptional Space to Examine Student Writing and Experiment with Different Pedagogical Practices

Because the number of students in studio groups at UAH was limited to fewer than 10, studio leaders were able to design and implement instructional plans specific to their students' writing needs without having to worry about the attention to classroom management procedures necessitated by larger classes. As Frost explained:

> Part of the beauty of Studio as a mentoring program for
> future teachers is simply that it is pretty delightful to teach
> a writing class with just 8 students. Never in America is that
> possible, as we are constantly fighting caps. . . . Some com-
> position classes now function at an utmost of 35 students, so
> one of the most beneficial aspects of the Studio program is
> that the GTAs get to be immersed in student writing, but in a
> small volume (personal communication, spring 2014).

Indeed, the small, intimate nature of the studio classroom immerses graduate students in student writing without overwhelming them. They learn from that writing how to identify the areas where their students need the most instruction and can experiment with different pedagogical practices in order to address those needs.

This process of practical application is captured in one GTA's reflection on teaching Studio:

> I learned more by teaching Studio than [from] the pedagogy
> class I took. It's a complete hands-on experience. And your
> students are more than willing to learn with you. They are

fine with it, and they like it. I would bring in my own writing in class. And that was great to be able to collaborate with everybody, and learn from other people's challenges and how they overcame it. A little stressful at the time, but I think the things I learned in Studio I'll take with me, because you were forced to learn it, really learn it.

Through their teaching experience, studio leaders gain the skills and confidence needed to feel comfortable teaching a regular-sized composition class in the future. Such confidence is apparent in one studio leader's admission that "the training and mentoring of the Studio program made me adequately prepared to deal with a classroom of 25 students because it caused me to meet with the students on an interpersonal level that I might not have ever considered if I did not work with such small groups on a daily basis." Another GTA commented on how being able to comment on a small volume of student papers helped him to see student writing differently, and this impacted his grading when he moved on to teach larger composition classes. According to him, the studio classes

> helped me engage with [his students'] writing on a smaller scale, which in turn helped me to learn to like what it was that my students were writing. This helped me to sharpen my skills of looking through what others might consider to be "bad" writing and find the great writers that my students could be in the midst of this. This has helped me when it comes to my larger classrooms because I shy away from that "these kids today" mentality and try to find the inner writer inside each of my students.

Clearly, the intimate setting of the Writing Studio allows GTAs the space and opportunity to really engage with and, in some cases, appreciate the approach to writing that uniquely characterizes each of their students.

4. TEACHING IN THE STUDIO ENVIRONMENT AFFORDS GTAS AN EXPERIMENTAL SPACE TO DISCOVER, REDEFINE, AND/OR DEVELOP THEIR OWN INDIVIDUAL PHILOSOPHY ON THE TEACHING OF WRITING

Perhaps the most obvious benefit to GTAs who participated in the UAH Writing Studio was the opportunity to refine and, in some cases, develop from scratch a unique writing pedagogy. Almost all of the GTAs came into the program without a solid grasp of how to teach writing: one admitted, "I didn't even know what a writing pedagogy was when I started teaching;" and another said, "We had to write a pedagogy for our writing pedagogy class, but it was all theory. It was not anything that I really strongly believed in or had put into practice." However, by the end of their studio experience, many of the GTAs shared that in addition to gaining a more confident and advanced instructional framework, their own pedagogical ideals about the teaching of writing began to take on a more definite shape. One commented on how "the theoretical and the practical merged as I taught more Studio," insisting that "Studio definitely influenced my pedagogy. I came into the program very uninitiated. This whole idea of pedagogy and pedagogical ideas is something that I've only been thinking about and playing with for the past year. I can assume that my pedagogy will continue to change and develop as I gain more experience."

Several of the graduate students realized that the only way to truly learn how to teach writing was by doing it, and Studio offered an ideal setting for this practical experience to take place. Summing up this revelation, a former GTA explained:

> Since there was not a lot of formal training up front, Studio kind of stands in and acts as that training. I don't think that you can really learn how to teach without doing it. You can read about and see great teachers, but you have to put that into practice. Emulating teachers that you've had in the past that you've liked [is] kind of how I approached the practice of teaching. You just have to practice over and over again until you find something that works, and I really think that getting that opportunity alone is what was the most beneficial. Having all of these students in a smaller setting helped to relax me and allowed me to ease into this new experience teaching.

All of the graduate students agreed that their time leading Studio taught them indispensable knowledge about instructional pedagogy. Perhaps more importantly, however, were the discoveries they made about the unique challenges that come with the teaching of writing.

One common realization among the studio leaders was that writing instruction demands a flexible approach. They talked about how they originally saw writing instruction as "teacher-centric," "sterile," and "formulaic," but discovered through their experiences as GTAs that the process was in fact "messy," "not linear," and "pragmatic." One graduate student in particular realized that writing is "not cut and dry . . . you have to step back as a teacher and let your students move through the writing process in whatever way they feel most comfortable." She learned, "You kind of have to be a good coach [through the writing process] rather than a teacher." Frost spoke to this point by referencing the studio space as one of experimentation and discovery: "One of the strengths of the Studio program and having the GTAs in that Studio is that each GTA has to solve their students' writing problems on the fly . . . I've seen people come up with creative ways to make sure that students understand the material being taught" (personal communication, spring 2014). Indeed, many of the GTAs commented on their responsibility to be flexible and "to react to the class' needs," a profound challenge for even seasoned instructors. One GTA noticed her teaching developing from "simply having to adjust to the dynamics of each of my different studio sections." She went on to explain, "While I would have the same goal or idea in mind for class, the way that I approached that idea would change based on the individual section. I learned to be adaptable and creative in thinking of ways to get the students involved and interested in the ideas. This was a challenge at first, but it was something that I think I got better at as the semester evolved." That these discoveries were made prior to the GTAs taking on the responsibilities of teaching a regular composition class is one of the great strengths of using the Writing Studio in this capacity.

Another strength of the GTA-led Writing Studio is that the small, flexible nature of the class allows studio leaders the freedom to try a range of teaching strategies. Since the studio sessions are supplemental to the regular class, GTAs are not required to stick to formulaic methods for teaching students content covered in the main class but can experiment to find out what works best for the students in their small sections. In the words of one GTA: "Studio functioned as somewhat of a testing ground to get a feel for teaching." This was a place where he would develop "mini-lesson plans . . . to convey the material [from the regular composition course] to students in new and exciting ways." In the process, the GTAs were constantly learning new things about how to teach writing. One noted a compelling change to her pedagogical practices:

> I realized that teaching can't be completely organized, that it
> can be very messy at times. Each student in your classroom
> is different, each classroom dynamic is different, so as I went
> through Studio I think I became much more student centered
> . . . I shifted from me being a ring leader, to pushing my stu-
> dents from the center.

This "student centeredness" is what now characterizes the teaching she does in her regular composition classes: "[Teaching Studio] completely changed the way I teach. From seeing teaching as this idea of professing knowledge, to asking questions, and getting them to tell you instead . . . it's almost like a different way of just leading a conversation, to get them to think" on their own. The immense amount of pedagogical growth experienced by the studio leaders at UAH suggests that this model of teacher training would also benefit the development of graduate student teachers and composition programs at other institutions.

CONCLUSION

Based on the evidence gathered from interviews with GTAs and English faculty, it is clear that the dialogue taking place within UAH's Writing Studio allows for the studio leaders to advance their writing and instructional abilities. Rather than being thrown immediately into teaching several freshman composition courses with little to no instruction or experience, the graduate students instead spend a semester acting as studio leaders before taking on the full responsibility of a composition course. This organization provides the graduate students with the opportunity to develop skills in classroom management, writing instruction, and lesson planning while not being overwhelmed with the responsibility of formally evaluating student work. Working in conjunction with a more seasoned instructor, graduate students learn strategies for teaching and assessing student writing, and also have the chance to see pedagogy in action. This unique setup allows both the students and the studio leaders to develop an academic relationship without the added pressure of strict assessments and furnishes a space for the graduate students to practice and experiment with different instructional methods. In the words of one GTA, "Studio was a safe space for me to discover my interest and ability in teaching with few dire consequences. . . . [It] functioned as something of a testing ground to get a feel for the teaching experience." Furthermore, for some graduate students, this experience helped to reinforce their own ambitions for work within the academy. Such reinforcement is clear in one GTA's revelation on the influence of the studio experience on her own scholarly development:

> I would not have felt the way I do now about teaching if I
> didn't have the chance to teach Studio. It is such an effective
> way to get a feel of what will be expected in the freshman
> composition classes. Not only that, but after teaching Studio,
> it reassured me that I in fact would like to do this [teach] at a
> collegiate level for the rest of my life. It is so refreshing when
> a student is able to understand and appreciate something and
> know that I am the reason for this level of comprehension.
> Coming to UAH to do what I love each day is never referred
> to as a "work day." I'm just having fun.

This mode of teacher training sends the studio leaders away from their first semester of graduate school with the makings of a working writing pedagogy, and in some cases, they leave feeling more fully solidified and confident in their individual career aspirations. Most importantly, after first facilitating a writing studio, GTAs find themselves better equipped to teach a freshman composition course of their own.

REFERENCES

Bly, B. K. (2000). Uneasy transitions: The graduate teaching assistant in the composition program. In T. L. Good & L. B. Warshauer (Eds.), *In our own voice: Graduate students teach writing.* (pp. 2–9). Boston, MA: Allyn & Bacon.

Ebest, S. B. (1999). The next generation of WPAs: A study of graduate students in Composition/Rhetoric. *Writing Program Administrators, 22*(3), 65–84.

Good, T. L. & Warshauer, L. B. (2000). Introduction. In T. L. Good & L. B. Warshauer (Eds.), *In our own voice: Graduate students teach writing* (pp. ix–xii). Boston, MA: Allyn & Bacon.

Grego, R. C. & Thompson, N. S. (1996). Repositioning remediation: Renegotiating composition's work in the academy. *College Composition and Communication, 47*(1), 62–84.

Grego, R. C. & Thompson, N. S. (2008). *Teaching/writing in thirdspaces: The studio approach.* Carbondale, IL: Southern Illinois University Press.

Report of the MLA task force on doctoral study in modern language and literature. (2014). Modern Language Association of America. Retrieved from http://www.mla.org /report_doctoral_study_2014.

Restaino, J. (2012). *First semester: Graduate students, teaching writing, and the challenge of middle ground.* Carbondale, IL: Southern Illinois University Press.

Schwartz, J. (1955). One method of training the composition teacher. *College Composition and Communication, 6*(4), 200–204.

Warshauer, L. B. (2000). Collaboration as a process: Reinforcing the workshop. In T. L. Good & L. B. Warshauer (Eds.), *In our own voice: Graduate students teach writing* (pp. 86–94). Boston, MA: Allyn & Bacon.

CHAPTER 9.

MULTIPLYING IMPACT: COMBINING THIRD AND FOURTHSPACES TO HOLISTICALLY ENGAGE BASIC WRITERS

Karen Gabrielle Johnson
Shippensberg University

Early in the spring semester, Cassie's[1] familiar face peeked around my office door. She was beaming with excitement, anxious to share her good news: She had just been offered a fulltime summer position in a nonprofit organization that would begin as soon as finals were over. As a writing center director who supervises studio programs, having a student visit three years later to share employment news is a bit unusual, and what makes Cassie's situation unique is that she began working for this nonprofit as part of a service-learning requirement in our basic writing course supported by Studio. Her connection to the organization was so strong that she continued to work for it even after her service learning course concluded, ultimately taking on an administrative role.

Of course, not all basic writers who enter a fourthspace, the place where students go to fulfill service, will connect so strongly with community partners, but Cassie's experience suggests deeper connections to university, community, classmates, and instructors can result when students reflect on service experiences in Studio. During studio sessions, Cassie and her classmates learned to link academic writing to their individual interests and experiences. Studio groups offer spaces for rich communication exchanges, and the addition of a fourthspace in the form of a service-learning site creates even greater opportunities for empowering writers to explore tangible, complex issues present in nearby communities while developing a network of relationships within and nearby the academy. Extending learning conversations to a fourthspace enriches thirdspace writing opportunities, further enhancing the learning atmosphere in the writing classroom. The synergy between thirdspace and fourthspace not only helps students

---

1   All students' name in this chapter have been changed.

improve their writing, it also extends possibilities for reflecting on interactions with classmates, studio leaders, instructors, and community partners. This additional reflection can create community and inspire writers to fully engage in complex issues embedded in their research writing assignments.

I begin this chapter by discussing the rationale for developing a different kind of Studio, a service-learning hybrid. Students enrolled in a basic writing course at a mid-sized comprehensive state-supported university located in the Mid-Atlantic region participated in the development and refinement of this hybrid program. Next, I review a process for setting up and institutionalizing a service-learning studio. Beginning with the first-year pilot, I give a year-by-year description of studio leader training and roles, classroom structure, service-learning requirements, writing assignments, assessments, and assessment results that guided improvements over a three-year period. I conclude with a discussion about how a centralized theme improved interactional inquiry, reduced service options enhanced community spirit and studio-classroom discourse, and redesigned leader trainings helped leaders build competency and networking opportunities.

RATIONALE FOR A SERVICE-LEARNING STUDIO HYBRID

ENGAGING THE WRITER

Designers of basic writing courses face nontrivial challenges to motivate and engage writers who are required to take noncredit, developmental courses. Although engaging and motivating basic writers can be difficult, student engagement is possible if instructors create meaningful contexts for writing and incorporate issues and experiences that centrally involve students (Rose, 1983). Essentially, writing contexts—discussions about ideas, writing spaces, and writing topics—can either stimulate or suppress writers' motivation to complete writing assignments.

At the same time, and even when classroom discussions spark lively discourse based on course readings and student experiences, basic writing students may still lack motivation to complete assignments. This lack of motivation may be related to diminished confidence in academic writing abilities. Helping basic writers gain confidence and become motivated to complete writing assignments may be accomplished through Studio. In Writing Studios, leaders can mentor, guide, and engage students in the writing process.

Service-learning also engages writers by challenging them to solve complex problems, research issues, and respond to the community through service projects. According to Light (2001), extending learning outside of class is vital, as four out of five students report that the most specific, critical incident or moment that profoundly changed them actually occurred outside the classroom. Composition courses that integrate service-learning can allow for connections to the kinds of outside experiences that improve students' motivation, satisfaction, and writing development. Through the dual pedagogies of service-learning and Studio, students can collaboratively examine service experiences before taking on the complex issues presented by writing process. This additional opportunity for reflection can position students to become more engaged and empowered, and thus more open to writing growth.

BENEFITS OF STUDENT ENGAGEMENT IN SERVICE-LEARNING

Pine (2008) believes that writing for and about the community, a type of service-learning described by Deans (2000), can help basic writers learn academic literacies, especially when basic writers develop a personal investment in service. She discovered that students used their sites of service as primary sources of investigation and integrated their experiences with secondary sources, which helped them develop more complex, less formulaic writing. Pine believes this model of service can academicize students' work in research writing, even if they have negative or less than ideal service experiences. However, Pine cautions instructors to make explicit connections between the service and course content "by and for students in multiple forms of writing and speaking" (2008, p. 53). She notes that service-learning has the potential to make basic writing coursework more meaningful, but care must be taken to help students link their experiences to classroom discussions and writing assignments.

A LAYERED APPROACH: SERVICE-LEARNING STUDIO HYBRID

Incorporating service-learning into a basic writing course appears to encourage writers' engagement and writing proficiencies (Astin, Volgelsand, Ikeda & Yee, 2000), but basic writers will still need additional support to help them develop academic writing skills. Studios provide writers a thirdspace for sharing experiences in smaller groups where they receive feedback on papers and learn from each other, yet unless writers find appealing topics that link academic writing to their interests, students may not fully engage in dialogue. Service-learning helps engage writers in exploring tangible, complex issues present in nearby communities. When writers participate in service events and later discuss and write about their experiences in studios, they can become more engaged and improve their academic literacies (Pine, 2008). To build a course that promotes engagement while helping students develop their writing, I developed a Service-Learning Studio hybrid for one class of 20 students. In this pilot, students participated in classroom-sponsored service projects and attended weekly meetings.

YEAR ONE: INITIATING A SERVICE-LEARNING STUDIO HYBRID

Funding constraints and the institution of a single studio class limited full adherence to Grego and Thompson's Studio. Like Mary Gray's (this volume) hybrid/studio for first-year writing that located online writing studios in the discussion board function for each writing class and required one undergraduate facilitator per class, I too could not draw students from multiple sections of basic writing. My pilot required one studio leader for my single course. In contrast to my fellow authors in this collection who received funding to launch initial studio initiatives, I began our first studio program without any funding at all. As a result, I had to deviate from Grego and Thompson's (2008) staffing model of an experienced teacher or graduate student. Instead, I recruited an experienced writing tutor, who volunteered his time through the AmeriCorps VISTA Scholar-in-Service program.

Before the semester began, we met for three one-hour sessions to discuss how he should lead interactive, small group discussions, manage groups, and participate in class. We also set up a schedule for half hour, biweekly meetings to discuss course material, student concerns, service-learning components, and studio strategies. Once the semester began, the studio leader attended class so he could better understand writing assignments and course content. Attending class allowed him to contribute to classroom discussions, teach selected lessons, and meet informally with students before and after class. He formed seven studio groups of two to three students who met for weekly one-hour sessions. Students were encouraged to remain in their initial groups but could change times if they encountered schedule or personality conflicts.

Throughout the fall semester, the leader built trust and fostered student interactions. Meetings were student-driven and led by their needs for guidance on completing writing assignments, service-learning requirements, or another writing assignment in a different course. A typical session encouraged peer reviews, helped students understand and interpret assignments, and provided feedback on drafts. According to the leader, the majority of sessions focused on the current writing assignment for the course, but his role was not limited to mere academics—students frequently discussed other concerns.

As a senior student, the leader also served as a mentor to provide "insider information," or rather, guidance about how to experience success in classes, study for exams, find information on the university's website, or how to register for classes. Similar to Gray's online studio, students received full course credit for fully participating as a writer and responder. Because attendance was required, the leader sent me a feedback form that briefly summarized students' activities. Students received full credit for sessions if they brought their writing assignments, engaged in peer review, and interacted in discussions. Attendance accounted for 10% of students' total course grade, which was calculated based on participation in 10 out of 12 possible weekly meetings.

THE SERVICE-LEARNING CLASSROOM

Students were required to serve for eight hours with an organization in a career field they were exploring. Most had not declared majors, so the service project gave students an opportunity to research a potential career while learning about a non-profit organization and the local community. During a regularly scheduled class session, students attended an annual Volunteer Service Organization Fair, organized by the university's Volunteer Service Organization, to meet community partners and select service projects. They met with community partners at the Volunteer Fair and committed to a project they could reasonably expect to complete in eight hours. Because the students and I were free to meet with community partners during class time, we discussed project expectations and determined the scope and breadth of projects. Service commitments were documented in a contract, which was signed by both parties. Students served at a variety of sites: a homeless shelter, an after-school program, an environmental agency, a local food bank, a fundraiser for cancer awareness, and a home for individuals with disabilities.

Course activities included readings and discussions focused on the value of engaging in service as well as specific instructions for carrying out service. Students interviewed community partners to learn about the organization, details for completing service projects, the partner's history and accomplishments with the organization, and additional information partners were willing to share. Using information gleaned from the interview, students wrote an oral history about their community partner. Students completed a number of other writing assignments closely linked to the service project: a rhetorical analysis essay on a service-learning article, an informal presentation about their service work, an annotated bibliography, and a final research essay that integrated experiences from their service-learning project. To complete this final essay, students conducted a literature review and developed a thesis and support for claims. Specifically, the instructions explained:

You will write a literature review where you will integrate three sources to provide background information about your organization, service, or a related topic. Following the literature review, you will discuss the service you fulfilled, results of your service, and the significance of your experience.

RESULTS OF THE STUDIO-SERVICE LEARNING STUDIO HYBRID, YEAR 1

Students had difficulty connecting research and service, but the Studio helped them explore ideas. The leader guided writers in developing their thesis and support, helping them grow in their ability to develop strong arguments via interactional inquiry. For example, one student who initially struggled in generating a thesis developed a strong argument after discussing her topic in Studio: "I am going to show you how much after-school programs mutually benefit the children as well as the workers." She then supported her thesis by using primary research from an interview with her community partner along with her secondary research.

EVALUATION OF STUDENT OUTCOMES

To argue for future funding, I needed several types of data to provide multiple perspectives on the studio's impact. An online survey provided feedback on students' perceptions. Academic writing growth was measured via a pretest-posttest assignment that required students to summarize an academic article, thus assessing growth in students' critical thinking and writing skills. Finally, a qualitative analysis of students' writing assignments and the leader's session notes provided insight concerning student perceptions of their experience.

Student perceptions

An anonymous, researcher-constructed Likert scale emailed to students during the last week of the semester asked them to rate their perceptions about their leader, future tutoring opportunities, and their personal growth as readers and writers. Scaled items ranged from the options of *Strongly Agree* to *Strongly Disagree* with values ranging from five for the *Strongly Agree* rating to one for the *Strongly Disagree* rating.

As Table 9.1 indicates, students positively perceived their leader, crediting him with their writing improvement. One interesting outcome was students' positive response concerning their interest in meeting with the leader in the subsequent semester (4.95) as this reveals their strong bond with the leader and his support. Students also seemed to be highly motivated (4.80) to complete writing assignments as they indicated putting an honest effort into their writing. Finally, the third highest score (4.70) reveals students gained confidence. Hence, these high scores suggest that relationships deepened, students remained motivated to complete writing assignments, and they gained confidence in their writing.

Open-ended survey questions confirmed Likert scale ratings and revealed additional benefits from Studio. Students' comments confirmed their enjoyment in working with the leader (Number 4) and credited him with facilitating their writing growth (Numbers 3 and 5): "He was really great with helping me to improve my writing." Yet, studio benefits stretched beyond writing growth; students also believed meetings nurtured the formation of friendships. As one student notes, the interactive nature of sessions contributed to friendship development: "[Studio sessions] helped me to meet new classmates, because we were all peer reviewing and talking to each other about assignments." Evidently, interactional inquiry benefitted students holistically in their social and academic development, deepening relational connections.

Table 9.1. Year one basic writing survey of student perceptions

Survey Statement	Mean Scores	Standard Deviation
1. My essays demonstrated a strong depth of analysis	4.25	0.44
2. I put an honest effort into writing my essay	4.80	0.41
3. As a result of my leader's work with me, I am more confident in my writing	4.70	0.47
4. I enjoyed working with my leader in our Writing Studio sessions	4.65	0.49
5. My leader has helped me improve in my use of grammar	4.55	0.51
6. My work with my leader has helped me in my other classes	4.55	0.60
7. I like it that my leader comes to class with me	4.60	0.60
8. I would like to work with my leader next semester with my papers	4.95	0.22
9. I was motivated to complete my writing assignments	4.55	0.69

Note. Sample size was 20 students with 100% participation rate.

Interestingly, survey results from our pilot strongly correlate with research from this collection. Two outcomes from Gray's survey findings are strikingly similar to ours, one of which includes the high ranking of student-perceived confidence. Gray's survey prompt, "I am confident in my writing ability," is remarkably similar to number three in our survey. Both of our results revealed high student confidence on the same five-point Likert scale, as 72.1% of Gray's cohort Strongly Agreed or Agreed they were confident in their writing ability while the service-learning hybrid ranked 4.7 out of 5.0 on a similar prompt. Such findings suggest that studio participation can increase student confidence across institutions and modes of delivery. The second area of similar findings includes students' perceptions of the facilitator. Though each hybrid used different prompts to determine students' perceived helpfulness of their facilitator, both groups rated facilitators highly in their ability to support them. The service-learning hybrid cohort even expressed a continued desire to work with the facilitator in the next semester. Thus, even though both groups were mandated to participate in Studio as part of a course requirement, students did not negatively perceive their sessions or facilitators. Third, Aurora Matzke and Kelsey Huising and I both established the importance of instructor-facilitator communication. Not only do our models of constant instructor-facilitator communication embody studio methodology, clarify facilitator roles, and help facilitators model studio communication in their groups, our constant communication contributed to students' positive experiences.

Academic Writing

Students summarized an academic article during the second and fifteenth week of classes. As a pretest measure, students summarized a research article without prior instruction. Students electronically submitted summaries, which I forwarded to a graduate assistant who coded them to eliminate identifying information. Posttest summaries were collected in the same manner, and both versions were scored when the semester ended.

To evaluate summaries, the Director of First-Year Writing and I developed a scale from one to five, with five ranking as the highest ability. Five criteria were used: (A) The summary is written in a coherent and consistent manner that reveals understanding about the topic; (B) The summary shows competence in the conventions of standard edited American English; (C) The article's main idea is clearly identified; (D) The summary contains only essential statements that relevantly support the article's main idea; (E) The summary is unbiased and does not contain the student's personal opinion. To maintain inter-rater reliability, we scored two essays together, compared ratings, and discussed our rationales for scores. After achieving reliability on two more essays, we scored the remaining essays. Scores were averaged and statistically calculated for differences by utilizing paired samples t-tests. Paired samples t-test results revealed an overall significant difference, $t(19) = 3.80$, $p<.05$, suggesting significant writing improvement.

Service-Learning Impact on Students

Results of the service-learning component were mixed. According to students' feedback on reflection activities, document analysis of research papers, and the leader's session notes, students enjoyed service events, although many struggled to generate research questions related to their organization and experienced difficulty integrating information from service experiences with research essays. Despite these connective complications, they remained motivated and wrote meaningful research essays. Three students expressed a desire to submit their research essays about service-learning to the university's undergraduate academic journal. One student's essay was accepted, and she introduced her essay with a reflective tribute about the value of her studio leader and service-learning project:

> My writing level . . . has drastically changed . . . Going into the class I had no faith in my writing skills . . . Never before in my life did I like writing as much as I did in this class . . . He [leader] was such a help to my writing skills and my confidence in my own work . . . In the class I got to work on writing skills, build relationships with new people, and do my service-learning project, while I was learning about myself as well. This class gave me insight into my own capabilities as a writer, as an overall student in any class, and more confidence with myself in any situation life may throw at me.

Two key points emerge in her reflection: the benefits of working with a leader and service-learning. She mentions thrice that the leader enhanced her confidence, an attribute important for helping students persevere in writing. Additionally, she attributes the development of her friendships, self-awareness, and skill development for other courses to the studio, class, and service activities. Her analysis reveals her deep connections to others, a peripheral benefit of this hybrid program.

Although direct measures indicated students improved in writing and higher order thinking skills, they struggled with integrating service experiences into their research essays. As Pine (2008) cautions, writing assignments must carefully and intentionally connect the service and writing. I revised my writing assignments and service projects for the second year to strengthen connections between service-learning and writing projects.

YEAR TWO: THE LAUNCH OF AN INSTITUTIONALIZED STUDIO PROGRAM

Miley (this volume) notes that success is not merely measured by students' development, but success is also measured by the number of newly formed partnerships because partnerships provide crucial funding for program survival. In my case, I found partnerships essential to program creation. I had an established partnership with the Director of First-Year Writing who desired to expand Studio to all basic writing courses. When we presented the assessment report to the Associate Provost in the spring, the Director of First-Year Writing appealed to the Associate Provost to fund all fall courses. I had merely hoped for funding one paid studio leader for my course, but the Associate Provost was thrilled with the results and granted seven *paid* leader positions. The following fall semester, I mentored six instructors who began integrating Studio while I continued incorporating the only service-learning studio hybrid.

STUDIO TRAINING FOR A LARGER COHORT

News of funded leaders came at the end of the spring semester, which did not allow time for development of a leader training program; however, selected leaders were trained tutors, so they possessed a pedagogical foundation. Throughout the fall semester, leaders attended six biweekly writing tutor training meetings, but most training topics discussed applications for one-to-one peer tutoring rather than studio groups. I met separately with leaders twice to address questions and concerns, but my limited availability prevented more frequent meetings. Meeting separately with leaders on a consistent basis would have been beneficial because even though leaders understood their studio roles, they still yearned for guidance in navigating complex situations. For example, some leaders struggled with engaging a group of students or managing a group peer review.

RESHAPING THE SERVICE-LEARNING STUDIO HYBRID

I revised the course from its original configuration by modifying the theme, class readings, and service sites. A new theme of *poverty* replaced the generic topic of *service-learning*, offering unique opportunities for exploring complex issues. Assigned readings explored factors that contribute to poverty, programs that seek to help individuals escape poverty, and attempts to improve the conditions overall. Additionally, service venues were limited to two sites in order to create more cohesive experiences and to cultivate stronger discourse in the classroom and Studio. Service sites were selected based on students' positive experiences in Year One. Finally, both the leader and I took a more active role by attending all service events with students. One service-learning trip, organized by the Catholic Campus Minister, was made to a privately-funded homeless shelter. At that site, students painted fences, cleaned houses, worked in a large community garden, and interviewed shelter residents and community partners. The second option, which had two separate service dates, included serving a free breakfast to townspeople in a church basement and interviewing community partners and individuals attending the event.

On class days following service events, class discussions served as reflective sessions. Students discussed the people they met and issues related to poverty. As students shared experiences, the classroom climate was noticeably different from Year One's discussions—some students were more subdued while others were more vocal, but they appeared alert and engaged in dialogue about the fourthspace. Students were affected by service experiences, and a cohesive classroom community began to emerge.

Similar to Year One, changes in students' thinking and development of relationships were not limited to the classroom. According to the leader, sessions following service events also became more engaging as students shared out-of-classroom experiences and applied learning to interview essays, annotated bibliographies, and research papers. Service-learning projects seemed to enhance student engagement and provide valuable experiences for conducting primary research that helped them traverse into the unfamiliar genre of academic writing.

EXAMINING WRITING GROWTH OF STUDENTS IN THE SERVICE-LEARNING STUDIO HYBRID

Because the service component had been redesigned, assignments were modified and shifted, which did not allow time for a summary assignment to be given early in the semester. To ensure that authentic writing growth was measured, students' original placement test, taken during the summer prior to admission, was used as a pretest. Students who scored below 445 on their SAT Writing subtest had taken a written placement test. They responded to a prompt and were evaluated on their ability to follow the prompt, write a coherent and reasonably well-organized essay, and control errors. Students were placed in basic writing if they received a score of 2 or below by both reviewers (See Figure 9.1 for ENG 050 Basic Writing Grading Rubric). If there was a lack of consensus between reviewers, a third evaluator scored the essay to break the tie. For the posttest, students retook the test under the same constraints at the end of the semester. Processes for collecting and coding essays, establishing inter-rater reliability, and scoring procedures remained consistent with the previous year's processes.

Scores were collected and statistically evaluated for differences through paired samples t-tests. Results indicated a significant difference between pretest and posttest scores, $t(19) = 12.46$, $p<.05$. Students' marked growth in writing skills seemed to have been a result of Year Two modifications. Students appeared more empowered to integrate information and service experiences into their research essays than they were in Year One, indicating that a more focused theme and fewer service sites may have improved their ability to integrate primary and secondary research into a cohesive research paper.

Assessed Skills	Score
Essay is short, disorganized, and filled with global errors.	1
Essay lacks overall structure and a clear focus.	
Ideas are incomplete and hard to understand.	
Writer tends to list benefits and drawbacks without taking a stand.	
Essay has some sentence level errors, but the focus is a bit stronger.	2
Writer tried to develop a clear thesis, but still fails to do so.	
Writers try to take a stand.	
Essay has a clear focus and not as many sentence-level errors.	3
Writer is able to create a thesis and developed at least 3 or 4 clear points/examples.	
Writer uses some interesting or useful examples to create a clear argument.	
Writer takes a clear stand, but not always.	
Essay has few or no grammatical errors, but the argument is especially compelling.	4
Examples are original and very persuasive.	

Figure 9.1. ENG 050 Basic Writing Grading Rubric.

Changes in Year Two's course and service-learning designs confirmed students' improvement in engagement, interactional inquiry, and learning. However, even though Year Two's design appeared effective, improvements needed to be addressed in leader training and on-going leader support. Providing leaders with studio-specific training could help them direct sessions while developing a supportive network of fellow leaders.

YEAR THREE: GROWTH OF SERVICE-LEARNING STUDIO HYBRID

BUILDING A STRONGER STUDIO

Although much of the structure of Studio remained unchanged, several modifications were made. First, the Director of First-Year Writing adopted the service-learning hybrid; therefore, in Year Three, three classes conducted service-learning projects. The three service-learning courses adopted a common syllabus, keeping the assignments largely the same as the previous year. All three classes traveled together on service days where they worked at homeless shelters, one to the same privately-funded shelter organized by the Catholic Campus Ministeries and the other to a publicly-funded, county shelter. Second, pre-semester training was improved to address leaders' need for more specific knowledge and skills. In this training, leaders read *The Bedford Guide for Writing Tutors* to gain an understanding of basic tutoring pedagogy. Before the fall semester began, leaders attended an all-day training co-led by the Director of First-Year Writing and me. Leaders learned how to help writers set goals, respond to student writing, and engage writers in dialogue and peer reviews. Leaders practiced directing mock studio sessions with participants who played the roles of basic writers with actual first-draft essays. Third, we held biweekly meetings with leaders to discuss tutoring methodology and troubleshoot difficulties, providing leaders with opportunities to circumvent problems and learn strategies for improving sessions' productiveness.

IMPACT OF SERVICE-LEARNING UPON STUDIO SESSIONS

Because studio classes were evenly distributed into traditional and hybrid groups, I wanted to determine if differences existed between groups. The Basic Writing Survey distributed in Year One was slightly revised to provide more specific prompts regarding student writing. One survey statement, which asked students if they would like to work with their leader in the subsequent semester, was deleted because some leaders would be unavailable for tutoring the following spring. As Table 9.2 shows, the Service-Learning Studio hybrid reported higher ratings on *all* items, with five of those significantly higher than the Traditional Studio groups. Almost all of the highest scores in the Service-Learning group are directly correlated with leader satisfaction, acknowledgement of leaders' assistance in helping students improve in writing, and students' positive relationship with the leader. These results mirrored Year One's scores, indicating that writer-leader interactions were strengthened during service activities and helped foster positive relationships.

Short-answer survey questions clarified students' perceptions. Students were asked if they believed meetings influenced their social interactions with classmates, both in and out of class. In the Service-Learning hybrid, 91% of students replied *yes* compared to 65% of students in traditional groups. This significant difference may be due to the early integration of fourthspace experiences into the course, allowing students to form friendships shortly after the semester began. One student explained that service-learning social interactions offered new opportunities for relationships at meetings: "I became more open and came to know my fellow classmates." Students' willingness to be "open" appeared to be a factor in the success of studio meetings.

Table 9.2. Year three basic writing survey of students' perceptions

Survey Statement	Mean	
	S-L	Trad.
1. I put an honest effort into writing my essays.	**4.53***	4.19
2. I will meet with a writing tutor for future essays.	**4.38***	4.01
3. As a result of working with my leader, I am a more confident writer.	**4.56**	4.31
4. I enjoyed working with my leader in our Writing Studio sessions.	**4.64**	4.41
5. My leader has helped me improve my use of grammar.	**4.64***	4.32
6. My work with my leader has helped me with my other classes.	**4.58***	4.00
7. I like it that my leader comes to class with me.	**4.62***	4.28
8. I was motivated to complete my writing assignments.	**4.13**	3.97
9. I usually make significant changes to my first draft of an essay.	**4.20**	3.99
10. In future papers I plan to incorporate the process of drafting, revising, and editing.	**4.32**	4.20

Notes. (1) S-L= Studio Groups that participated in Service-Learning. Trad. = Traditional Studio Groups. (2) Higher scores are indicated in bold font. (3) Sample size was 122 students with 95% participation rate. (4) * Indicates a significant difference between groups: 1. $t(120)=2.09$, $p<.05$; 2. $t(120)=2.00$, $p<.05$; 5. $t(120)=2.39$, $p<.05$; 6. $t(120)=3.02$, $p<.05$; 7. $t(120)=2.19$, $p<.05$.

SPRING CONVERSATIONS

In the spring, we held follow-up interviews to further research student perceptions of Studio. Two students responded to an email solicitation and consented to a digitally-recorded interview. Both interviews were transcribed and analyzed. One student, Adam, discussed how his leader helped him develop his writing skills by pushing him to "interpret [events] more clearly" and helping him to learn "writing techniques to become more professional." Adam believed that writing about his service-learning experience improved his writing because he "became more descriptive, wanting people to feel like they are there." Adam maintained motivation to refine his discourse to enhance reader interpretation of his ideas.

Another student, Bruce, noted the change in the classroom environment after service trips. He credits the service experience for facilitating his development of relationships:

> Before we went to the shelter, (laughing) I did not like some people in the class. At the shelter, we built connections and friendships. We got closer as a family, joked around together. I could be myself in class and learned a lot.

Working together, eating together, traveling together, and listening to stories of tragedy and triumph transforms not only the spirit of the classroom, but these experiences also invigorate dynamics in studio sessions and lead to better conversations about writing.

Overall, results from surveys and interviews suggest service-learning students rated their academic growth more highly, viewed their leader more positively, developed more interactions in the Studio and classroom, and carried their learning into the new semester. Engaging in whole-class service-learning projects synergized classroom and studio discussions, creating community and inspiring writers. Lastly, service impacted leaders as they enjoyed service activities and leading discussions about service experiences.

MULTIPLYING THE IMPACT OF THIRDSPACE-FOURTHSPACE COLLABORATIONS

The thirdspace of the Studio can be enriched by a fourthspace: service-learning. Even so, combining service with Studio requires thoughtful planning. In this hybrid, three components enhanced studio experiences. A centralized theme, poverty, improved interactional inquiry because students learned different perspectives about their common topic when listening to peers. Building service experiences that coincide with complex issues cultivates interactional inquiry even further, ultimately helping writers become more engaged in writing, improve their writing skills, and apply learning to written assignments. Fourthspace conversations about poverty and direct involvement in service to organizations that work with individuals who live in poverty can help writers build stronger writing connections. The centralized theme helped students transport their ideas and experiences from the fourthspace to the thirdspace, enhancing interactional inquiry and their understanding of inquiry-based research.

Reducing service options to create shared service experiences enhanced the classroom's community spirit and cohesive studio-classroom discourse. In short, *collectively* listening to personal stories of committed volunteers dedicated to improving the conditions of the homeless or of a homeless man's advice to college students surely draws classroom members together in engaging discourse. Working side-by-side with writers at service events also impacted leaders, which undoubtedly spilled over in studio conversations. Stories enter our human soul and provide meaningful, rhetorical contexts. Leaders connected with writers in fourthspace events, and later on, provided students with much more than help with writing assignments—leaders also gave advice, provided insider information about the university, and created a caring, safe environment. By serving together in fourthspaces, students began to develop relationships with leaders where they openly discussed ideas and requested feedback on writing projects. Students who participated in fourthspaces rated their leaders more positively and put more effort into their writing assignments than those without fourthspace experiences.

Finally, leader training must be uniquely designed, address theoretical foundations for practice, and establish protocols for studio sessions. Gray (this volume) highlights the investment of time and effort needed to support studio programs, arguing for the Writing Center's central role in developing and implementing Studio. Writing Center directors are uniquely positioned to educate facilitators and provide training opportunities to help facilitators build competency, ask specific questions, and provide networking opportunities where facilitators can form friendships, adding to *their* satisfaction. Regular staff meetings in our Writing Center provided leaders with support in working out complex situations, a forum for exchanging ideas, and a place to make their own knowledge, becoming a space for interactional inquiry. As Grego and Thompson (2008) note, staff meetings can keep participants "in touch with issues of conducting groups, while also bringing to the table issues related to student participants, making us all more reflective about the patterns and interactions that we are a part of" (p. 171). These ongoing communications help leaders become more effective in their roles.

Teaching with a service-learning component is time-intensive and requires coordination with community members. Coupling Studio with a service-learning project can be even more challenging, but after years of observing changes in students and leaders, the benefits of these combined spaces seem too compelling to relinquish. Students learn the discourse of the academy and use real world experiences to link research with writing, a process that helps them internalize important components for holistic success in college—engagement, critical thinking, and writing. Yet, benefits are not limited to students' learning and success; students' service-learning and studio experiences offer opportunities for expanding their understanding in new venues they will remember long after they leave the academy.

Before the Third Year ended, Andrew popped in my office to ask me to join him for coffee in the nearby Starbucks. Andrew, a first-generation student from South Philadelphia, struggled with writing in our course. I quickly closed my laptop and joined him in a celebratory coffee chat. He had successfully passed all his first-year courses and was planning on studying abroad in the fall. We discussed how to access online writing support while he was overseas, and then suddenly, his thoughts flipped to a completely different topic: "I'd really like to go back to the shelter. Are you planning another trip?" With my heart dancing at his interest yet disappointed that I could not support a summer service project, I answered, "Not until the fall, Andrew, but if I come up with a project before then, I'll let you know."

REFERENCES

Astin, A. W., Volgelgesand, L. J., Ikeda, E. K. & Yee, J. A. (2000). *How service learning affects students*. Los Angeles, CA: UCLA Higher Education Research Institute.

Deans, T. (2000). *Writing partnerships: Learning in composition*. Urbana, IL: National Council of Teachers of English.

Grego, R. & Thompson, N. (2008). *Teaching/Writing in thirdspaces: The studio approach*. Carbondale, IL: Southern Illinois University Press.

Light, R. J. (2001). *Making the most of college: Students speak their minds*. Cambridge, MA: Harvard University Press.

Pine, N. (2008). Service learning in a basic writing class: A best case scenario. *Journal of Basic Writing, 27*(2), 29–55.

Rose, M. (1983). Remedial writing courses: A critique and a proposal. *College English, 45*(2), 109–128. https://dx.doi.org/10.2307/377219.

Ryan, L. & Zimmerelli, L. (2010). *The Bedford guide for writing tutors*. New York, NY: Bedford/St. Martins.

CHAPTER 10.

WRITING STUDIOS AS COUNTERMONUMENT: REFLEXIVE MOMENTS FROM ONLINE WRITING STUDIOS IN WRITING CENTER PARTNERSHIPS

Michelle Miley

Montana State University

We hear the warning cries all around us: The shift to the new corporate university is leading to the crumbling of the humanities (Arum & Roksa, 2011; Berlin, 1996, 2003; Bérubé & Nelson, 1994; Bousquet & Parascondola, 2004; for example). With its focus on efficiency, production, and profits, the corporate university erodes what many see as the intangible value of a liberal education. Recognizing the need to find our place in this new era of higher ed, some argue that rhetoric and composition, with our resistance to the static consumption of knowledge, provides a necessary counter perspective to the monument of the corporation. But Paul Butler (2006) argues that despite our efforts to subvert the calcified models of education inherent in a corporate model "through innovative teaching practices," the difficulty of working for generative change within the university creates an "impasse," and writing programs can quickly become "monolithic or static in their evolution" (p. 11). Butler uses the metaphor of the "countermonument" as a defense against fossilized programs. Drawing from James Young's analysis of countermonuments as "self-conscious memorial spaces" (p. 11), Butler asserts that finding countermonuments to our programs can help us "examine their fundamental reason for being," resisting impasse as "[they] assume a more protean and thus more viable shape" (2006, p. 12).

The idea of a countermonument provides a nice metaphor for the structural risks necessary for innovation. Butler notes that countermonuments require a great amount of self-assessment and reflection and, importantly, a willingness to allow viewers to share authority in the construction of identity (p. 15). The necessity of a countermonument's "willingness to open itself to its own violation" (p. 15) suggests to me the openness of Edward Soja's (1996) thirdspace where multiple perspectives collide, where the clash between our lived experiences and idealizations become visible. Soja notes that exploring these spaces requires a "strategic and flexible way of thinking" (p. 22). Donna Qualley's (1997) reflexive spaces speak both to Soja's necessary flexibility for thirdspace exploration and Butler's reflection and willingness to share authority in construction of identity. Qualley (1997) defines reflexive spaces as those where we see our own ways of knowing reflected back to us through another's perspective. She notes how often times our understanding of teaching grows from the limited focus of an individual perspective rather than a holistic view (1997, p. 23). I believe that by creating reflexive and reflective spaces, countermonuments reveal thirdspaces and provide new angles of vision necessary for creating innovative environments that resist fossilization. I experience Writing Studios as offering those angles of vision. Through the development of writing studio partnerships at the University of Houston's Writing Center, I encountered thirdspace and experienced both the reflective and reflexive moments Butler's and Qualley's metaphors allow us to envision.

The University of Houston Writing Center's Writing in the Disciplines (WID) program was birthed out of the university's desire to provide "writing instruction that meets the diverse needs of a student population at undergraduate, graduate, and professional levels" ("The Writing Center at UH; Mission Statement"). A large, metropolitan commuter campus touted as the second most diverse research institution in the United States, the university provides rich opportunity for educators to teach students writing within their disciplines, both as a means to join their professional discourse communities and as a way to become active creators of knowledge within their professions. Because of the diversity of students and large class sizes, these educators rely on the Writing Center for help providing effective writing instruction. Those of us working within the Center understood our charge, but also understood how easily we could give in to the pressure to become the "saviors" of writing for professors in large lecture classes who are not schooled in teaching writing. As the Assistant Director of Writing in the Disciplines, I felt this pressure. I also knew that our standard approach, one meeting between a tutor and a student, could not provide the rich, rhetorical understanding of writing I wanted students to experience. Looking for an approach that would resist the static consumption of knowledge that can occur in the context of large, lecture-oriented disciplinary classes and would draw on the resources available through the Writing Center, I turned to the Studio method. Although, as the chapters in this volume suggest, the Studio method began in and is often associated with basic and first-year writing, I saw in the Studio model an opportunity to build a countermonument to what I saw as the limited structures in place for supporting Writing in the Disciplines at our institution.

The first studio partnerships were connected to traditional face-to-face courses. Those enrolled, for example, in the Hospitality Law course were assigned to a studio group of five to seven students. That group, which stayed consistent throughout the semester, would meet every few weeks with a Writing Center tutor to discuss their writing. The tutor would facilitate the discussion and then would give me feedback on the process. As our partnerships expanded to include online and hybrid courses, we encountered the need to move the studios into online spaces. These online studios, which began with a partnership in the College of Technology, led to a large-scale partnership with the composition program and the development of hybrid sections of first-year composition. (Mary Gray discusses the development of the first-year writing program in her chapter in this volume.)

In this chapter, I use Butler's metaphor of the countermonument and its possibilities for creating reflexive spaces to describe my experience with online Writing Studios both in a WID partnership and in the larger first-year composition partnership. The chapter draws from data gathered between fall 2009 and spring 2013 (Miley, 2013), and includes analysis of archived online writing studio conversations from both fall 2009 and spring 2010, email conversations outside of the studio space, and written facilitator reflections. In addition, I interviewed the instructors and the facilitators involved in the project in spring 2013. From these sources, I trace the adaptation of the Studio approach into an online, hybrid setting for a College of Technology class, showing how that class' online studios helped those of us in the partnership rethink both our ways of and motivations for teaching writing. I then discuss the expansion of the online studio approach into a hybrid first-year composition course model, describing how the online studios made visible moments of resistance to innovation influenced by disciplinary discourse and institutional relationships. Through these partnerships, I discovered that the writing studio collaborations provided what Grego and Thompson (2008) describe as "an institutionally aware methodology" (p. 21), serving as a counter not only to the institution but also to disciplinary knowledge. The chapter concludes by suggesting how online Writing Studios can help writing teachers resist disciplinary calcification and work within and against the institution. This discussion also illustrates how studios make visible the moments when, without the willingness to take the structural risks that Butler calls for, we become "monolithic or static" (2006, p. 11) despite our motivation to be innovative.

BUILDING THE COUNTERMONUMENT: ONLINE STUDIOS FOR A WRITING IN THE DISCIPLINES COURSE

Writing center history includes a long list of scholars who creatively envision writing center work as much more than the remedial service it was originally imagined to provide. But, as Butler argues, the generative change of countermonuments is not easily accomplished. One difficulty in re-envisioning the possibilities for writing center work lies in the center's place in the institution. Situated as student service centers with tenuous funding, writing centers often agree to ignore tensions between the institutional expectations of writing centers and what is actually possible and theoretically sound because they need a "sense of authority and expertise" in order to survive (Pemberton, 1995, p. 120). Pemberton uses the relationship between WID programs and writing centers to exemplify the often fossilizing tension between expectations and possibilities for writing center work. Historically, WID programs have involved collaboration between those in the disciplines and those in writing center work, but much of it has been in the form of WID instructors sending students to the center for one-on-one tutoring sessions, in a sense "outsourcing" the teaching of writing. This model of collaboration seems to benefit both parties. Those in writing centers gain identity and purpose, and those sending their students to us get the help they need teaching writing. We become complicit in what Pemberton terms "administrative expediency" (1995, p. 117).

In an environment where the management of the university draws more and more on a corporate model that measures success by continual expansion, I know the dangers of falling into a service identity, of the writing center becoming the outsource for someone else's teaching. I must admit, in fact, that the development of online studios in the University of Houston Writing Center began with my own fear that if I did not provide a new service to meet the needs of my WID partners, I would become irrelevant in my institution. Although my initial impulse for implementing Studios was as a means to provide the innovative learning environments that worked against the large lecture classes the institution imposed, I was also working under the pressure of the institution to continually grow the number of students served in the Writing Center. When I began developing studio partnerships, my success was measured not simply by the development of the students I was working with, but also by the number of new partnerships I formed. I knew that if I did not expand the studio partnerships to other courses, I would not continue to receive the funding I needed to survive. In an attempt to expand, I asked Micah, the Assistant Dean of Assessment in the College of Technology, if he knew any faculty members who might want to partner with me.

At about that same time, Morgan, an assistant professor within the College of Technology, had gone to Micah expressing frustration at the "incomprehensible" writing in her senior-level, undergraduate Quality Improvement Methods course. In her course, Morgan asked students to investigate real world problems, to apply the tools and methods they were learning in class to these problems, and then to summarize their findings in a technical report. Morgan specifically designed her assignments to include a written report that would provide students with an opportunity to practice articulating ideas in written form, a skill "especially important in the decision sciences where effective communication is needed to make well-informed decisions within organizations" (Kovach, Miley & Ramos, 2012, p. 367). Morgan had become increasingly frustrated by these reports as she began to recognize that "students' written communication skills made it extremely difficult to identify whether students understood the course material" (Kovach, Miley & Ramos, 2012, p. 368). When Micah sent out the offer for assistance from the Writing Center, she responded, hoping that "the [W]riting [C]enter would help to copy edit my students work, so it would be better and I wouldn't have to do it" (personal email conversation, 13 March 2013).

Both Morgan and I were falling into the "administrative expediency" Pemberton warns against. Certainly, Morgan communicated her anxiety about responding to writing with the all-too-familiar excuse that because she did not have time to teach writing, the Writing Center could do it. I accepted this identity, knowing I needed to increase my partnerships. But the countermonument I was building, the face-to-face Writing Studios, were too static for the new environments of teaching at the university. Immediately, the partnership with Morgan provided the reflexive moment necessary to counter my fossilized ways of thinking about where and when writing instruction can and should occur. Within the first semester of working together, our online writing studio collaboration made visible my static ways of thinking about teaching with technology. In fact, the online environment provided a material space for those of us teaching writing to view the learning that we simply trusted was happening in the face-to-face environment. Figuring out how to provide the best learning environment for Morgan's students, we moved toward a collaboration that was less like what Pemberton describes and more like the "ethical collaborators who developed 'shared agency'" that Ritola, et.al (this volume) describe.

REFLEXIVE MOMENT: RESISTANCE TO ONLINE EDUCATION

As noted above, students in the original version of Studio met face-to-face in a space designed to facilitate conversation. The space provided what I believed was a counter to the large lecture classes in which they were enrolled and provided a means to foster both conversation and community. In my mind, online education fostered neither conversation nor community, and was simply a means by which the institution could continue to increase course enrollment. However, Morgan's Quality Improvement Methods course is a hybrid course, like many courses in the College of Technology. Our first semester, Morgan immediately asked if we could develop the Writing Studios in an online environment. I reacted with an emphatic "no." I argued that the studios had to be face-to-face; the conversation and relationships essential to the practice depended on it. Because the course is a hybrid and students are typically non-traditional, however, Morgan countered that students would not participate if we did not find a way to put the writing studio space online. She also noted that being technology students, online was a comfortable place for them to be.

I do not completely know why I resisted moving the Studios online. In many ways, the Studio approach and online writing instruction (OWI) grow from the same theoretical family tree. As Gray notes in this volume, Hewett and Ehmann (2004) root OWI "strongly in the social-constructivist epistemology, wherein knowledge is understood to be dynamic, provisional, and developed and mediated socially as people operate within various 'communities' of knowledge" (p. 33). Citing theorists like Vygotsky, Kuhn, and Bruffee, Hewett and Ehmann provide a strong argument for the success of online writing instruction. In addition, Scott Warnock (2008) goes so far as to connect OWI to the Studio model, stating that "[t]he continuous writing environment [of OWI] makes it ever possible for students to learn through their own work in a studio-like environment" (p. xii). Remembering that Grego and Thompson (2008) assert that Studios should be "highly adaptable," formed from "a configuration of relationships that can emerge from different contexts," I finally agreed to develop online writing studios for Morgan's class (p. 7).

INNOVATING: CREATING THE ONLINE STUDIO ENVIRONMENT

Our development started with the creation of a "space" in Morgan's Blackboard shell where we created discussion forums for the studio groups using the group function. We divided the students into groups of five to seven and assigned a Writing Center peer tutor to facilitate each group. We asked students to "post" a draft of their writing along with a paragraph telling the group where they were in the process and what they would like for the group to focus on. The others in the group would have four days to come into the space and respond to their peers' questions, concerns, ideas, and drafts. The Writing Center tutor would come in and out of the space, responding to writing, facilitating questions, and guiding the conversation.

As it turns out, transitioning studios to an online environment not only "worked," it had real benefits. Because the conversation is asynchronous, writers could come back into the boards at any time to ask or answer any questions posed. Students communicated through writing throughout the entire process.

Our commuter student population had the added benefit of being able to work in the studios at the time most convenient for them. And, somewhat selfishly from a researcher's standpoint, I had every conversation "captured" for current and future analysis.

In addition, because of our partnership, I was exposed to a new environment for teaching writing. In my conversations with Morgan, I discovered that she, too, found a new way of teaching. She had never thought to use Blackboard's "discussion" tool. Because of our partnership, she now includes discussions not just in her online teaching environment but also in the classroom environment.

Discussion, a staple in the composition classroom, was a new tool for teaching decision sciences. Through the analysis of the online conversations, Morgan, the tutors, and I could better understand both the process students were undergoing as they wrote the assigned technical reports and the ways our interactions with the students shaped their understanding of their writing processes. Because we could see the conversations between the students in the online studio groups, those of us in the teaching role had a new view from the student perspective. Drawing from new insights gained, Morgan revised how she teaches her class, and the peer tutors and I revised how we interact with the students. Like the reflective properties of the countermonument, the online environment provided the time and the space necessary to "see" what the conversations in our learning environment reveal.

Reflexive Moment: The Importance of Articulating Innovation

It was not simply in the online space that we discovered insights. The conversations surrounding setting up the online writing studio partnerships provided rich reflexive moments as well. In fact, like Dan Fraizer (this volume) argues, we found our dialogue between facilitators, teachers, and administrators to be essential for the success of the studio program. It was in our dialogue that our discovery for the need for a clear orientation occurred. For writing studios to succeed, I had to articulate their purpose and logistics to both professors and students. Writing studios are, indeed, innovative, and new ideas require some explanation. Describing the logistics of creating this space to students and professors becomes even more important when the Studio is moved online. If those participating do not grasp what the studio environment can provide or how the Studio will function, the online space remains empty. We cannot reach through the screen to draw people in.

In the College of Technology, PowerPoints with graphs and charts are a standard medium for communicating. So, when Morgan began putting together the class in which we would introduce studios to the students, she asked me for a slide set to explain the studio process—a chart, a graph, or some sort of illustration. Working from my own standards in teaching, I responded, "I think I'll just talk to the students and explain to them the conversation in Studio." In my mind, Studios were all about conversation and relationships, a model that could not be translated into a graph. In response to my refusal to understand studios in another way, Morgan developed a graphic of her own, one that, because she was working from her discipline, I thought missed all of the important aspects I wanted to communicate.

Here was the reflexive moment: If I did not find a way to bridge the disciplinary discourses, my students and my disciplinary partners would try to make meaning using the resources they had. As a rhetorician, I had to accept my responsibility for figuring out how to communicate in a way that my audience would understand. If that meant the best means of persuasion was an illustration, I should think through the possibilities of how to illustrate the process. If I am aware of the disciplinary differences, then I have to come to the conclusion that they are as uncomfortable with my words as I am sifting through all their charts and graphs. My encounter with Morgan made my responsibility for bridging discourses visible. I created a PowerPoint to visually represent the studio process, and in the end, that visual representation bridged our discourses in ways that I could not by simply using my disciplinary vocabulary.

Reflecting on what I have learned about bridging discourses, I asked Morgan about her experience in trying to communicate her discipline to me. She immediately acknowledged that she, too, felt the discomfort of collaborating with someone who speaks a different disciplinary language, describing the feeling as being "paralyzed:"

> When I gave you something in a graph and you kept saying
> I don't understand this, I was paralyzed. I didn't know what
> else to do to try and help you understand it because . . . the
> form I put it in was perfectly understandable to me. And so I
> think that's a challenge in communication—I mean it relates
> to writing, but communication in general—is when you think
> something is so clear the way you are saying it from your
> perspective, it is so hard to draw yourself out and put yourself
> in that other person's shoes and then try to translate in a . . .
> different format that they would understand. (Personal communication, 1 March 2013)

Recognizing the "paralysis" within my ways of communicating may create open spaces to new ways of communicating. Because I had to bridge disciplinary discourses, I had to learn to translate my ideas into other ways of thinking and speaking. This is not only good for my students; it is also good for my teaching.

REFLEXIVE MOMENT: DISCIPLINARY WAYS OF SPEAKING

I find that bridging disciplinary discourses is both one of the most rewarding and most challenging features in writing center and WID work. Those in writing center work know the discomfort of finding ourselves in a disciplinary conversation that is not our own. Of course, this discomfort, as Pemberton (1995) points out, can be a way for us to make productive the tension between writing center theory and the foundations of Writing in the Disciplines. Pemberton suggests that when we work with students in other disciplines, we have the opportunity to empower them in a way they cannot be in the classroom. When students come to the writing center, those of us working with them can allow them to claim authority over their subject matter while giving them the security of someone who "knows writing" to help guide the writing process (Pemberton, 1995, p. 123–125). The Studio approach provides a similar rebalancing of power. As Grego and Thompson (2008) note, "in a thirdspace like Studio groups, the usual scripted responses on which teachers base their authority, as well as students counterscripting moves, don't quite fit, because in this space teacher-student power relationships are not as rigidly determined by institutional scripts as in the typical classroom" (p. 75).

When we first developed Writing Studios for the WID partnerships, the facilitators and I were aware of the disciplinary differences and hoped to use that to empower the students to take ownership of their own work. To acknowledge the students' expert knowledge within the discipline, the facilitators (including myself, the first semester) consciously reminded the students that we would be able to help them with their writing, but they would need to rely on one another for responses to the graphic representations of their tools and measures. Even with that acknowledgement, we immediately found our language was not always easily accessible to the students. In fact, sometimes it confused the situation.

The pilot year of the partnership, I facilitated a studio group for Morgan's course. As I finished my first round of reading the students' work, I wrote a general comment to all the studio members reminding them that I was not "versed in the tools" and would be relying on them to give feedback on the use of the diagrams and charts. In my mind, the graphic representations existed "apart" from the writing. I was naïve to think this. Another interaction makes this clear. One student, David, struggled with articulating the specific problem he was analyzing. He asked the studio members to make sure that the process he was analyzing came through. I commented on his text, making suggestions about his description of the process he was writing about, but not pulling in the diagrams and flowcharts he had attached. David read my response and responded with "I am confused." No wonder. Because of the online space, I can reflect back on my comments, which suggest to me now that I was reading his writing as somehow being separate from his content. But I gave him no suggestions as to how to join those two.

Thankfully, one of his studio group members was able to translate for me, to join the content with the form, and to understand David's charts and graphs as essential to his communicating. In the same thread, Jason responded:

> David—I think that I understand what Michelle is saying. Look back through your IAR's [individual activity reports] starting with #1, and make sure that you focus on the process to resolve your problem. That process is what goes into the FMEA [the diagramming tool learned in class]. I believe you looked at the causes that can affect getting to your goal and not the process itself. . . . Hope this helps! –Jason

The studio space allowed Jason and David to work through my way of speaking about writing and to begin to contextualize my language into their discipline. And, in this particular moment, the studio space empowered the student writers with disciplinary authority so that they could begin to help one another rather than simply relying on the "writing expert" for help.

Another student, Alex, made this comment to David: "[E]ven though your classmates may know how to read the PDPC [a diagramming tool learned in class], without any arrows or lines, someone outside of the course may have difficulty understanding the diagram." The studios provided the space for these students to begin to reflect on how their ideas communicated to audiences both within their discipline and without. Perhaps more importantly, the studios provided an environment for both me and the Writing Center staff to see our own ways of communicating with students through their eyes, Qualley's reflexive stance. We were able to take what was made visible in the online environment and use it in our face-to-face work. For example, after a training meeting in which we used the online studio groups to look at the differences in our discourse communities, one tutor excitedly rushed into my office. She had just finished a face-to-face studio with an Art History group during which she realized she was having trouble "talking their talk." So she used her own discourse, telling them how a poet would break down the assignment, and then asked them to translate that for her into their own disciplinary voice. By making visible her disciplinary discourse, she gave her students the necessary vocabulary to begin describing their own.

ENCOUNTERING RESISTANCE TO INNOVATION: MOVING ONLINE STUDIOS INTO FIRST-YEAR COMPOSITION

Through the Writing Center's studio partnerships in WID, those of us collaborating experienced reflective and reflexive moments. Those moments were not always comfortable. There were disruptions in all of our ways of thinking about writing. But through the disruptions, real work was accomplished. So when the success of the online WID hybrid/studio model with Morgan resulted in a hybrid first-year composition course using the online Studio model, I was ecstatic. Now not only was I getting to work with the Studio model, but I would be partnering with people in my own discipline, with those who know writing, who understand the importance of invention, of revision, of audience. As the partnership developed, however, I realized that negotiating the disruptions studios can bring would challenge me in brand new ways. Certainly the studios did provide a space where we could experience the generative, creative, dynamic, and disruptive forces Morgan and I experienced. But there were moments when I found myself at an impasse, looking in the disruptions for clarity, understanding, and growth, unable to act on the insights made visible through the studio work. In this partnership, I did not as often experience the collective banding together that Ritola, et al. (this volume) advocates for, nor the productive collaboration that Fraizer (this volume) describes.

CALCIFICATION: PROCESS BECOMES PRODUCT

The first disruption dealt with the separation of spaces necessary for studio work. Because our first rendition of the online studios linked directly into the Blackboard class shell, I technically could not keep the instructors out of the studio space. The course shell belonged to the instructors, and by software design, instructors have access to all groups. So, from the beginning of the first-year composition Studio, knowing the importance of keeping a process space separate for the students, those of us in the Writing Center and in the English Department emphasized keeping the studio space exclusively for the students, one in which they did not have the authority figure of the instructor lurking over them while they worked through the messiness of their writing process.

But the need to know what was happening in the studio was incredibly hard to resist for most of the instructors. In addition, unlike the WID class, instructors attached a high percentage value to the students' participation in Studios, some as high as thirty percent of the grade. We took "attendance," a task that quickly became troublesome for some of the facilitators as the instructors gave them detailed instructions about when a student should get full credit and when they should not. Some instructors wanted a breakdown of how many words each student post-ed, the quality of the response, and how developed each draft was. The facilita-tors would complain to me about the feeling that instructors were like helicopter moms: stalking the studios online, wanting information about students, specifical-ly if they had attended on time. As I began thinking about why I was having these particular problems with this particular course and not with Morgan's, I began to realize that Studio, a place for process, was quickly becoming another graded task for the students. Our process was becoming our product.

Theoretically, those of us in composition espouse the importance of allowing for different processes in writing and for the recursive nature of writing. Focus-ing on process, after all, is one way we resist what we see as calcified thinking about writing. But because we have studied process and know it, we also want to teach it and control it. This need to control can actually backfire so that we make "process" the actual "product," thus a little bit negating the "process." I see this in myself. When I first started working with studios online, I insisted on a "prompt" to get the conversation going. By "prompting" conversation, many times I created a checklist of items for students to produce in this space that should be open to their individual processes. My prompt was a desire to force them into a process space. My facilitators soon pointed out to me the prompt was limiting their ability to facilitate what the students brought to the Studio.

The answer, of course, is not simply to "let go" of things like prompts and attendance points. We do, in fact, need structures in place in order for organic learning to occur. But the balance between structure and fluidity is a tenuous one, one I am constantly trying to keep from tipping. Both Morgan and the facilitators seemed to accept this need for balance. The resistance to allowing space for the fluid nature of Studios came specifically from instructors teaching first-year composition. Every semester, we revisited the conversation about what protocols needed to be put in place to make sure students who were not "par-ticipating" did not get credit. I argued that the students' papers should be the product measured. The instructors wanted assurance that the studio space would include required assessments. The tension to control was great, and the desire to, as one instructor said, "crack the whip" was ever-present.

In the first-year composition project, my ideal of student engagement and allowing the writing process to develop was disrupted when the Studio illu-minated how my discipline uses that process to control. Xin Liu Gale (1996) astutely notes that "compositionists are simultaneously abandoning authority and re-claiming authority," and that this "paradoxical phenomenon . . . indicates the irresolvable conflict between the progressive teachers' desire to democratize teaching for social justice and equality and the violent dimension of teaching, which . . . demands the teacher's authority to ensure students' obedience and participation" (p. 33–34). In the first-year composition hybrid/studio project, those of us in the teaching spaces collided with the irresolvable conflict that Gale describes. Because the Studio model is a collaborative environment, the teacher's authority has to be reconceptualized. The online writing studio environment made the tension of teacher identity and authority, particularly for those teaching within our discipline, visible.

Risk and Resistance: Relationships with the Institution

The impasse I just described likely occurred because in this partnership, we were all working within the same discipline. The spaces were not as easily separated as in WID projects, where we all clearly come with our own authoritative identity. Reflexive moments were harder to identify because what was reflected back was my own discipline's ways of thinking. But I believe that the relationship with and status of the instructors within the institution explains the fossilization in the project even more than disciplinary identity does. The first-year composition project was built on the foundation of contingent labor, labor rife with tensions that both support and often hide the collisions between the reality and ideology of composition work. The effects of labor became particularly clear when I compared this partnership to the one with Morgan.

I initially understood the impasses in composition with Barbara Shapiro's (2009) astute observations of composition's disciplinary identity being intertwined with our teaching, and therefore with our relationship with students. I believe this intertwining would explain why Morgan would not feel the same need to know specifically what was occurring in the studio space. When I asked her about it, though, I discovered that while disciplinary identity did have something to do with her ability to create an instructor-free zone, the way she viewed her relationship with the students was very much shaped by her identity within and relationship with the institution.

Morgan first referenced an email I sent her that included a paragraph from an essay I had written in a rhetoric class. In the essay, I discussed Elio Frattaroli (2001), a Freudian psychoanalyst, who relates that physicians often have a tendency to become irritated and intolerant of patients who do not cure easily. He notes that Freud called this tendency "furor sanandi—'the rage to cure'" (2001, p. 121). Frattaroli explains that this need to cure his patients may come from a need to prove his own worth rather than a concern for his patients. The rage is not necessarily a bad thing; in fact

> [i]t is both an essential ingredient and a universal problem in
> the motivation of all who are drawn to the helping professions,
> and one of the primary reasons why all psychotherapists and

> psychiatrists need psycho-therapy for themselves. Until they
> learn to recognize and come to terms with this rage to cure,
> therapists generally have trouble distinguishing their own needs
> from their patients' needs. (Frattaroli, 2001, p. 121)

I have used this passage to calm many facilitators who become frustrated at their students' seeming lack of improvement. "The rage to cure" has become a common phrase in our studio training. I do not remember why I shared it with Morgan; I believe it was after a conversation during which we had been bemoaning the slow pace of student development. She remembered it, though, and noted how the concept helped her reflect on her relationship to students and the effects of the tenure process on that relationship:

> When you shared that that was like a big wake-up because I
> realized that all this pressure that I was under—here we go
> back to tenure—that I felt like I had to be perfect and if I
> was anything less than perfect I wouldn't get tenure . . . and I
> think that was translating into the classroom . . . my students'
> projects could not be anything less than perfect, and so I was
> like super hard on them. . . . [It is] not that I didn't care about
> their learning, because I thought that through this process [of
> writing] they would learn, but I think it backfired because it
> was too, too much. (Personal communication, 1 March 2013)

Morgan understood how her identity as a pre-tenured faculty member shaped her teaching. Her comment that students were the "means" by which she would get tenure mirrors Rhoades and Slaughter's (1998) observation about the changing relationship between universities and students: "Students are neither 'customers' or 'consumers.' They are the 'industry's' 'inputs' and 'products.' The purchasers of the products—private, corporate 'employers'—are the customers. The push, then, is to improve (standardize) the product by 'improving' the input" (p. 39). But the tenure relationship with the institution also gave Morgan the security of time necessary to take risks. Because of that security, and because the studios provided an opportunity for research (and thus for publishing), she was willing to confront the reflexive moments and adapt her teaching. She was willing to risk innovation because she could channel the knowledge about teaching into research and a publication toward tenure.

The instructors in the first-year composition partnership were all contingent faculty, on year-to-year contracts without the security of time. Rather than understanding the course as one in which they could reflect and make changes, the instructors felt the pressure to please administration, to have high grades and high participation. They were not rewarded for new ways of thinking that resulted in research. Unlike Morgan, who, as a tenure-track faculty member, felt secure in knowing that she would be teaching each year, and who was motivated to research and explore new methods because of the pressures of tenure, these instructors taught each year not knowing if funding would be available in the next. They were the "disposable teacher[s]" Bousquet, Scott, and Parascondola (2004) describe. One instructor described the experience as surreal:

> If I want this job, it has to succeed. It has to succeed on multiple levels. The surreal nature is not lost on me that I am the most contingent of contingent faculty. One whip and I'm gone. (Personal communication, 6 March 2013)

Fraizer (this volume) notes that "[s]tudio faculty members can 'see' and 'be seen' by others as we work together to understand each other's goals and meet student needs." Through my experience working with adjunct instructors in the studio partnership, I wonder if the increased visibility of studios can be too risky for those who do not have the security of tenure in today's corporate university. I also wonder, and do not have an answer to, how this visibility might have been more risky because it was occurring outside of the home department of these home instructors.

What is interesting is that, despite this instructor's fear, because of the popularity with administration to offer hybrid first-year composition courses, the number of sections continues to grow. With the growth, the Studio model has become the monument. The need for innovation is constant in order for our educational environments to thrive. Online studios provided one means for innovation, but we cannot imagine that they are the only one.

CONCLUSION

In moments of disruption, we have opportunity for innovation that can lead to new ways of understanding. Grego and Thompson developed Writing Studio out of a crisis moment. The development of online writing studios at the University of Houston was not so clearly a crisis moment, but there was a sense of needing something new. The online writing studio partnerships hosted in the Writing Center allowed both me and my partners to resist calcified pedagogies. In addition, the Studios provided institutional-, disciplinary-, and self-awareness by making visible institutional relationships and providing reflexive moments that broadened self-understanding. In fact, one of the greatest strengths of the online writing studio model was that by working with one another across disciplines and across programs, we could provide more spaces for innovation.

But, as countermonuments can do, the studio partnerships also revealed that sometimes structural risks are frankly too risky, particularly for contingent faculty. The corporate monument looms large and casts a long shadow. Resisting it may lead to self-destruction. Our work requires us to live in the spaces of tension. Butler is correct. Being willing to take those risks of instability, being willing to find reflexive moments and to question our very reason for being, is necessary for us to continue to remain vital. Finding and creating innovative practices, practices like the Studio method, allows the fluid nature of creativity and learning to occur even within the fossilized environments of the institution. Online writing studios are indeed an innovative method for teaching, but the true lesson of online writing studios has been this: The danger of calcification and the necessity of innovation means that we have to conclude with a commitment to being open to the countermonuments that help us to see both the possibilities and limitations within our work.

I am now at an institution where I serve as the Director of the Writing Center. I find that the insights gained from my writing studio partnerships affect not just my development of new studio partnerships but also my overall understanding of writing center work. Although I cannot ignore the pressures of the institution to develop writing center partnerships to "serve" more and more students, I can be aware of the dangers of "outsourcing," and I can look for partnerships like mine with Morgan that allow for reflexive moments both for me and for my tutors. Working in a non-traditional learning space with peer tutors, with non-tenure track faculty members, and with students unsure of their academic status, I am aware of the risks I am asking of people who may not feel empowered to take those risks. But I am also aware of the necessity of reflective space, of reflexive space, and of constant innovation. And I am open to the possibilities innovative spaces like Writing Studios can provide. It is in these innovative spaces where we can resist the erosion at work within the academy.

REFERENCES

Arum, R. & Roksa, J. (2011). *Academically adrift: Limited learning on college campuses.* Chicago, IL: University of Chicago Press.

Berlin, J. A. (2003/1996). *Rhetoric, poetics, and cultures: Refiguring college English studies.* West Lafayette, IN: Parlor Press/Fort Collins, CO: WAC Clearinghouse.

Bérubé, M. & Nelson, C. (1995). *Higher education under fire: Politics, economics and the crisis of the humanities.* New York, NY: Routledge.

Bousquet, M., Scott, T. & Parascondola L., (Eds.). (2004). *Tenured bosses and disposable teachers: Writing instruction in the managed university.* Carbondale, IL: Southern Illinois University Press.

Butler, P. (2006). Composition as countermonument: Toward a new space in writing classrooms and curricula. *WPA: Writing Program Administration, 29*(3), 11–25.

Frattaroli, E. (2001). *Healing the soul in the age of the brain: Why medication isn't enough.* New York, NY: Viking Penguin.

Gale, X. L. (1996). *Teachers, discourses, and authority in the postmodern composition classroom.* Albany, NY: State University of New York Press.

Grego, R. & Thompson, N. (2008). *Teaching/writing in thirdspaces: The studio approach.* Carbondale, IL: Southern Illinois University Press.

Hewett, B. & Ehmann, C. (2004). *Preparing educators for online writing instruction.* Urbana, IL: National Council of Teachers of English.

Kovach, J., Miley, M. & Ramos, M. (2012). Using online studio groups to improve writing competency: A pilot study in a quality improvement methods course. *Decision Sciences Journal of Innovative Education, 10*(3), 363–387.

Miley, M. (2013). *Thirdspace explorations in online writing studios: Writing centers, writing in the disciplines, and first-year composition in the corporate university.* (Doctoral dissertation). Retrieved from Dissertations & Theses at University of Houston, ProQuest. (3574470)

Mission Statement. (2011). *About Us.* University of Houston Writing Center. Retrieved from http://www.uh.edu/writecen.

Pemberton, M. (1995). Rethinking the WAC/writing center connection. *The Writing Center Journal, 15*(2), 116–133.

Qualley, D. (1997). *Teaching composition as reflexive inquiry.* Portsmouth, NH: Boynton/Cook.

Rhoades, G. & Slaughter, S. (1998). Academic capitalism, managed professionals, and supply-side higher education. In R. Martin (Ed.), *Chalk lines: The politics of work in the managed university* (pp. 33–68). Durham, NC: Duke University Press.

Shapiro, B. (2011). Negotiating a third space in the classroom. *Pedagogy: Critical Approaches to Teaching Literature, Language, Composition and Culture, 9*(3), 423–439.

Soja, E. (2006). *Thirdspace: Journeys to Los Angeles and other real-and-imagined places.* Oxford, UK: Blackwell.

Warnock, S. (2009). *Teaching writing online: How and why.* Urbana, IL: National Council of Teachers of English.

CHAPTER 11.

SOMETHING GAINED: THE ROLE OF ONLINE STUDIOS IN A HYBRID FIRST-YEAR WRITING COURSE

Mary Gray

University of Houston

In a 2013 policy brief titled "First-Year Writing: What Good Does It Do?," the National Council of Teachers of English (NCTE) argues for the relevance of first-year writing courses in light of the contemporary push to accelerate the student college experience through more online instruction, dual credit courses, MOOCs, and other non-traditional alternatives. Research cited in the NCTE brief supports conclusions that first-year writing (FYW) contributes to outcomes of retention, rhetorical knowledge, metacognition, and responsibility, all important for institutions and student development, and as the brief suggests, all at risk if current trends continue. The authors argue that the traditional first-year writing experience is uniquely suited to producing these outcomes and that "none of the alternatives can provide the sustained attention to developing the habits of mind and strategies fostered in FYW" (2013, p. 14).

Despite NCTE's strong evidence for the value of traditional first-year writing courses, institutions continue to move rapidly toward new modes of online course delivery. Recent data suggest that approximately one-third of college students are now enrolled in at least one online course, and administrators believe that number will grow over the next five years to include a majority of students (Allen & Seaman, 2013, p. 20). Reasons for this institutional wave, or what David Brooks (2012) has called "the campus tsunami," range from budget-driven cost and efficiency concerns to student needs for more flexible learning environments. The field of composition, long engaged in the theory and praxis of online writing environments within a traditional class, has acknowledged this wider adoption of online course delivery with its own recent statement of best practices for online writing instruction (Conference on College Composition and Communication, 2013).

The hybrid writing class, which blends face-to-face and online instruction, now holds growing acceptance as an effective alternative to the traditional classroom. In an overview of the current state of online writing instruction published in the field's flagship publication, *College Composition and Communication,* June Griffin and Deborah Minter (2013) report the field seems "poised to pivot, along with the rest of higher education" (p. 140) to broader adoption of online and hybrid, or blended, classes. Writing studio methodology, shown to be effective in face-to-face settings, may also have a role to play in transposing writing classes to fully online or hybrid spaces. With its pedagogical emphasis on sustained interactive support, writing studio methodology should hold promise for online adaptation, as a vehicle for both retaining essential outcomes of first-year writing and responding to institutional pressures for alternative course deliveries. In this chapter, I introduce a model for integrating online Writing Studios into a hybrid first-year writing course and point to ways the model supports those outcomes NCTE warns might be compromised or lost entirely in the online landscape.

OVERVIEW OF THE UH HYBRID/ STUDIO-SUPPORTED MODEL

As the result of a successful pilot project in 2010/2011, first-year writing students at the University of Houston (UH) have the option to enroll in a hybrid first-year writing class supported by a fully online Writing Studio. The University of Houston, a public institution of approximately 40,000 students, serves a student body whose demographics reflect the city's broad diversity. Over three-quarters of the student body live off campus, and a majority of those students report being employed during the academic year, therefore making the hybrid format an attractive option to help balance the complicated demands of work and commuting (*U.S. News & World Report,* 2014). To fulfill core communication requirements, students currently enroll in a two-semester sequence of first-year writing taught largely by English Department teaching assistants enrolled in graduate programs of literature, creative writing, or rhetoric/composition/pedagogy. Both first-year courses feature a rhetorical approach, emphasizing expository writing in the first semester and argument in the second, culminating with a substantial research-supported argument at the conclusion of the second semester.

In fall 2010, the Department of English, in partnership with the UH Writing Center, initiated first-year writing classes in the hybrid format with online Writing Studios as an integral part of the class. Offered in addition to traditional face-to-face classes, the hybrid/studio-supported classes addressed needs of students, graduate student instructors, and administrators by 1) creating flexible scheduling for the large commuter student population, 2) training graduate instructors in hybrid pedagogy and delivery, and 3) relieving scheduling pressure for overcrowded classroom space. Students meet once a week in the traditional face-to-face classroom setting, led by either faculty or experienced TAs, with the remainder of the class conducted in the university's course management system, Blackboard. The online portion of the class consists of two components: 1) on-line instructor-directed activities such as blogs, journals, quizzes, or discussions; and 2) regular participation by all students in an online Writing Studio space conducted through the discussion board function in Blackboard. Depending on individual course plans for the week, students might engage in one or both of these online spaces.

GUIDING THEORY AND SCHOLARSHIP

The UH model draws from theory and research of online writing instruction (OWI) as well as studio theory and practice. As writing programs continue adopt and evaluate hybrid classes, researchers are increasingly finding learning in a hy-brid class equivalent to that of a traditional class. Researchers at Brigham Young University found that student writing in a hybrid first-year writing course com-pared favorably with student writing in the face-to-face courses and concluded "the hybrid format did not damage student learning; if anything, it made their writing more consistent" (Waddoups, Hatch & Butterworth, 2003, p. 278). In terms of student perception and writing outcomes, the hybrid can represent a successful balance between fully online and face-to-face formats (Sapp & Simon, 2005; Young, 2002).

To provide ongoing support for the writing process, instructors and Writ-ing Center partners envisioned transposing Grego and Thompson's theoretical and practical model of the studio thirdspace (2008) into the online portion of the hybrid class. In the Studio model, drawn from theories of place and space (Reynolds, 2004; Soja, 1996) as well as Burke's (1960) conception of "scene," small groups of students, with guidance from a trained facilitator, mutually en-gage with their developing ideas and texts. As Grego and Thompson outline, Studios do not entail end-stage editing or even the traditional peer review ses-sions writing instructors commonly practice, but constitute a more organic "safe house" (2008, p. 74) where alternative power relationships and student-centered conversations resist institutional scripts and make possible unexpected, genera-tive student counterscripts (p. 23). Because Studios meet students at all stages of the writing process and transpire over time, they also offer a place for think-ing about ideas, and more importantly, for thinking about how to think about writing, and as such, might be a site to further support emerging metacognition outlined in the NCTE brief.

Unlike Studio's theoretical constructs, theoretical perspectives guiding OWI are best understood as a range of relevant possibilities. Hewett and Ehmann

(2004), in their guide for OWI instructors, convincingly advocate a position where instructors and writing program administrators may call upon varied approaches and "ground their practices *fluidly* and eclectically in more than one theory" (p. 54, emphasis in the original). Depending on instructional goals, theories underpinning any effective pedagogical approach—social constructivism, expressivism, post-process, critical pedagogy—can inform a successful online writing class (Hewett, 2014, p. 197). Most relevant to the hybrid/studio-supported class, however, are the perspectives of social constructivism and expressivism.

OWI scholarship has its strongest ties to social constructivism (Hewett, 2010; Hewett & Ehmann, 2004), which posits that language, knowledge, and even identity are constructed through a dialogic interchange between the individual and her social context (Bruffee, 1984, 1986; Fulkerson, 2005; Halasek, 1999; LeFevre, 1987). Composition theory continues to emphasize contextual meaning-making in collaborative settings where students become co-creators of knowledge, whether through small group activities, peer reviews, or publishing their texts online. The collaborative small-group exchanges online are a natural embodiment of social constructivist tenets and offer opportunities for conversations and community building unique to the studio experience. Research further suggests, and the NCTE brief argues, connections made in the writing class can keep students engaged and enrolled (Braxton, 2000; Tinto, 1997, 2000).

For both OWI and online studio methodology, important elements of expressivism—assigning primacy to the writer's individual thoughts, expressions, and development—also inform pedagogy, particularly the foundational work of Peter Elbow in *Writing without Teachers* (1970) and Donald Murray's (1982) practices for reaching and teaching the student writer's "other self." As Grego and Thompson (2008) point out, Elbow's work has a natural affinity with Studio's emphasis on small groups of writers engaged with their texts and each other through ideas, drafting strategies, and reflections (p. 51). In their epilogue to *Teaching/Writing in Thirdspaces*, Grego and Thompson (2008) mention Elbow's own support for the role of studio interactions in diffusing frustrations student writers face when encountering new settings and unfamiliar academic expectations (p. 206).

Christopher Burnham, in his bibliographic work on expressivism, further cites student interactions as a central strategy of expressivist pedagogy which "employs freewriting, journal keeping, reflective writing, and small group dialogic collaborative response to foster a writer's aesthetic, cognitive, and moral development" (2003, p. 19). In the online instructional setting and in online studios, where these dialogs take place textually, Hewett and Ehmann (2004) explain expressivism's relevance to OWI: "Both traditional instruction and OWI engage in the expressivist approach through a focus on higher level concerns

(HLC) over lower-level concerns. OWI teaching interactions question and prod writers to dig deeper into an idea and to consider the implications of what they think" (p. 57). Studio methodology encourages facilitators and group members alike to model this practice.

The UH pilot project further drew on scholarship of teaching online in a hybrid setting. First, the planners looked to the work of Scott Warnock (2009) to conceptualize how the online portion of a hybrid class might be designed and to determine what resources and tools could be employed for class-related online activities and online Writing Studios. Warnock's reliance on asynchronous message boards for much of the online portion of his class also rests on the social constructivist theory expressed by Bruffee (1984; 1986) as well as theorist M. M. Bakhtin who found the "dialogic response" key to "active and engaged understanding" (Bakhtin, cited in Warnock, 2009, p. 68). The message board schema Warnock describes—giving students a two-part obligation for primary and secondary posts, with an accompanying two-part deadline (2009, p. 82)—also meshed with plans to require hybrid studio group members to post their ideas or drafts-in-progress and then solicit responses from peers. Through studio participation and other class online activities, multiple online writing opportunities might offer students a "complexity of audiences" (Warnock, 2009, p. 70) and a deepening sense of rhetorical situations. In their discussion of the current state of OWI, Griffin and Minter (2013) also stress the importance of "structuring occasions through which a group of students learns to work productively together on writing and responding to writing across the span of the course" (p. 150). Warnock further cites studio methodology as contributing to a "continuous writing environment [that] makes it ever possible for students to learn through their own work" (2009, xii).

Second, as a guide to developing online studios in a hybrid setting, research on a local model was already in place. In 2009, the UH College of Technology, in partnership with the Writing Center, adapted the principles of face-to-face writing studios for online delivery in an upper division hybrid quality improvement methods course. With guidance from undergraduate Writing Center facilitators, students in the methods course followed the post/response framework outlined in Warnock (2009), posting ideas or work-in-progress by a certain date/time, then responding and continuing the online conversation until the studio's end date/time. Students received regular online studio support throughout the semester on multiple writing assignments. Michelle Miley (this volume) details this model's development using Paul Butler's concept of "countermonument" as a metaphor for studio's capacity to disrupt institutional norms and open generative spaces. Her reflections, encompassing instructor, facilitator, and Writing Center partner perspectives, trace the trajectory of UH online Studios.

At the end of the semester, researchers assessed the technology methods class by 1) measuring student attitudes toward writing and the online Studios and 2) evaluating student writing samples with a holistic rubric. Results were compared across semesters to a previous class conducted without writing studio support. Comparative results showed significant improvement in student attitudes toward confidence and competence in writing as well as a willingness to revise their work (Kovach, Miley & Ramos, 2012, p. 376). In terms of writing performance, students in the studio-supported class scored one rubric level higher on the final assignment than students without studio support (Kovach, Miley & Ramos, 2012, p. 376), prompting the researchers to conclude online studios "[were] associated with improved student performance and enhanced perceptions about the writing process" (p. 380).

SHAPING THE UH HYBRID/STUDIO-SUPPORTED CLASS

The UH hybrid/studio-supported class was therefore created through a marriage of theory and scholarship surrounding both hybrid writing instruction and Writing Studio. Aurora Matzke and Bre Garrett (this volume) draw on the notion of bricolage to describe how new studio programs spring from raw materials tied to local contexts. To define new programs, partners engage in a recursive process of adapting existing concepts and practices through "uptake," while clarifying through "not talk" what the program should not include. In Matzke and Garrett's terms, the UH partners approached the project as bricoleurs, fortunate to have positive materials for "uptake" while identifying elements to avoid through "not talk." As instructors began the pilot semester, they began by transposing or, in Warnock's terms, "migrating" (2009, p. xiii) familiar course plans to the new format with an important revision arising from "not talk" surrounding the course arc. Students had been asked to write three major argumentative essays, with the third being a "substantial research essay" normally unconnected to the first two essays. Instructors agreed that focusing on a semester-long research process, rather than the traditional end-of-semester researched argument, would better suit the hybrid format and thus adopted a theme-based syllabus that made research the primary motive for the course. To enact a more recursive process of writing and research, the assignment sequence led from topic development to exploration to annotated bibliography to final research-supported argument. This plan allowed students time for false starts, revisions, and reflection, enabling the reiterative research and writing process to develop over time, particularly within the online studio groups. Within the context of a theme-based class, students might share sources, or point struggling researchers to appropriate databases, or question other writers at the level of ideas or conclusions.

STUDIO PROTOCOLS

Along with developing the research-based arc of the course, the online Studio structure took shape following Grego and Thompson's model. Aside from taking place online, however, the UH model departed from Grego and Thompson (2008) in two important aspects. First, logistics at the project's inception required locating the online writing studios within the discussion board function of the Blackboard course shell; therefore, the Writing Studio could not be fully "outside but alongside" (Grego & Thompson, 2008, p. 22) the writing class. Additionally, unlike students in Grego and Thompson's Studios, who were drawn from multiple sections of basic writing, all students in each hybrid section are divided into small online studio groups and interact only with classmates who are working on the same assignments.

As students begin to work on major assignments, the online studio space provides ongoing support for the drafting process over the course of two or three weeks before each major assignment due date. In the studio group, students asynchronously post messages and drafts of their work to a small group (five to six students) of their peers, developing ideas, synthesizing their ideas with others, revising their work, and responding to peers' works-in-progress. Importantly, as a means to foster continuity and community, students remain with their same studio group throughout the semester. In the pilot year, groups were facilitated by undergraduate facilitators who studied group facilitation and writing pedagogy under the supervision of Writing Center staff. Table 11.1 summarizes this model.

Table 11.1 Structure of the hybrid/studio-supported writing class

Course Component	Component Description
Face-to-Face Class (1 day per week)	Traditional face-to-face instructor-led activities, e.g., lecture, group activities, individual student presentations, in-class peer review
Online Class Activity (Blackboard)	Weekly instructor-directed online activities, e.g., online blogs, journals, discussions, quizzes, instructor-created or outside videos, research activities
Online Writing Studio (Blackboard)	Additional writing support in facilitator-guided online Writing Studios. Small groups of students (5–6) asynchronously post and respond to each other's works-in-progress during a week-long studio session (2–3 studios per major assignment; 6–8 studios per semester).

Online Writing Studios are scheduled in two- or three-week cycles; for example, Studios 1-A and 1-B, each lasting one week, might precede the due date for Major Assignment One, followed by Studios 2-A, 2-B, and 2-C supporting Major Assignment Two. Table 11.2 provides a fuller description of the week-long studio process, as presented to a hybrid class meeting face-to-face on Tuesdays.

Table 11.2. Sample online studio pattern for hybrid students in a face-to-face Tuesday class

Day(s) of Week	Studio Activity
Tuesday—1:00 p.m. *Class Day*	Studio opens. Check out your facilitator's message; see where the discussion will begin.
Wednesday—11:59 p.m.	You should be engaged in the studio discussion.
Thursday, Friday, Saturday, Sunday	Keep reading the group's ideas, questions, drafts, frustrations, successes, and responses; answer questions, provide guidance, feel sympathy, and respond thoughtfully; follow up with any new questions, revisions, or additional comments you have. Your facilitator will be responding, too, and guiding the conversation. More talk = better studio. Studio content depends on your needs.
Monday—11:59 p.m.	Conversation for this studio ends. Your facilitator will open a new studio tomorrow at 1:00 p.m.

The weekly pattern would be the same for a class meeting on another day. Studios begin on the face-to-face class day and end at 11:59 p.m. the night before the next face-to-face class. Students receive the studio schedule, along with all assignment due dates, as part of an in-class orientation by Writing Center staff and facilitators. At this session, students also have a one-time opportunity to meet their facilitator in person. The studio pattern was inspired by a facilitator who suggested the metaphor of a vortex to describe how Studios should whirl about, always circling back as they move forward. Students have dates and times to engage with thoughts, ideas, or drafts, then a date and time for the conversations to cease, regroup, and continue. Studios pause briefly between the close of one studio and the beginning of the next; the conversation takes a small collective breath, and then whirls on.

While engaged in studio conversations, students assume dual roles of writer and responder, and must fulfill both responsibilities to receive full studio credit. In the writer role, each group member accesses the facilitator's opening comments and general guidelines, available on the discussion board at the day/ time Studio begins, then posts ideas or work-in-progress by a deadline. Acting as responder, each writer replies online to all other members with comments, questions, or suggestions by a deadline. The facilitator also acts as a responder to each writer, encouraging further discussion with questions and comments. In a productive studio session, asynchronous conversation will continue over the course of the week with students responding, asking follow-up questions, or submitting revised work, always guided by the facilitator.

For facilitators and students alike, sustaining a dynamic online dialog comes with challenges as well as opportunities. For example, the linear arrangement of Blackboard's discussion board appears to march down the page in a vertical list of posts requiring multiple clicks to open, thus preventing the conversation from appearing spontaneous and circular. To mitigate this effect, facilitators, following the advice of Hewett and Ehmann (2004) to "respond as a reader" and "ask probing questions" (p. 79), focus on turning the conversation back to students. Illustrating this practice is the following sample response from a facilitator to a student who had found a new, more credible source: "[Student name], it's wonderful that you're considering the credibility of your sources in the context of your ethos in the paper. Excellent work there, and it sounds like you've found some much better sources with this more specific research question. Now, can you tell us how you'd answer your research question? What's your tentative thesis?"

Questions like these may spur further response from the student and lead to additional comments from other students. Such questions can also facilitate brainstorming activities or prompt students to clarify assignment prompts for the group. Because students remain in their same studio groups for the entire semester, they may become more comfortable with each other and more willing to engage in conversation. Facilitators, with their own responses to student writing, can model productive commentary and highlight possible revisions for the group.

While the asynchronous online conversation can pose challenges, for some students it can offer distinct advantages and opportunities. Although the online Studio lacks face-to-face immediacy, it affords time for students to think more carefully about posts and responses. For some students, having time to "compose" makes the process less daunting. Mark Warschauer (1997), for example, has reported increased participation in computer-mediated language classes, especially among students who might hold back from class discussions. Because computer-mediated environments allow time to compose and distance to respond, he explains, they have the capacity to be "more equal in participation than face-to-face discussion, with those who are traditionally shut out of discussions benefiting most from the increased participation" (1997, p. 473).

Also important to note are opportunities for studio groups to see each other in the face-to-face portion of the hybrid class. In face-to-face studio models where students are drawn from different classes (e.g., Grego and Thompson's model), students might not know or interact with each other outside the studio setting. Students in the UH model, however, have chances to meet each other during class time. While studio conversations are purposely kept out of the face-to-face class to preserve studio boundaries, instructors will sometimes use studio groups to organize other in-class, small-group collaborative activities, thus giving studio groups a chance to reinforce their relationships.

THE INSTRUCTOR/FACILITATOR RELATIONSHIP

In this model, the instructor/facilitator relationship differs from the more familiar instructor/TA relationship in that studio facilitators are not directly responsible to the instructors. Facilitators remain under the supervision of a senior Writing Center staff member who acts as buffer and conduit between facilitator and instructor. Instructors, therefore, do not guide facilitators in the same way they might if facilitators were present in the classroom or explicitly carrying out the instructor's wishes online; however, all parties work to maintain communication without compromising the integrity of the studio's safe thirdspace. Instructors meet regularly as a group and share syllabi, prompts, and brief class plans with the Writing Center supervisor, who then distributes them to facilitators. Facilitators also participate in regular group meetings in the Writing Center to compare experiences, raise questions, and discuss pedagogical approaches. Twice during the semester, instructors join these meetings to interact one-on-one with their facilitators.

Teaching in this model requires a good deal of surrender, since the instructional team works in partnership to create a positive learning environment. Expectations and practices are laid bare, and because much of the teaching and learning process occurs within Blackboard, they are permanently archived. The transparency of processes and pedagogies, however, can create a productive opening for student learning and the opportunity for "interactional inquiry," described by Grego and Thompson (2008) as the intersection of inquiry and action made possible by the collaborative studio environment (p. 22). However, as Miley (this volume) explains, a studio partnership with an English department reveals an inherent tension surrounding authority over writing instruction, that is, whether instructors can cede the writing ground to facilitators. She correctly asserts that the Freudian "rage to cure" is strong among writing teachers, who must allow themselves to let go and trust students' studio experience creates a different but equally valuable opportunity to develop their thinking and writing.

STUDENT VOICES FROM THE PILOT YEAR

At the conclusion of the pilot year's fall and spring semesters, students were invited to participate in a voluntary, anonymous survey designed to assess student attitudes and beliefs concerning items related to course goals. The survey contained both closed-ended items on a five-point Likert scale (1=Strongly Disagree; 5=Strongly Agree) and open-ended short-answer questions that allowed students to more fully describe their feelings toward the class. Closed-ended items on the survey targeted three important concepts: 1) student attitudes toward confidence in writing; 2) student attitudes toward the hybrid format; and 3) student attitudes toward the role of the online Writing Studio. Because online studios comprised a significant portion of the class and students participated in multiple studios for each major assignment, the studio experience necessarily shaped student perceptions of writing, the hybrid format, and the Studios themselves.

Closed-ended Likert Scale Items

An analysis of the survey suggests students left the course with a positive assessment of all three targeted concepts. Table 11.3 shows the mean responses for the three targeted concepts along with the average reliability co-efficient (Cronbach's alpha).

Table 11.3. Descriptive statistics for individual targeted concepts fall 2010/ spring 2011 end-of-semester surveys

Targeted Concepts	End of Semester Fall 2010 (N=122)		End of Semester Spring 2011 (N=106)		Average Reliability Co-efficient*
	Mean	SD	Mean	SD	α
Confidence in Writing (4 items)	3.89	.860	3.83	.861	.87
Attitudes toward the Hybrid Format (4 items)	3.92	1.030	3.82	1.094	.83
Attitudes toward the Writing Studio Method (6 items)	3.88	.890	3.89	1.003	.90

Note: * Cronbach's alpha

Table 11.4 reports the items associated with the target concepts for each semester, as well as the percentage of students who indicated agreement. In the actual survey, items were shuffled to appear in random order.

Table 11.4. Summary of individual items arranged by targeted concept showing percentage of students responding "Agree" or "Strongly Agree"

Targeted Concept/Survey Item	Fall 2011 (N=122)	Spring 2011 (N=106)
Confidence in Writing (4 items)		
I am confident in my writing ability.	72.1%	71.6%
I can easily find meaningful things to say in my writing.	70.5%	68.9%
I can easily express what I want to say in my writing.	64.8%	59.4%
I am confident writing for my university courses.	77.9%	76.4%
Attitudes toward the Hybrid Format (4 items)		
The hybrid class makes managing my schedule easier.	82.8%	74.5%
I prefer hybrid classes to traditional face-to-face classes.	57.4%	57.5%
The hybrid course format is as effective as a traditional face-to-face format.	66.4%	62.3%
Students can learn the same amount in a hybrid class as in a face-to-face class.	76.2%	65.1%
Attitudes toward the Writing Studio Method (6 items)		
The writing studio discussions keep me connected to the class.	79.5%	77.4%
The writing studio group helps me become a better writer.	61.5%	63.2%
The writing studio provides valuable feedback throughout the writing process.	78.7%	72.6%
The writing studio gives me an audience to develop my ideas.	79.5%	77.4%
I am more likely to revise my writing after feedback from the studio group.	75.4%	74.5%
Responding to my studio group helps me improve my own writing.	67.2%	67.9%

The results illustrate a consistency between the two semesters, with the greatest area of agreement on items associated with the online Writing Studios. Responses also indicate students feel confident in their writing, a belief shown to make "an independent contribution to the prediction of writing outcomes" (Pajares, 2003, p. 145) and view the Writing Studio as a place to interact with an authentic audience and receive constructive feedback. Students further reported they are likely to revise after studio feedback, a finding in line with results in Kovach, Miley, and Ramos (2012). Karen Gabrielle Johnson's data (this volume), based on a studio-supported writing/service learning class, also demonstrate Studio's role in building confidence and a willingness to revise. Her findings, which also show facilitators' influence on student learning, suggest the Studio method can yield positive results across different contexts.

Responses linking online Studios with a connection to the class are especially relevant considering the NCTE brief and research into the relationship between the freshman classroom and student persistence. The NCTE policy brief stresses the role of first-year writing courses in "fostering engagement (a sense of investment and involvement in learning) along with persistence" (2013, p. 13). The first-year classroom has further been singled out by researchers as the site where student engagement begins and institutional ties are formed (Tinto, 2000, 1997). Moreover, connections made in those classroom communities have been shown to be "reliable predictors of student persistence" (Braxton et al., 2000, p. 569).

OPEN-ENDED SHORT ANSWER ITEMS

While a majority of responses indicated agreement on the survey's targeted concepts, it was not possible on the scaled items to gauge why students might have agreed or disagreed. The following open-ended short answer items allowed students to more fully express their attitudes toward their writing processes, the hybrid format, and the online Studio method. Analyzing responses in light of the NCTE brief suggests the online Studios reinforced important elements of the first-year writing class. Responses, however, also point to places where the online space created barriers and sites of dissatisfaction.

How Did Your Writing Practices in this Class Differ from Other Composition Classes You Have Taken?

When prompted to discuss how their writing practices in the hybrid class differed from other composition classes they had taken in either college or high school, 75% of respondents in fall and 69% of respondents in spring pointed to elements of the online Studios as making a positive difference in their experiences. Most frequently mentioned were creating multiple drafts, staying on task through the online writing obligations, and increased confidence in writing. Another emerging theme highlighted the communal nature of writing, as expressed by the following student:

> In other composition classes, you only focus on your own
> writing and follow the teacher's prompt in your own thought,
> so sometimes in the writing process, you don't know that if
> you are on the right track toward the goal of the assignment.
> But in this class, I get to view other's writing and others give

> me feedback on my writing during the writing producing
> stage. This helps me to know if I am on the right track in the
> writing, and I get to receive others' ideas, not just my ideas.

The student emphasizes the difference between composing as a solitary writer and being part of a collaborative process, signaling the value of shared texts with the phrase, "I *get* to view other's writing" (emphasis mine). Yet another student expressed difference in terms of the solitary vs. the communal: "My writing has become something I don't dread doing. I can feel confident in my essays because I have constant feedback from the board post. I am not alone and have constant help at the touch of a computer." This student implies a causal connection between online group support, the pedagogical embodiment of social constructivism, and a shift from dread to confidence.

Other students saw the difference in terms of a safe space to work through the writing process, echoing Grego and Thompson's definition of the studio setting as "a 'safe house' for risk taking on the part of both students and teachers" (2008, p. 74). One student described the studio space as such a safe environment, saying, "I like how everyone shares their opinion with no fear. It gave people the courage to be completely honest, which in turn is very helpful." Another seemed to reinforce Warschauer's (1997) conclusions that computer-mediated learning environments may hold benefits for the student hesitant to participate in class discussions: "It allowed me to be critiqued without being embarrassed or shy to say what I wanted or for people to respond as they wanted." For some students, the difference in the hybrid class and other writing classes lay in producing more writing. The hybrid format alone demands a greater reliance on writing, and text-based online studio conversations—posting, responding, questioning, revising, and reflecting—only multiply occasions for writing. "I was always writing," explained one student; "the more writing, the better I got."

How would You Describe the Role of the Studio Group in Your Writing Process?

When asked to describe the role of the online studio group in their writing process, 69% of respondents in fall and 84% of respondents in spring described the studio group as beneficial to the writing process. While some students focused on the Studio's role in keeping them "on track" and preventing procrastination, many other students expressed the importance of having an immediate audience for their ideas and drafts. One student, for example, characterized the Studio as a place that "gave me more insight into my writing and also allowed me to consider my audience more." The NCTE brief stresses the importance of audience awareness in developing rhetorical knowledge transferable to other disciplinary settings (2013, p. 14). Students sharing different ideas, styles, and methods in the studio setting can foster that deepening sense of audience.

Not all students, however, were satisfied with their online studio group. Most often mentioned in negative responses were complaints about meeting deadlines, poor group attendance, and the quality of peer responses. Peer responses, one student mentioned, were completed only to "fulfill a participation grade," so group members often did not treat the studio conversations seriously. Instructors and Writing Center staff acknowledge the tension inherent between maintaining a safe, non-judgmental studio space and eventually ascribing a value to student participation. In decisions about grading policies, instructors tried to strike a balance for rewarding responsible participation and providing penalties for irresponsible participation by assigning holistic grades based on facilitator notes for full, partial, or no studio participation.

In addition to complaints about studio participation, another student felt that feedback offered online was not as effective as feedback offered face-to-face: "[F]eedback about someone's work, in my opinion, is best given face-to-face on a personal level. Emotions do not read well through text, so I do not think that feedback through the studio was terribly effective." Although this perceptive response reflects a personal preference, it exposes the persistent challenge of making the online, text-based environment as accommodating as possible for students with diverse learning styles.

How Would You Describe the Role of Your Studio Facilitator in Your Writing Process?

Students registered the strongest positive responses when prompted to describe the role of the studio facilitator, with 85% of respondents in fall and 90% of respondents in spring describing the facilitator in terms of helpfulness and support. Students often mentioned the role of facilitators in giving constructive feedback, as illustrated by the following: "She explained and answered questions in a way that was easy to comprehend. Best of all, sometimes she understood where my paper was heading better than I did, which in turn gave me more ideas for what to write about and how to write it." One respondent characterized the facilitator as an "excellent mediator," while still another cited the facilitator's influence in a successful first-year transition, responding, "[He] helped me bridge the gap between university and high school level writing."

Responses to the facilitator's role in the online Studio also indicate evidence of two important elements of the NCTE's defense of first-year writing: 1) emerging metacognition and 2) responsibility. The NCTE brief notes that metacognition, or "the ability to reflect on one's own thinking" (2013, p. 14), enables students to adapt their writing for different contexts and genres. Students, the authors point out, "often become 'locked' in the genre constraints of what they learned in high school" and assume "that a five-paragraph theme is the best response to any writing context" (p. 14). One student expressed how his thinking about writing had changed over the course of the semester by saying, "In high school, I was taught a certain structure of writing, which confused me for years. So, I had to learn how to be more open when writing." This step in cognitive development indicates the student might be open to adjusting rhetorically to a new writing context, in essence to think about how to think about the assignment and thus less likely to fall back on old, established patterns.

The NCTE brief concludes with the claim that first-year writing increases responsibility, a trait that goes "hand-in-hand" (2013, p. 14) with metacognition and enables students to "become empowered as agents responsible for their own learning when they are given the *time and space* to develop their meta-awareness as writers" (p. 14, emphasis in the original). Studio methodology requires facilitators to act as guides, not instructors, and, as an outgrowth of expressivist epistemology, facilitators are trained to turn the conversation back towards students to encourage them to take ownership of their own writing processes and the productivity of the group. Student descriptions of the role of facilitators and the studio group often reflected this process in action:

- "She really helps me to see flaws in my writing and pushes me to find ways to make it better on my own."
- "Gave good advice, and listened attentively to questions we had regarding the papers. Led us in the right direction (or back on track), and provided questions to further our thought processes."
- "The studio group allowed me to question myself and my writing in order to make necessary changes for improvement."
- "I like how this class taught me to be more confident in my writing and not to lean so much on a teacher or peer for help."

The above responses represent a range of perceptions regarding the facilitator/student relationship, but all point to developing agency, self-awareness, and personal responsibility toward writing. Interesting also is the suggestion by one student that the Studio constitutes a conversation, with the facilitator "listen[ing] attentively" to questions.

What Was Your Greatest Obstacle (Academically, Technologically, or Otherwise) to Completing Your Assignments? Please Explain.

Responses to this question, as a whole, reflected the range of challenges faced by first-year students, from struggling with more rigorous academic demands, to overcoming work/study obstacles, to becoming more proficient writers. Also, and unsurprising in a university with a large contingent of international students and multilingual learners, gaining writing proficiency in English posed the greatest challenge for one student: "My greatest obstacle was to express my ideas in right words, in correct grammar, and in a smooth way in English. And it took a lot of time to produce the correct expression of my thoughts in writing." For students grappling with English language acquisition, online Studios may hold special potential through ongoing informal, low-stakes writing to an authentic audience of peers and facilitator guides.

Other responses, however, addressed technological difficulties particular to the online environment, such as temporarily losing internet service. Several students cited the regular online writing obligations as obstacles, but often faulted their own tendencies toward procrastination and forgetfulness for missing assignments or deadlines. More troubling, however, were the few students who expressed issues of proficiency and access in comments such as, "I am not around a computer at that time," or "I am a slow typer and had a hard time finishing the assignment in time sometimes," or "I don't have the internet at home and live 25 miles from campus," or "The studio group was well thought out if you can handle computers all the time. I found it to be a little frustrating because I'm not computer savvy. I like to write everything down that flows from my mind." While these students may not have fully understood the implications of a hybrid class, their frustrations suggest our assumptions about students' technology proficiency should still be questioned and concerns regarding access remain valid (see, e.g., Kirtley, 2004; Moran, 1999, 2003).

REVISION, REFIGURATION, AND A PATH TO SUSTAINABILITY

As the tale of the studio program at the University of South Carolina (Grego & Thompson, 2008) makes clear, even well-planned and effective studio programs may face elimination for institutional reasons beyond instructors' or facilitators' control. It was unclear after the pilot year whether this model would survive as well. Threatening its continuation was the unavoidable fact that its structure required more resources than a traditional face-to-face class, and in the face of shrinking budgets, its future was uncertain. Saving the project in its second year, however, was the award of a university grant supporting courses aligned with the university's Quality Enhancement Plan (QEP), which emphasizes a commitment to undergraduate research. Because the hybrid/studio-supported classes focused on a semester-long research process, the project already shared many QEP goals. The research-based arc of the course, along with Writing Center and research-based library partnerships, therefore led to a successful grant proposal.

The project's third year saw several important developments that created a more secure future. First, the English Department, with support from the university's administration, substantially revised the first-year program for incoming graduate teaching assistants. In their first year as teaching assistants, new graduate students had been expected to be fully responsible for teaching one course in the fall and two in the spring, and then assume a full teaching load of two classes per semester thereafter. In the third year of the hybrid project, however, the incoming class of GTAs moved out of the classroom entirely and into the Writing Center as studio facilitators for both hybrid first-year writing classes and Writing Center studio projects in other disciplines like art history. This change represented strong administrative support for the hybrid project and for GTAs, who now spend their first year working closely with students across the academic spectrum, facilitating online and face-to-face Writing Studios in classes ranging from first-year writing to senior-level disciplinary courses. Kylie Korsnack (this volume) shares a similar evolution at the University of Alabama-Huntsville, where GTAs now serve as studio facilitators for a year before assuming full instructional duties. Much like the graduate students Korsnack (this volume) describes, first-year GTAs at UH faced all the pressures and insecurities of full classroom management, including grading, after a single week of orientation coupled with a pedagogy seminar. They now receive ongoing support for their year-long studio experience, take the pedagogy seminar before they enter the classroom, and view teaching writing from the unique facilitator perspective.

Second, the project expanded to include the first semester writing course, which allowed students to take the two-semester sequence in the hybrid/studio-supported format and facilitators to view the processes and products of the entire first-year writing program. Shifting the facilitator role from undergraduate writing consultants to graduate teaching assistants also marked an evolution toward a more autonomous facilitator, one more able to provide "an openness to student concerns and determination of the group's agenda on the basis of student concerns and needs" (Grego & Thompson, 2008, p. 74). Teaching assistants have the latitude to frame studio conversations in ways that respond more directly to specific contexts and the group's immediate needs.

Along with a change in the facilitator role in the third year, a change in the configuration of the Blackboard space allowed Studios to be situated outside the class Blackboard shell. With help from the university's Blackboard support staff, the online Studios moved from the discussion board function within the instructor's course shell into a separate Blackboard space. Now, when students log into Blackboard, they see a separate Writing Studio link in their course listings and enter a separate studio space, thus replicating online the way they might leave a face-to-face classroom and go to the Writing Center for a face-to-face studio. Instructors had always exercised care to reassure students that the studio space was an instructor-free zone where ideas and writing processes were not subject to instructor observation or judgment; however, as long as studios were situated within the course shell, it was possible for instructors to peer into the studio space. As Miley (this volume) explains in her discussion of the origins of UH online Studios, this arrangement can be challenging for facilitators to navigate and tempting for instructors to innocently or actively trespass. That option, however, no longer exists as the space now belongs exclusively to students, facilitators, and Writing Center staff.

In a final logical progression implemented in the project's fourth year, graduate student facilitators now have the option, with departmental approval, to become hybrid instructors after completing their year as Writing Center facilitators. As former facilitators, they come to the instructional cohort with a history of reflective practice gained through a year's experience in the facilitator community, and they transfer that practice to the instructional community. Viewing student writing processes from the inside out now shapes their pedagogy, whether in practical matters like assignment design or commenting on student work, or in more global considerations like creating a teaching persona or understanding student motivations. Also informing their pedagogy is an understanding of the different audiences and expectations students encounter in other disciplinary settings. From a programmatic perspective, the creation of a predictable pipeline for qualified and capable hybrid instructors has further stabilized the project. Hybrid/studio-supported offerings have expanded each year and grown from enrolling 372 students in the 2010/2011 pilot year to over 1,100 in 2016/2017.

FINAL CONSIDERATIONS

As with any methodology, the hybrid/studio-supported model may not be suited for all students; however, the online studios allow students to communicate through writing to multiple audiences and to think, draft, and reflect on class assignments in ways that wouldn't happen otherwise. Survey responses also indicate online Studios promote the outcomes of engagement and retention, rhetorical knowledge, metacognition, and responsibility outlined in the NCTE brief. Moreover, as more writing classes move online, the need for online writing support will only increase. The Conference on College Composition and Communication position statement on OWI best practices (2013) argues that online instruction (either hybrid or fully online) should be accompanied by online writing support through an online writing lab. Based on UH results, the online

Writing Studio deserves consideration as an effective alternative to the online writing lab. Online studios might be attached to either hybrid or fully online classes, either as stand-alone credit-bearing courses or integrated into individual classes as in our model.

For those considering adapting an online writing studio component in their own contexts, the UH experience further illustrates successes and challenges of online Studios. As a whole, students reacted positively to the online space and expressed satisfaction with the Studio's community and role in their writing. Online asynchronous interactions were shown to be advantageous for some students, such as shy or withdrawn students who may be reluctant to join face-to-face conversations but become thoughtful and "talkative" responders online. On the other hand, some students find the online space uncomfortable, for example, in responding or accepting feedback when they cannot gauge expression or body language. Students may also resist the recurring deadlines inherent in online studio participation. Since online Studios require an initial post, then responses to other group members, students must keep two deadlines in mind and check in and out of their Studio over the course of a week. Making studio obligations clear, consistent, and predictable, however, can assist students in adapting to the asynchronous rhythms of online studios. Adopters of any online writing model must also remain alert to the persistent possibility that students may struggle with technology's dependability and access or may lack the proficiency we too often assume.

Perhaps the biggest challenge for adopting online studios lies in their added layer of complexity. Online studios, whether inside or outside the class structure, require not only knowledge of facilitating first-year writing, but knowledge of facilitating first-year writing in an online setting. The complexity of online studios therefore poses additional challenges in terms of training instructors, facilitators, and staff, as well as in creating course structures and partnerships that will support studio success. Each of these elements requires an investment of time and effort for both individuals and departments. The classes discussed here, for example, could not have been sustained without the Writing Center's role as the site for studio development and implementation.

Although the UH hybrid/studio project seems stabilized for now, its future cannot be guaranteed. Administrations change, and priorities shift. Sustaining the complex system of the hybrid model further requires constant internal reassessment of its practices and results. Regardless of its future, however, it may offer a model for retaining important elements of traditional first-year writing courses that might be diminished or lost in the rush to new delivery methods and credit alternatives. The hybrid course supported by online Writing Studios may hold the potential to mitigate those losses and realize unexpected gains.

REFERENCES

Allen, I. E. & Seaman, J. (2013). *Grade change: Tracking changes in online education.* Babson Survey Research Group. Retrieved from https://onlinelearningconsortium .org/survey_report/2013-survey-online-learning-report/.

Braxton, J. M., Milern, J. F. & Sullivan, A. S. (2000). The influence of active learning on the college student departure process: Toward a revision of Tinto's theory. *The Journal of Higher Education, 71*(5), 560–590.

Brooks, D. (2012, May 3). The campus tsunami. *The New York Times.* Retrieved from http://www.nytimes.com/2012/05/04/opinion/brooks-the-campus-tsunami.html?_r=0.

Bruffee, K. (1984). Collaborative learning and the "conversation of mankind." *College English, 46*(7), 635–653.

Bruffee, K. (1986). Social construction, language, and the authority of knowledge: A bibliographical essay. *College English, 48*(8), 635–653.

Burke, K. (1960). *A grammar of motives.* Berkeley, CA: University of California Press.

Burnham, C. (2003). Expressive pedagogy: Practice/theory, theory/practice. In G.Tate, A. Rupiper & K. Schick (Eds). *A guide to composition pedagogies* (pp. 19–35). New York, NY: Oxford University Press.

Conference on College Composition and Communication. (2013). Position statement of principles and best practices for online writing instruction. Retrieved from http://cccc.ncte.org/cccc/resources/positions/owiprinciples.

Elbow, P. (1973). *Writing without teachers.* New York, NY: Oxford University Press.

Fulkerson, R. (2005). Composition at the turn of the twenty-first century. *College Composition and Communication, 56*(4), 654–687.

Grego, R. C. & Thompson, N. S. (2008). *Teaching/writing in thirdspaces: The studio approach.* Carbondale, IL: Southern Illinois University Press.

Griffin, J. & Minter, D. (2013). The rise of the online writing classroom: Reflecting on the material conditions of college composition teaching. *College Composition and Communication, 65*(1), 140–161.

Halasek, K. (1999). *A pedagogy of possibility: Bakhtinian perspectives on composition studies.* Carbondale, IL: Southern Illinois University Press.

Hewett, B. L. (2010). *The online writing conference: A guide for teachers and tutors.* Portsmouth, NH: Boynton/Cook.

Hewett, B. L. (2014). Fully online and hybrid writing instruction. In G. Tate, A. R. Taggart, K. Schick & H.B. Hessler, (Eds). *A guide to composition pedagogies* (2nd ed., pp. 194–211). New York, NY: Oxford University Press.

Hewett, B. L. & Ehmann, C. (2004). *Preparing educators for online writing instruction.* Urbana, IL: National Council of Teachers of English.

Kirtley, S. (2005). Students' views on technology and writing: The power of personal history. *Computers and Composition, 22*(2), 209–229.

Kovach, J.V., Miley, M. & Ramos, M. A. (2012). Using online studio groups to improve writing competency: A pilot study in a quality improvement methods course. *Decision Sciences Journal of Innovative Education, 10*(3), 363–387. https://dx.doi .org/10.1111/j.1540–4609.2012.00349.x.

LeFevre, K. (1987). *Invention as a social act.* Carbondale, IL: SIU Press.

Moran, C. (1999). Access-the "a" word in technology studies. In G. E. Hawisher & C. Selfe (Eds.), *Passions, pedagogies and 21st century technologies* (pp. 205–220). Logan, UT: Utah State University Press.

Moran, C. (2003). Technology and the teaching of writing. In G. Tate, A. Rupiper & K. Schick, (Eds), *A guide to composition pedagogies* (pp. 203–223). New York, NY: Oxford University Press.

Murray, D. (1982). Teaching the other self. *College Composition and Communication, 33*(2), 140–147.

National Council of Teachers of English. (2013). First-year writing: What good does it do? *Council Chronicle, 23*(2), 13–15. Retrieved from http://www.ncte.og/library/NCTEFiles/Resources/Journals/CC/0232-nov2013/CC0232Policy.pdf.

Pajares, F. (2003). Self-efficacy beliefs, motivation, and achievement in writing: A review of the literature. *Reading and Writing Quarterly, 19,* 139–158.

Reynolds, N. (1998). *Geographies of writing: Inhabiting places and encountering difference.* Carbondale, IL: Southern Illinois University Press.

Sapp, D. A. & Simon, J. (2005). Comparing grades in online and face-to-face writing courses: Interpersonal accountability and institutional commitment. *Computers and Composition, 22*(4), 471–489.

Soja, E. W. (1996). *Thirdspace: Journeys to Los Angeles and other real-and-imagined places.* Cambridge, MA: Blackwell.

Sutton, M. (2010). Messages to and from the third space: Communication between writing studio and classroom teachers. *Open Words: Access and English Studies, 4*(1), 31–45. Retrieved from https://www.pearsoned.com/wp-content/uploads/Sutton-Open_Words-Spring_2010-5.pdf.

Tinto, V. (1997). Classrooms as communities: Exploring the educational character of student persistence. *The Journal of Higher Education, 68*(6), 599–623.

Tinto, V. (2000). Linking learning and leaving: Exploring the role of college classroom in student departure. In J. M. Braxton (Ed.), *Reworking the student departure puzzle* (pp. 81–94). Nashville, TN: Vanderbilt University Press.

U.S. News & World Report. (2014). Education: Rankings and reviews—University of Houston. Retrieved from http://colleges.usnews.rankingsandreviews.com/best-colleges/university-of-houston-3652.

Waddoups, G. L., Hatch, G. L. & Butterworth, S. (2003). Blended teaching and learning in a first-year composition course. *The Quarterly Review of Distance Education, 4*(3), 271–278.

Warnock, S. (2009). *Teaching writing online: How and why.* Urbana, IL: NCTE.

Warschauer, M. (1997). Computer-mediated collaborative learning: Theory and practice. *The Modern Language Journal, 81,* 470–481.

Young, J. R. (2002). "Hybrid" teaching seeks to end the divide between traditional and online instruction. *Chronicle of Higher Education, 48*(28), 33–34.

CONTRIBUTORS

Suzanne Biedenbach is Associate Professor of English and chair of the English Composition Committee at Georgia Gwinnett College, where she teaches developmental writing, first-year composition, advanced composition, rhetoric courses, and professional writing courses. In her approach to teaching writing, she strives to employ a variety of teaching strategies aimed at assisting her students in becoming self-regulated independent learners who understand the connections between and are able to maneuver back and forth through the various discourse communities in which they find themselves.

Alison Cardinal is a doctoral candidate at the University of Washington and a Senior Lecturer at the University of Washington Tacoma. She is also an Affiliate Researcher at the University of El Paso's Sites of Translation: A User Experience Research Center. Her community-engaged work uses participatory approaches to generate collaborative research and user-centered design. Her work has appeared in *Composition Forum* and *Communication Design Quarterly*.

Dan Fraizer is Professor of Composition and Rhetoric at Springfield College. He teaches first-year composition, writing studio, advanced composition, and writing for the professions, and he also works with faculty across the disciplines to improve writing assignments and evaluation tools in a program called Faculty Writing Fellows. His publications have added to conversations about the textbook industry, service-learning, writing about war, and most recently knowledge transfer, where his research on studios as locations of transfer appeared in *WPA: Writing Program Administration* and his research on teaching for transfer in cross-disciplinary courses appeared in *Composition Forum*. He introduced writing studio to Springfield College in the late 1990s, making it an early adopter of Studio.

Bre Garrett is Assistant Professor and Director of Composition at the University of West Florida, where she teaches a range of writing and rhetoric classes across the curriculum. Her research investigates the intersection of rhetorical theory and composition pedagogy. She has an article that links writing studio and disability studies in *Composition Forum*, and she has conducted additional research on embodied composing and curricular design, on institutional studies and writing program administration, and on multimodal composing.

Mary Gray is Visiting Assistant Professor of English at the University of Houston, where she coordinates and teaches hybrid first-year writing supported by online studios. In partnership with the UH Writing Center, her work includes training and supervising new hybrid instructors as well as conducting program assessment.

Christine Weber Heilman is currently a part-time faculty member in English composition at Miami University of Ohio, where she teaches first-year writing. She has been teaching college writing for nearly thirty years at both two-year and four-year colleges. As Assistant Professor of English at Georgia Gwinnett College from 2011 to 2013, she served as Coordinator of the Segue Initiative, which piloted ALP (Accelerated Learning Program), a learning community that blends mainstreaming, acceleration, and studio models for developmental writers and allows them to earn college credit. Her research has focused on the interconnection between two fields: working-class studies and college student intellectual development as it relates to college writing.

Karen Gabrielle Johnson is Associate Professor at Shippensburg University, where she directs the Writing Studio. Karen is Co-editor of the *Writing Lab Newsletter: A Journal of Writing Center Scholarship* and a member of the Executive Board of the International Writing Centers Association. Her scholarship has focused on service-learning and writing assessment, while her editorial work includes guest-editing a special issue on tutor pedagogy in *The Writing Lab Newsletter*. Her most recent work is an open-access digital book, *What We Teach Writing Tutors: A WLN Digital Edited Collection*, which was co-edited with Ted Roggenbuck in 2018.

Kelvin Keown is the English Learner Specialist at the University of Washington Tacoma, where the focus of his work in the Teaching and Learning Center is tutoring and teaching multilingual students. His professional interests include language teaching and learning, sociolinguistics, and the history of English.

Kylie Korsnack is a doctoral candidate in English at Vanderbilt University, where she teaches undergraduate writing courses in the English department and facilitates graduate seminars as part of the Vanderbilt Center for Teaching's Certificate in College Teaching Program. Her research focuses on contemporary literature, speculative fiction, and digital pedagogy.

Michael Kuhne began his educational career as a high school English teacher in Minnesota and Colorado before earning a Ph.D. in English at the University of Minnesota (1998). Since 1995, he has taught English at Minneapolis Community and Technical College. His research interests include game-based learning and racial justice. He has published in *Teaching English in the Two-Year College*, the *Minneapolis Star Tribune*, the *Minnesota English Journal, Communitas*, and *Antipodes*, and he has contributed chapters to numerous books.

Robert LaBarge is an English Language Arts instructor at Piñon High School on the Navajo Nation. A former linguist, his current research interests include literacy and development in rural and under-served areas and the rhetoric of Marian apparitions.

Jane Leach has taught English at Minneapolis Community and Technical College since earning her Ph.D. in English at the University of Minnesota in 1999. Her primary interests are developmental writing, first-year composition, and critical literacy. She has taught Developmental English for more than 15 years and was awarded a Minnesota State Board of Trustees Outstanding Educator Award in 2012.

Aurora Matzke is Associate Professor and Co-Director of the English Writing Program at Biola University, where she teaches first-year writing, embodied rhetorics, digital pedagogy, and writing in the disciplines courses. Her work may be found in such collections as *Bad Ideas about Writing* and *Feminist Challenges or Feminist Rhetorics?: Locations, Scholarship, and Discourse*.

Michelle Miley is Assistant Professor of English and Director of the MSU Writing Center at Montana State University. Her articles have appeared in the *Writing Center Journal* and *WLN: A Journal of Writing Center Scholarship*. Her current research uses institutional ethnography as a lens to map perceptions of the work of academic writing and writing centers from the standpoint of students.

Cara Minardi-Power teaches at Florida Southwestern State College in La-Belle, Florida. When she taught at Georgia Gwinnett College (GGC), she was one of the six-member team who worked on the state's project to transform remedial writing instruction through a grant from Complete College America, which developed into GGC's Segue Program. Her research areas include scholarship on teaching and learning as well as feminist rhetorics. She has published articles in *Peitho, thirdspace*, and *Pedagogy & Practice*, and has co-edited five textbooks for first-year composition.

Tonya Ritola is Teaching Professor and Chair of the Writing Program at University of California, Santa Cruz, where she teaches lower-division writing and provides pedagogical training for graduate student instructors. Her publications and research focus on teaching for transfer, equity in writing program assessment, and organizational rhetoric.

Shirley K Rose is Professor and Director of Writing Programs in the Department of English at Arizona State University. She is a Past President of the Council of Writing Program Administrators and is the Director of the WPA Consultant-Evaluator Service. She regularly teaches graduate courses in writing program administration and has published articles on writing pedagogy and on issues in archival research and practice. With Irwin Weiser, she has edited four collections on the intellectual work of writing program administration, including *The WPA as Researcher, The Writing Program Administrator as Theorist, Going Public: What Writing Programs Learn from Engagement*, and *The Internationalization of US Writing Programs*.

Christina Santana is Assistant Professor of English at Worcester State University, where she serves as Director of the University Writing Center. Her work on collaboration and community engagement has been focused on both writing and conversation and includes her dissertation project as well as articles that have appeared in the *Community Literacy Journal* and *Currents in Teaching and Learning*. She regularly teaches courses in community writing, professional/business writing, and writing consultancy.

Mandy Sepulveda is Associate Professor of English at Georgia Gwinnett College. She has been teaching college courses in various departments and disciplines for the last 13 years. Her areas of specialty are teacher training and adolescent learning. She worked as a graduate teaching assistant (GTA) in Auburn University's English and Educational Psychology Departments for 5 years, teaching courses in rhetoric and composition, basic research methods, and adolescent development, learning, assessment and motivation. She received a Master's of Liberal Arts in 2005, a Master's of English with a concentration in rhetoric/composition in 2008, and a Ph.D. in Educational Psychology in 2010. As one of the six charter members of the Segue Taskforce at Georgia Gwinnett College, she is involved with transforming remediation of first year writing courses, introducing students to yoga, and promoting a holistic approach to learning.

INDEX

A

Accelerated Developmental English (ADE) 115, 116, 117, 118, 119, 121, 122, 123, 124, 125, 126, 127, 128, 129

Accelerated Learning Program (ALP) 4, 31, 32, 38, 62, 65, 70, 80, 115, 117, 118

Access 33, 34, 35

Accuplacer 128

Action research 7, 13, 58, 69, 128

ACT Test 48, 71

Adams, Peter 30, 32, 62, 70, 80, 118, 119

Adjunct faculty 16, 39, 48, 49, 55, 58, 69, 82, 90, 104, 122, 179, 180, 181, 182

Adler-Kassner, Linda 17, 27, 28, 99

Administration, college 14, 16, 17, 19, 27, 28, 29, 37, 38, 39, 40, 44, 45, 47, 48, 50, 55, 58, 59, 62, 64, 66, 67, 69, 70, 72, 74, 75, 79, 81, 97, 101, 119, 158, 170, 173, 185, 186, 204

Advisement 54, 55, 82, 83, 84, 85

Aljaafreh, Ali 34

Allen, I. Elaine 185

Armstrong, Lloyd 15

Arum, Richard 167

Asmussen Research and Consulting 116

Assessment, Studio programs 7, 20, 36, 37, 38, 44, 50, 51, 55, 56, 72, 105, 107, 110, 111, 127, 157, 160, 163, 190, 201

Assignments, writing 6, 35, 36, 92, 93, 94, 99, 104, 133, 150, 151, 152, 153, 154, 155, 157, 161, 162, 164, 189, 190

Astin, Alexander 151

Athens Technical College 64

Attendance 6, 20, 21, 49, 55, 56, 64, 70, 89, 91, 93, 97, 98, 99, 100, 103, 105, 107, 108, 109, 110, 111, 112, 120, 137, 153, 177, 178, 199

Attrition, student 70, 108, 126, 127

B

Bakhtin, Mikhail 189

Balay, Anne 86

Bartholomae, David 80

Basic writers 5, 8, 30, 31, 32, 37, 61, 79, 149, 150, 151, 161

Basic writing 4, 5, 8, 19, 22, 28, 30, 38, 39, 54, 61, 64, 65, 66, 70, 71, 75, 80, 87, 88, 89, 115, 116, 117, 118, 121, 123, 125, 126, 127, 128, 129, 131, 132, 135, 136, 149, 150, 151, 152, 158, 159, 191

Bawarshi, Anis 30, 36, 87

Beaudette, Pascael 64

Beaufort, Anne 32

Bell, Derrick 28

Benedict College 7, 14

Bergmann, Linda 28

Berlin, James 167

Berrett, D. 16

Bérubé, Michael 167

Biedenbach, Suzanne 18, 61, 207

Biola University 43, 44, 48, 51, 57, 58

Bly, Brian 138

Bollinger, Laurel 136

Bousquet, Marc 68, 167, 181

Braxton, John 188, 197

Bricolage 18, 39, 43, 44, 45, 46, 47, 50, 51, 53, 57, 58, 104, 118, 190

Bricoleur 43, 45, 46, 190